TRACK
AND
FIELD
FOR
COACH
AND
ATHLETE

TRACK AND FIELD FOR COACH AND ATHLETE

second edition

JOHN M. COOPER
Associate Dean
School of Health, Physical Education, and Recreation
Indiana University

with

JAMES LAVERY
School of Health, Physical Education, and Recreation
Ohio University

WILLIAM PERRIN
Athletic Department and Assistant Track Coach
University of Wisconsin

Prentice-Hall, Inc., Englewood Cliffs, New Jersey

PRENTICE-HALL INTERNATIONAL, INC., *London*
PRENTICE-HALL OF AUSTRALIA PTY. LTD., *Sydney*
PRENTICE-HALL OF CANADA, LTD., *Toronto*
PRENTICE-HALL OF INDIA PRIVATE LTD., *New Delhi*
PRENTICE-HALL OF JAPAN, INC., *Tokyo*

Printed in the United States of America

FOREWORD

Dr. John M. Cooper and his co-authors, James Lavery and William Perrin, have displayed the knowledge of and have had such distinguished experience in track and field as to make this an outstanding track and field publication.

Dr. Cooper collaborated with Jesse Mortensen, then head track coach at the University of Southern California, now deceased, in the writing of the First Edition of this book. He has also served as a national consultant to two of the Olympic Development Institutes in track and field. For many years in the southern California area before coming to Indiana, he presented workshops and lectures to coaches on the various phases of track and field. Internationally, he recently presented a scientific paper on the "Kinesiology of High Jumping" at the first International Seminar on Biomechanics held in Zurich, Switzerland in August, 1967.

In addition, he has written several articles on the subject of track and field for selected sports magazines. He is considered a profound scientific student of this sport.

James Lavery and William Perrin bring to this tri-authorship the aspect of practicality. Each is a veteran coach in his own right. Each is also very much interested in applying scientific methods to the study of their athletes' performances, to the end of bringing about improvement. This is a happy blend of a track scientist and two coaches.

I commend this book to all those who wish to know more about this great universal sport.

JOHN R. ENDWRIGHT
Dean, School of Health, Physical Education
and Recreation
Indiana University

PREFACE

This is the Second Edition of *Track and Field for Coach and Athlete*. Since the advice and opinions of many track coaches, especially at the high school and junior college levels, were previously solicited, the basic format of the First Edition has not been changed appreciably. However, all sections have been extensively updated. Chapters on cross-country, steeplechase, and hammer throw have been added.

The consensus of the coaches consulted was that such a book should suggest means of discovering potential performers, minimize the historical phases, analyze in simple language the actions of top performers, present sequence pictures of some of the best performers in each event, give sample workout schedules, present the best known way (or two ways, at most) to perform an event, give helpful hints to performers (consequently giving information that would aid coaches), and summarize in understandable terms appropriate research findings. We have attempted to preserve these concepts in this publication.

This edition contains discussions of all the major events in track and field. Not only has the material been updated, but, in addition to the new sections, the information on the pole vault and relay racing has been completely rewritten. No one area is emphasized over another. However, certain special features are worthy of mention, notably the sprints, high jump, pole vault, and cross-country. The chapter dealing with the discovery and selection of performers was placed to precede the information about the events. In the Appendix, sections on motivating and handling track athletes and track and field strategy constitute another major emphasis.

The information contained in this edition is written for the coach and athlete who have had some experience with track and field activities. In most instances, they should at least be familiar with the terminology associated with the various events. However, the language used in the book is so clearly stated that beginners should be able to understand the meaning without difficulty.

No attempt is made to discuss rules, except in rare instances in which such is needed to understand the performance desired. Consequently, there is no discussion of infractions as such.

The drawings of the various events, made from motion pictures and film strips of performances of leading athletes, are an important feature of this book.

Every track and field book that has been published represents in part the writings and the findings of others. This debt to the past is acknowledged here as well as in connection with some material in most of the chapters of the present book, especially as concerns the historical phases. On the other hand, the authors take responsibility for having selected certain well-established actions and ideas for presentation herein, as well as for whatever may be new and unique.

The book contains the best that the authors know concerning successful performances in track and field. They recognize that today's ideas and beliefs will change as findings from research and experience lead to improved procedures and techniques. Thus, the authors encourage coaches and performers to be experimental and openminded, and to have the courage to try new ideas and procedures when circumstances permit. Only in such ways will track and field continue to advance and performers continue to improve.

The authors wish to thank Charlianna Cooper and Peggy Edwards for helping in the preparation of the manuscript. We also wish to express appreciation to all performers and coaches who helped in any way in the development of ideas mentioned in the text.

JOHN M. COOPER
JAMES LAVERY
WILLIAM PERRIN

CONTENTS

PART THREE HURDLES

PART FOUR JUMPS

ILLUSTRATIONS

TRACK
AND
FIELD
FOR
COACH
AND
ATHLETE

DISCOVERY AND SELECTION OF PERFORMERS

Most college and university track coaches are usually aware of their potential performers before the season begins. Occasionally they are without a top athlete in some events and need to discover a capable performer. Sometimes a boy with little or no previous experience develops into a fine runner, jumper, hurdler, or thrower with proper training and good coaching. On the other hand, the high school track coach is often confronted yearly with the problem of determining who will be his performers for the coming season in many track and field events.

In an attempt to aid the high school coach (and even some college coaches) who will be trying to discover performers for his team, a few suggestions for the various events are offered.

short sprints

1. All boys interested in becoming sprinters should be invited to report for practice. Although many of those who report will not be-

come sprinters, they may become middle- or long-distance runners, hurdlers, jumpers, or other track performers.

2. Any reports of fast runners in the school should be investigated, and the performers encouraged to report for the team.

3. Speed shown by athletes in other sports should be observed. Some of them may be encouraged to try out for the track team in the spring.

4. An effort might be made to have all of the fastest boys in school run together in a race the length of the football field. The 5 or 6 fastest runners from this group might become top sprinters.

5. There is no definite body build to look for in the sprints. However, leg speed is one of the essential factors in fast running.

6. A 3- or 4-week track and field program in the physical education classes (if required of all boys in school) should include instruction and competition in the sprints. It is possible to discover the fastest runners by recording the best times made in 50-, 100-, and 150-yard runs.

7. Class and intramural track meets, time trials of all potential runners, and all school meets conducted prior to the regular track season, may help uncover the best runners.

440-yard dash

1. Light, thin-boned individuals whose speed is better than good may become good 440 dash men. Although, as in the short sprints, there is no definite body type preferred, extremely stocky, short, heavy-legged, or large individuals are not usually successful in this event. The most successful performers are thin, wiry, and of average height. There are, however, some notable exceptions.

2. The strongest and oldest boys from the sprinter group should be selected to try this event. An older boy in high school, because of greater strength and endurance that comes with age, will often defeat a younger, faster boy in the 440. It appears that effective combination of speed and endurance requires training, experience, and maturity.

3. Boys who have speed and endurance should be successful in the 440.

4. Athletes able to run fast but still able to relax and keep up their speed past a 220-yard run have potential in the quarter-mile.

5. All 220 and 440 aspirants should run 330 yards early in the season. The most successful ones may become good quarter-milers.

6. All sprinters and 880 men, along with the 440 men, should run the 440 against time 3 or 4 times in early season to help discover all potential 440 men.

7. Class and intramural track meets, time trials of all potential runners, and all school meets conducted prior to the regular track season, may help uncover the best runners.

880-yard run

1. Tall, long-legged runners with average speed may become good 880 men. Usually the taller, heavier quarter-milers who lack great speed can be successful runners in this event. Boys who have reasonable speed for 330 yards and the endurance to run 660 yards without undue strain should be considered.

2. Time trials in the 880, in which the 440, 880, and mile runners compete, should be held early in the season. Possibly some of the 220-yard dash men should be asked to enter these time trials in order to discover their ability in this middle distance race.

3. Individuals who have displayed potential ability previously, and have the patience to run long distances, should try out. It should be kept in mind that the 880 is the beginning of a type of event that lasts long enough for the participants to experience "running by themselves." It takes a certain type of personality—one who enjoys running for a long period, often by himself—to be successful. This is, of course, more pronounced in the long-distance races.

4. Boys who are not extremely socially inclined may be successful. A boy who likes to play team games finds it harder to adjust to running distance races than one who has the opposite traits. (There are, however, many notable exceptions to this statement.)

5. The age of the participant should be considered when deciding on his potential ability. In high school an older boy may force himself to run harder than a younger boy.

one mile

1. The ideal miler is a slightly built individual who has a loose striding running action.

2. He must like to run just for the fun of it.

3. Boys with a slow normal pulse rate probably have an advantage. Max Truex, one of the top former college distance runners in the United States, had a normal pulse rate of 54 beats per minute, as compared with the average of 72.

4. Individuals who do not stop when their arms get tired or when they get a "stitch" in the side during distance running have some of the

requisite qualities. However, tolerance to the stress of running can be developed.

5. A certain amount of speed is necessary and should be considered. A long-legged boy with average speed and not much body weight, but a desire to run, should also be considered.

6. Early season time trials in the mile with 440, 880, 1- and 2-mile runners participating might uncover some potential milers.

7. Information about boys who run a considerable distance to school should be of interest to the coach. Ray Conger, national champion and conqueror of Nurmi, the great Finnish runner for 12 years, ran and walked 2 to 3 miles each day to public school.

8. Scheduling runs of 660 to 1,320 yards in regular physical education classes may help in discovering boys with distance running ability.

long-distance

1. Long-distance participants are usually the smallest runners on the track team.

2. Establishment of a long-distance course with participation optional for all boys in the school helps create interest and discover ability. If records are kept and attempts to break them encouraged, more boys will participate.

3. A tradition that a certain school always has good long-distance runners will help in encouraging runners to report for the event.

4. All 880 and 1-mile runners should be timed over the longer distances a few times in early season.

5. A small boy with a fierce desire to make some school team should be encouraged to try the long distances.

6. As in the mile, a boy must be willing to run alone in training for a considerable length of time. He must enjoy just running.

7. Ability to withstand physiological stress that may result from continuous running is a factor that should also be considered.

cross-country

1. The long-distance runners are usually the competitors in this event.

2. However, men and boys of all shapes and sizes often compete. Some coaches have all track runners not out for another fall sport participate in cross-country.

3. Requirements for running cross-country are basically the same as those for distance running. The main ones are ability to withstand physiological stress, to enjoy the challenge of running alone, and to compete against oneself.

4. All boys in school should be encouraged to try out for cross-country. Many potential track runners are discovered in this manner.

steeplechase

1. The steeplechaser is primarily a distance runner and secondarily a hurdler. First consideration should therefore be given to the selection of long-distance runners for this event.

2. Candidates should have legs long enough to clear the barriers with ease. Since the barriers are only three feet high, all but the very small men should be encouraged to try out for this event.

3. Track aspirants who desire to compete in a distance run that offers some variety in its environment may be challenged by this event.

4. Perhaps all distance runners should be encouraged to try this event, since it is known that practice in this event prepares one for long-distance running in general.

low hurdles

1. Fast runners, even the very best sprinters, should be encouraged to try this event. It is a speed event and great skill in hurdling is not essential. Only extremely short-legged runners should be discouraged from attempting the low hurdles.

2. Since long jumpers, pole vaulters, and others practice running the low hurdles, their times should be recorded to see if they have potential ability.

3. Quarter-milers are another potential source of possible participants. They have the speed and endurance necessary for running the low hurdles.

4. Participants' abilities displayed in school and class meets and physical education classes should be sought and evaluated.

5. Age is a factor to consider in seeking low hurdlers. The older boys in high school usually have more strength and endurance for this event.

6. Frequently boys who display speed and agility in other sports, such as football and basketball, may become good low hurdlers.

intermediate hurdles

1. The 440-yard runners are the most logical to encourage toward competition in this event.

2. Usually competitors in this event are not too tall (about 6 feet in height), but have long legs in order to be able to hurdle effectively.

3. Many hurdlers with enough endurance to run a quarter of a mile in acceptable time are potential competitors.

4. Older boys in high school who have both speed and endurance could be good performers.

5. Since hurdling skill in this event is second to endurance, individuals who possess a combination of speed and endurance qualities can learn the skill of hurdling in a relatively short time to perform reasonably well.

high hurdles

1. Tall boys, or at least ones with long legs and good flexibility in the pelvic region, form a potential source of material. However, since the high school hurdles are only 39 inches high, as compared to the 42-inch college hurdles, shorter high school boys may prove to be successful.

2. High jumpers with average speed and good leg flexibility should be encouraged to try this event.

3. Boys in physical education classes should be taught how to go over the high hurdles so they will know enough to want to try out for the event.

4. A football end with good flexible legs should be asked to practice high hurdling. It takes the same kind of courage to attempt the high hurdles as it does to crash through blockers.

5. Class meets may help in discovering potential performers.

shot put

1. Boys with explosive arm and leg power, usually in the heavyweight class, should be encouraged to try for this event.

2. Instruction in shot putting should be given to all boys in the physical education classes, and records made of their best puts.

3. A boy with the proper physical attributes who enjoys achievement in an individual event may develop into a successful shot putter.

4. Football tackles, ends, and guards are the greatest source of potential performers.

5. Discus throwers may become good shot putters.

6. This is not entirely a strength event; speed and agility are also important. A big, slow, strong boy may not be successful.

7. Good competitive spirit is necessary.

8. Class meets and preseason tryouts often reveal potential performers.

long jump and triple jump

1. The jumps of all sprinters, low hurdlers, and pole vaulters should be measured to determine their abilities in this event.

2. Class meets should be held to discover potential performers.

3. Triple jump contests in physical education classes may help to discover a good long jumper or triple jumper.

4. A nimble and quick football halfback should be encouraged to try for these events.

5. Boys who display ability to spring forward and sideward in other sports, including tumbling, may become good long jumpers and triple jump performers.

high jump

1. Tall boys with good vertical spring should be especially encouraged to try out for high jumping.

2. The high hurdlers' abilities should be determined in this event.

3. Centers and other basketball players who are considered good rebounders may become good high jumpers.

4. Physical education class students who score high in the jump and reach test should be invited to try out.

5. Class meets should help to discover potential high jumpers.

pole vault

1. Rope climbers, parallel bar specialists, and gymnastics apparatus performers in general are a source of potential performers.

2. Boys who perform even reasonably well in the pole vault in physical education classes and class meets should be invited out.

3. Boys who have jumped ditches with poles as youngsters, as well as those who have a vaulting setup in their backyards, should be asked to report.

4. The individual of average or better height who has some speed and a strong upper body may have potential ability.

5. This is such a specialized event that boys who appear to have ability in this area should be placed in a special group for instruction as early as the freshman year in high school.

discus

1. Boys with long arms and considerable weight should be encouraged to attempt this event.

2. Football tackles and ends and basketball centers often have great potential.

3. Several years of practice are needed to learn this skill, so prospective performers should begin early in high school to learn how to throw the discus.

4. Slow, tall boys may be able to throw the discus a reasonable distance.

5. Shot putters may be able to compete successfully in this event.

javelin

1. Boys who have good throwing arms should be best in this event.

2. Long passers in football and baseball outfielders with good throwing arms are the best source of potential javelin throwers. The whiplike arm action used in these sports is similar to that of javelin throwing.

3. Boys who threw sticks and spears as youngsters may have ability to throw the javelin.

4. Since many high schools do not include the javelin in the track program, college coaches have had to find potential performers among their freshmen. Since it usually takes four years for a promising boy to become a good performer, the college coach must invite prospects to try the event as early as possible.

5. All track performers may be asked to attempt a few throws early in the season to discover if they have any ability in this event.

hammer throw

1. Young men who are strong and have explosive power should be effective in this event.

2. Most competitors are of the heavyweight variety.

3. Shot putters should be encouraged to try this event.

4. While this is a strength event, speed and good footwork are essential. A young man who is strong but slow may not be successful.

5. Football tackles, football guards, and discus throwers are potential performers.

6. Interested candidates should be given the opportunity to receive instruction in this event.

The health and physical condition of every boy trying out for the team should always be considered. A coach should never let a boy perform in any event unless he has had a proper health examination and been given approval, by a physician, to take part in track and field events. If the coach knows a boy is not physically able, because of poor health, to perform in the event of his choice, he should be withheld from participation until he has recovered fully.

Finally, the average coach must not sit back and wait for a "natural" to report. Reasonably good performers may be developed from "average" boys who might never experience the fun of participation or be able to help their schools if only the best are invited out. Occasionally a great performer arises from the "average" group. The coach should encourage as many boys as possible to participate in track and field events. This encouragement may take the form of bulletin board displays, assembly programs highlighting track and field, all-school field days, or any other activity that brings the sport to the attention of the student body. Active recruitment of boys who aren't out for any sport may prove worthwhile, especially in the distance runs.

ONE

SPRINTS

SHORT SPRINTS

Sprinting is a type of running in which the participant runs the entire distance at near maximum speed. It differs from fast running in that the stride is usually longer, the number of strides per second is greater, and the force of the driving leg against the ground is less. In other words, it is an all-out effort by the contestant to move as fast as he can over the indicated distance in as short a time as possible.

a glimpse at past performances

Ever changing styles. The ancient Greeks had a short race (reportedly 220 yards) as a part of their Olympic Games, and it is interesting to note that they used starting blocks for their runners. The evolution of running styles has been slow; concepts of proper performance techniques have changed from one period to another, and there has been a frequent return to the opinion of an earlier era on how best to sprint.

The ancient Greeks may have had modern concepts with regard

to the value of arm action. Aristotle [1] wrote, "runners run faster if they swing their arms, for in extension of the arms there is a kind of leaning upon the hands and wrists."

The starting stances in modern sprinting have varied from use of very small distances between the feet to a wide distance between the feet and currently back again to the short distance between the feet. The height of the hip and the distance of the front foot from the starting line have also varied from time to time.

The bunch start, in which the feet are placed close together, was popular during the 1920's and 1930's. Then research findings disproved earlier claims of the superiority of this stance. However, when the starting rules were changed so that the starter held the runners in the "set" position for less than 2 seconds, the bunch start returned to favor. While the sprinter using the bunch start has always been able to move faster off the blocks, the elongated start seems the most efficient for sprinting when the runners are held in the set position longer than 2 seconds.

Man's quest for speed and new records is increasingly evident in this space age, as goals and achievements of travel mount almost daily. Certain goals in track and field have always been set and reset; championship times were formerly much slower than they are today. Many high school dash men now exceed the times of college men of a few decades ago. A college performer who does not run faster than the "good" times of yesterday is not considered a good sprinter.

H. W. Stevens of Williams won the first I.C.A.A.A.A. 100-yard dash in 11 seconds in 1876. John Owens, competing for the Detroit Athletic Club, was one of the first to break the 10-second 100-yard dash time when he ran the distance in $9\frac{4}{5}$ seconds in 1890. Since then there has been a steady assault upon this and subsequent world records. Mel Patton set a world record of 9.3 seconds in 1948, but this record has been broken several times since. The record is now 9.1, held jointly by several men. Arthur Duffey of Georgetown University was the first to break John Owens' record when he ran the distance in $9\frac{3}{5}$ seconds. Many years later, in 1930, University of Southern California sprinter Frank Wykoff negotiated the distance in 9.4 seconds. This same Wykoff competed in three straight Olympiads.

Previously, Howard Drew from Springfield, Massachusetts, who later competed for the University of Southern California, had tied Duffey's record of $9\frac{3}{5}$ seconds, and ran the 220 in the record time of $21\frac{1}{5}$ seconds.

Charles W. Paddock, University of Southern California, consid-

[1] Aristotle, *Parts of Animals, Movement of Animals, and Progression of Animals,* trans. L. A. Peck and E. S. Forster (Cambridge: Harvard University Press, 1945).

ered by some as the fastest sprinter of his era (1918-1926), tied or set many records. He ran the 100-yards in 9⅗ seconds and the 220-yards in 20⅘ seconds. Jackson Scholz of Missouri also was a great sprinter during this period, and one of Paddock's toughest competitors. Roland Locke of Nebraska set a 200-meter record of 20.6 in 1926.

In the 1930's, in addition to Wykoff, there were two black sprinters, Eddie Tolan of Michigan and Ralph Metcalfe of Marquette. This trio, along with George Simpson of Ohio, were the best sprinters of that day. Tolan set a new record of 10.3 seconds in 100-meters and Metcalfe tied Locke's 200-meter 20.6-second record. They all ran the 100 in 9.4 seconds.

Jesse Owens of Ohio State, acclaimed the greatest track athlete from the period 1900 to 1950, tied the then 100-yard 9.4-second record and ran the 220 in 20.3 seconds in 1935. He also set a world record in the 220 low hurdles and in the broad jump. Other sprinters such as Clyde Jeffry of Stanford, Barney Ewell of Penn State, and Hal Davis of California turned in excellent times from 1939 to 1942.

Mel Patton, University of Southern California, who held the 100-yard world record of 9.3 seconds and the 220-yard world record of 20.2 seconds, and Harrison Dillard, great hurdler who won the 100-meter Olympic race in 1948, were among the greatest sprinters immediately after World War II. Two other sprinters, Bobby Morrow of Abilene Christian College, winner of the 100-meter and 200-meter races in the Olympics at Melbourne, Australia, in 1956, and Dave Sime of Duke, former record holder of 220-yards in :20, had demonstrated the ability to beat the world's best.

The United States has continued to develop a large number of world class sprinters. One was the electrifying Bob Hayes in the 1964 Tokyo Olympics, who charged his way to three gold medals. The smooth efficient running of Henry Carr, Arizona State world record holder of the 220-yards, was another. New sprint sensations in the late 1960's were Charlie Greene of Nebraska, Jim Hines of Texas Southern (1968 Olympic champion), Ronnie Ray Smith of San Jose State, all with pending times of :09.9 in the 100-meters, and Tommy Smith of San Jose, whose great stride and speed lowered the world record for 220 yards straightaway to :19.5 (:18.9 for 200 meters). There are also many promising young sprinters who should be capable in the next few years of running world class competition; they include Mike Goodrich of Indiana, Herb Washington of Michigan State, and Jim Green of Kentucky. John Carlos of San José has now attained this status.

Evolution in starting. In the early 1930's, the accepted technique for the sprinter was to take several short fast steps as he left the blocks. This technique prevailed until after World War II, when top sprinters began to increase the length of strides made as they left the blocks. It now appears that the sprinter who can take a reasonably long stride, and still not slow down his leg speed appreciably, is using the most effective method both at the start and throughout the race of 100 yards. However, the first few strides after leaving the blocks are considerably shorter than those taken during the remainder of the race.

Since starting blocks were used by the ancient Greeks, it might be assumed that they also used some form of crouch start. Although the crouch start may have appeared in the United States earlier, it was probably not employed until 1887. After several years this stance replaced the old standing start and has gradually become the established stance for all sprinters, hurdlers, and quarter-milers.

As late as 1930, some sprinters at the big meets dug holes to start from; others used starting blocks. However, those who used starting blocks were warned that, if they won, their times would not be considered as records. For example, in 1929 in the N.C.A.A. championships, George Simpson of Ohio State won the 100 in 9.4 seconds, but his record was disallowed because he used starting blocks. It was not until 1930 that blocks were officially approved and their use made legal by mention in the official N.C.A.A. track and field rule book.

characteristics of the sprinter

Body build. Sprinters appear to be the least distinguishable of track and field participants. There are tall, short, heavy, light, and medium-sized sprinters. Extremely short-legged sprinters often have difficulty holding their own with taller sprinters in 220-yard and longer sprints.

Probably the ideal body build for a sprinter would be a height of about 6 feet with light bones, good musculature, especially around the thigh region, light musculature in the calf of the leg (at least not thick ankles and heavy calf muscles placed low on the leg), and long, slender feet. Nevertheless, a boy with physical characteristics that would seem detrimental to his performance may become a fast runner, because he: (a) has very fast muscular movement of the legs, called *leg speed;* (b) uses good body mechanics; (c) has a long stride; (d) has confidence in his ability; and (e) has determination to train and to win.

Temperament and age. The sprinter is often nervous and high-strung. Whether this results from experience in an explosive, competitive situation or is a natural condition is debatable. Certainly such qualities alone will not create a potential sprinter, but having favorable physical characteristics to go along with such a temperament may be an advantage. Evidence in relation to age seems to indicate that speed belongs to youth, but some great sprinters have been able to keep their speed until the age of 30 or longer. However, this is only possible when they train regularly every year.

Sprinters' attributes.   Fenn [2] has found that the faster runners have the following movement characteristics: (1) longer length of stride; (2) faster number of steps (strides) per second; (3) greater height in front leg lift; (4) ground contact with a larger angle with the horizontal, therefore less wasted energy in forward pressure on the ground; and (5) less up-and-down movement of the body's center of weight.

After a 6 year experimental program conducted on sprinting during the years 1950-1954 at the University of Southern California, the following still applicable conclusions were drawn: [3]

1. When starting, the stronger leg should be placed on the front block. Fifteen untrained sprinters achieved better time in a 5-yard sprint by using the stronger leg against the front block.

2. Response time to the starting signal does not appear to be an important factor in the time required to run a given dash distance. There is a great difference between quickness of movement and speed of movement when starting and in sprinting. It is important to use proper running form off the blocks and throughout the race.

3. Removal of the rear block so that the sprinter starts with use of only the front block adversely affects starting speed. This research was done to test the importance of the rear block in starting.

4. The optimum time for holding a sprinter at the "set" position is slightly beyond $1\frac{1}{2}$ seconds. The response time to the starting gun is slower when the holding time is longer than 2 seconds.

5. The medium elongated starting stance was found at the time of

---

[2] Wallace O. Fenn, "Work Against Gravity and Work due to Velocity Changes in Running: Movement of the Center of Gravity within the Body and Foot Pressures on the Ground," *American Journal of Physiology*, XCIII (June, 1930), 433-62.

[3] This information was drawn from the conclusions found in the following studies, conducted under the direction of one of the authors (J.M.C.):

Robert Hager, "Experimental Study on the Effects of Various Foot Spacings in the Sprint Start" (Master's project, University of Southern California, August, 1957; original data collected in 1950).

Samuel R. Nicholson, "Study of the Factors which Contribute to Decreasing the Starting Time of Trained Sprinters" (Unpublished report, January, 1952).

————, "Study of the Relationship of the Removal of the Rear Starting Block to the Starting Time of the Sprint Start" (Unpublished practicum, University of Southern California, June, 1952).

Joseph M. Reeves, "A Study of the Relationships of Various Factors in Track Starting" (Unpublished report, University of Southern California, January, 1953).

Dale O. Nelson, "A Comparative Study of the Difference in Using the Left Foot Forward and the Right Foot Forward in the Track Start" (Unpublished report, University of Southern California, January, 1954).

the program to be best. Now the bunch starting position (mean distance 10.9 inches or slightly longer between the blocks) appears to be the most effective.

6. There appears to be no relationship between the amount of pressure exerted against the blocks and the time recorded in running a specified distance (5 yards in this case). The greatest force exerted against the blocks did not yield the fastest time for the performer.

7. When starting, the average good sprinter's rear leg exerts considerably more force than the front leg on the blocks, but the force from the front leg is applied for a longer time. *It would seem from the findings in this study that the runner should attempt to get the rear foot into action against the ground as soon as possible.*

starting positions

Modern types of starting positions vary considerably. The most common are described below.

Bunch starting position. This position is determined by having the runner place the toe of the back foot opposite the rear edge of the heel of the front foot. Use of this position usually means the blocks are placed from 10 to 13 inches apart. Many top sprinters are using the bunch start today. It usually enables the sprinter to leave the blocks faster than in the other starts. In the bunch start, the sprinter's hips are high and he tends to leave the blocks very fast. However, it is a very difficult position to maintain if the starter holds the runner in the "set" position beyond 2 seconds (*see* Fig. 2-1).

Medium starting position. This position is determined by having the runner place the knee of his rear leg opposite the end of the front foot. This fairly popular position is one of the more effective stances.

Medium elongated starting. This position is not determined by a fixed distance between feet, but by a varying one, and experimentally has been shown in the past to have been the most effective, but is not considered so today. To determine this position the runner places the knee of his rear leg opposite the foot of the front leg at *any place beyond the line opposite the toe of the front foot and up to, but not including, a position opposite the heel of the front foot.* The average position would involve the knee of the rear leg being opposite the middle arch of the front foot. The sprinter determines the best position for his own use through experience or by going to an experimental running track, where devices test his speed for a given distance using various starting distances.

Elongated starting position. This position is the extreme opposite

FIGURE 2–1.   The "set" position. The sprinter is using a bunch start with the
rear leg extended. Most top sprinters are tending toward use of a partially or
fully extended rear leg. Note that the body weight is well forward and the hips
a little higher than the shoulders. The head is relaxed and the eyes focused on a
point just below the head.

of the bunch start. The method used to determine the distance between
blocks is to have the runner place the knee of his rear leg opposite the
back of the heel of the front foot, or at any location beyond this distance. Very few sprinters use this starting stance, since the feet are placed
at too great a distance apart for almost all sprinters. The runner is unable to cause his body to fall forward fast enough to give him a fast start.

starting and sprinting procedures

Based upon coaching experience and experimental evidence, the
following starting procedures are suggested.

1. The blocks should be set at the sprinter's preferred distance.
It is recommended that the bunch or medium position be used by most
sprinters, with the blocks 11 to 15 inches apart.

2. If the distance of the front foot from the starting line has not
been determined through experience, a beginning reference point may
be found by placing the front block the distance of two full hand
"spans" from the front line. Modification of this distance should be
made as experience and study dictate. This would mean that the rear
block would be about 25 to 30 inches from the starting line. The front

leg in a starting "set" position in the past formed an angle of about 80°. It was thought that this leg angle enabled the front leg to support the rear leg effectively as it swung through for the first step. However, many good sprinters have recently tended to extend completely or nearly the rear leg when they are in the "set" position. This position tends to make the sprinter go forward more easily during his first step.

3. A standing position immediately behind the blocks is assumed.

4. One or two moderately deep breaths are taken when the starter says, "Go to your marks."

5. A position directly in front of the blocks is taken, the hands placed on the ground, and the feet backed into the starting blocks, placing first the front and then the rear foot against the blocks. (If sufficient training has not been experienced, it is suggested that the stronger leg be placed in front. If leg and foot strength devices, such as dynamometers, are not available, a crude method may be used to determine the stronger foot. The sprinter stands erect with both feet together. Someone gently pushes him from the rear in the small of the back. Usually he will support his weight with his stronger leg, thus stepping forward with the weaker leg in the first step.)

6. The hands are then dusted off and the rear knee is kept on the ground.

7. The hands are now placed on the ground and the wrists rotated outward so that the thumb and index finger are just behind the starting line, spread and parallel. The body weight is borne on the fingers; only the finger tips and thumb tips of each hand should be in contact with the ground. (Where finger strength is too weak to permit the sprinter to be up on his finger tips, special types of fingertip push-up exercises should be used to strengthen them. The fingertip position increases the forward lean and enables the runner to get off faster.)

8. The arms should hang in a perpendicular line from the shoulders to the ground, with the two thumbs about 8 inches apart. (Some sprinters may prefer to have the hands slightly wider than shoulder width. Some few even use a very wide hand spread of as much as 20 or more inches.)

9. The head should be loose, relaxed, and allowed to hang down.

10. At the command "set," one quick breath may be taken before the body weight moves upward and forward over the hands, so that all that is necessary is to pull the hands out to the side to start to fall forward. The legs then move fast enough to keep the body from falling. (Enough weight should be felt on the front foot to permit a firm application of force against the block. There is no felt weight kept on the rear foot.)

The sprinter should be less balanced in the "set" position if the starter holds him for less than 2 seconds. (When he is held for 2 seconds or longer, he will have assumed a more stable position—that is, with feet placed farther apart in the blocks.) He must have such an unstable position in order to fall forward when he releases his hands as support. His attention should be focused on *sound,*[4] and any little noise would cause him to start immediately. He should concentrate, after hearing the sound, on moving off the blocks as soon as possible.

11. The hips at "set" are raised to a point slightly above the shoulders, so that as the runner leaves the blocks he lifts his shoulders just above the hips. The force from the legs is then directed forward and only slightly upward. The idea of having the force from the legs go through the center of the body and continue in a straight line to the finish tape points out to the sprinter the importance of being in a forward-lean position at "set," and of letting the legs continuously catch the body before it falls in its progress to the finish line, in a rhythmical, smooth motion. However, to set an initial goal of a short distance (such as 5 yards) only enables the runner to reach that particular point rapidly. Often the sprinter fails to maintain his pace from that point on because his body is too far forward. When practicing sprint starting, the goal selected should be a distance of more than 20 yards.

12. The eyes at "set" are focused on a point on the ground directly in front of the body, so that the head hangs down and is relaxed. Some coaches contend that the sprinter should look at a point 3 to 20 yards down the track preparatory to starting. However, it is suggested that the raised head in the "set" position is tense.

13. The runner should concentrate on taking the first step as rapidly as possible.

These 13 points are shown in Fig. 2-2.

LEAVING THE BLOCKS

The following additional points are presented for the sprinter to follow as he leaves the block.

1. At the sound of the gun, the slightly bent arm, opposite the stepping leg (rear leg at start), is quickly, but gently, thrust forward at shoulder level, but not as far as possible. The other arm is moved vigorously toward the rear so that the arms will move in opposition to the legs. The first actual movement in starting is the cocking of the rear foot preparatory to taking a step. The front foot is then cocked (flexed) just before the arms start their movement. The arms are actually hang-

---

[4] This statement was corroborated by Franklin Henry, "Track Men Should Abandon Old Idea," *Science News Letter,* August 17, 1957, p. 98.

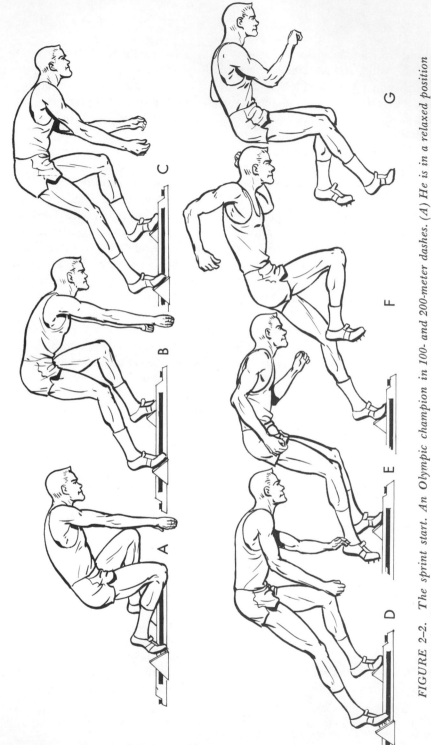

FIGURE 2-2. The sprint start. An Olympic champion in 100- and 200-meter dashes. (A) He is in a relaxed position on the blocks. (B) This is an example of an almost perfect "set" position. (C) Note that he is pushing off with both feet. (D) and (E) His lead arm is starting forward. (F) and (G) These are an almost perfect example of good body position and arm action.

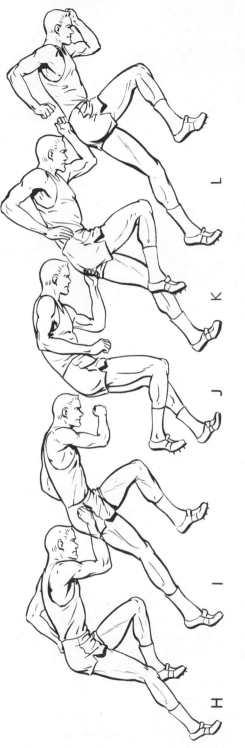

H   I   J   K   L

FIGURE 2-2 (cont.).   The sprint start. (H) through (L) His high knee and relaxed rear arm action is seen. The eyes are looking down and the head is not raised for the first 10 yards.

23

ing in front of the body when the first step is taken. This position keeps the body weight in front of the feet.

2. The first step should be 18 to 30 inches from the starting line and slightly inward from a straight line down the track. The foot taking the first step should still be behind the weight center line of the body, and should barely clear the ground in moving forward. Any lifting of the foot upward throws the body of the sprinter upward and prevents him from moving forward rapidly.

3. The foot is pointed almost straight ahead as it strikes the ground (exception: on the first step, the foot is turned slightly inward). Excessive toeing inward or outward decreases foot and leg action. However, knee position is the real key to the sprinter's ability to direct his body in as straight a line as possible. The knee must be pointed in the direction of the run in order for the sprinter to move linearly. Slight toeing-out may not be as disadvantageous as once thought if the knee is pointed straight ahead. In fact, young Mike Goodrich of Indiana, as well as Charlie Greene of Nebraska, run with a definite toeing-out action.

4. The head should be raised *gently* as the runner leaves the block so that he focuses on a spot 20 to 30 feet down the track ahead of him as he moves forward.

5. The sprinter should slowly come to a completely upright position. Each succeeding step should be longer until he reaches this upright position. For most sprinters, this means that they have covered a distance of 10 to 15 yards before attaining their upright running position. If it were possible to have a higher effective starting position, full running stride could be achieved more rapidly. Short-legged sprinters reach this position sooner than long-legged ones.

6. The first few strides after leaving the blocks are fairly long, but not exaggerated in length. Short choppy steps should not be used.

Reaction time off the blocks is not correlated with speed in the sprints. However, the better start each runner gets, the greater is his opportunity for running an ideal race. Probably the two most important factors are that the sprinter gets a firm, fast start and attempts to maintain top speed as long as possible.

7. Upon reaching full running position, the sprinter should pull his hips under him and attempt to roll his hips as he runs, thereby increasing the length of each stride. Since a sprinter reaches his maximum speed at approximately 65 yards from the start, or in approximately 6 seconds, the sprinter who is among the leaders at this point will win the race if he can come closer than the others to maintaining *this* speed for the remainder of the race.

8. The use of proper arm and leg action is obviously extremely important. Going off the blocks, the sprinter should have strong arm

action, with the movement to the front and rear made as fast as possible. As the sprinter reaches his full running position, the arm action should be rapid but executed somewhat more in front of the body. The movement of the bent arm to the front is rapid, but easy, so that the body will not react to the front arm movement with a backward motion. The arms should move slightly in toward the middle of the body, but not much higher than shoulder level. This slightly inward swinging motion is necessary for smooth, relaxed action because of the anatomical connection of the arm with the rest of the body, and the way in which the chest muscles pull the arms forward and inward. If the sprinter tends to tense his arms as he runs, it may be better to have him cut down the action of the arms, and swing them gently and easily in rhythm with the legs for balance purposes only.

9. During the sprint, the hand should be slightly cupped with the thumb pushing against the forefinger. Ability to relax the arm is an important factor in enabling the runner to secure entire body relaxation while running. Pushing the thumb against the forefinger helps prevent the arm from becoming tense.

10. The legs, from the first step until slightly beyond the upright running position, are moved vigorously with a high knee lift. The high knee lift should be continued throughout a 100-yard sprint, but the foot action against the ground is not as vigorous when the sprinter uses longer strides.

Observation of the marks made on the ground by the feet of top sprinters (shoes covered with white chalk) has shown that there are deep holes in the ground after the first 5 or 6 strides, with the heel plainly visible. After that, the holes are much smaller, with the heel hitting very lightly and the marks barely visible. The movement of the leg to the rear is such that the foot goes somewhat higher than the knee. However, too much kick up in the rear appears to be unnecessary, does not add anything to the speed of movement, and results in loss of time.

The knee lift in front should be high, almost even with the top of the hip. The leg and foot are extended forward so that a long stride is taken, with the foot striking the ground in a pawing-like action. The sprinter should move his legs as fast as he can and still take as long a stride as possible. However, leg speed should not be unduly sacrificed for a longer stride.

11. The body lean forward at the start is extreme (almost as far as the sprinter can lean without falling). This angle of lean gradually decreases until the vertical position is assumed as the runner reaches his upright running position. While running, the leg of the rear foot, at the point of fullest extension, should be in a straight line with the back and the head. Some top runners have even been found to lean slightly

backward during the latter portion of the race. However, it is impossible to run forward without having the rear leg and foot, the motive force, exerting effort from the rear of the center of the body weight.

It is essential that the head be kept up during the run. Many beginning sprinters hold their heads down during the first few strides after leaving the blocks, especially those who have a tendency to stand up at the start. This gives them a false illusion of gradually coming up to an erect running position. Unfortunately, they are working at a mechanical disadvantage and may lose because of their poorer initial form.

12. The running form throughout should be smooth and seemingly effortless. Galloping, rolling of the head and body from side to side, excessive movement of the hands and arms, and clenching of the teeth, which makes the neck and face muscles bulge, will decrease running speed.

13. The feet and ankles move rapidly in a bounce-like action to increase the speed of leg and foot movement.

By way of summary to this point, after the sprinter has come to an upright running position, he should run with a long unexaggerated stride varying according to his leg length and general build—probably somewhere between 6 and 9 feet (from right foot to left foot). He should use a high leg lift, employ fast arm action, and keep a straight back, as shown in Fig. 2-3.

SOME SPRINT ESSENTIALS

Several additional comments about sprinting should be made. The great sprinters of the past learned to relax when they ran. One step in accomplishing relaxation is to let the swinging leg move partially unchecked until just before the vigorous thrust of the foot against the ground. Using the arms in such a manner that the forward motion is extremely easy and not under control of the muscles except as necessary for fast backward movement also helps in relaxing the runner. The back and the rear and front of the neck are among the areas apt to show most strain.

To alleviate this strain, which often begins in the hands and arms, it is necessary for relaxation to begin in the hands and face. Rolling the lip outward, or letting the lower jaw sag by opening the mouth, aids in relaxing the front of the neck and the face. The head and neck may be relaxed by keeping the head in line with the back. Lifting the head high at the start tends to tense the neck and back muscles.

During the time the runner is accelerating, and especially while he is attempting to maintain his speed, it is important that he not overexert himself. This is not an easy skill to learn. Every runner has a maximum rhythm of leg movement beyond which he cannot go. Trying to exceed this rhythm of movement slows and "ties up" the runner.

Two breaths taken at the start of a sprint, and another as the runner gets "set," as previously mentioned, enable the runner to hold his breath during part of a 100-yard race, usually for the duration of a 60-yard sprint. Taking one or two breaths at the beginning of a race also tends to relax the runner before he leaves the blocks. At the 80-yard mark in the 100-yard sprint, one breath should be taken for a good supply of oxygen and to enable the runner to relax and run more easily at the finish. For distances beyond 100-yards, breathing normally seems to be the best technique, but the runner should take one or more breaths at the start. Almost all runners hold their breath during an all-out effort, such as the last 25 yards of a long race.

The sprinter who attempts to leap, jump, shrug, or twist as he finishes a race is actually diminishing his speed with these extra motions. He should run through the tape and *go beyond it* about 10 yards before slowing up. An extra motion at the last moment may sometimes attract the judges' eyes, but if the finish of the race is photographed, the runner who continues running through the tape shows to greatest advantage in a close finish. If any extra movement at the finish is necessary, it should be accomplished during the last stride (*see* Fig. 2-4).

special comments about 220-yard dash

The records reveal not only that the time for the 220 has been gradually decreased during the last 60 years, but that more and more runners are able to equal previous "best" records. This is a race in which the contestant should attempt to run the entire distance at near maximum speed, and which calls for both top speed and more endurance than does the 100-yard dash. Certain special running techniques should be employed to enable the runner to maintain speed as long as possible.

The physical qualifications of the 220-yard sprinter are the same as those for the 100-yard sprinter, with only a few differences. Although there are exceptions, it is possible for an extremely short, heavy, quick runner to make a reasonably good 100-yard dash man, even a top one. Most of this physical type have difficulty in running a fast race beyond this distance because of weight and lack of length of stride. Occasionally, a fast runner who also competes in field events can run a good 100-yard race, but because of lack of training does not have the endurance to run an effective 220. Since the 220-yard dash is run on a curve, the runner must be able to sprint under control throughout the turn.

Age is often a factor to consider in selecting participants for the

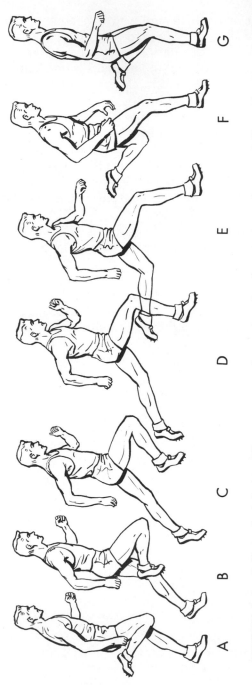

A   B   C   D   E   F   G

FIGURE 2–3. Full-speed sprinting. These are an action series of a former top sprinter at full speed. (C) and (D) Especially note the high knee action and the push-off with the toe of the trail leg. (G) The heel is seen to lightly touch the ground at the beginning of each full foot support phase.

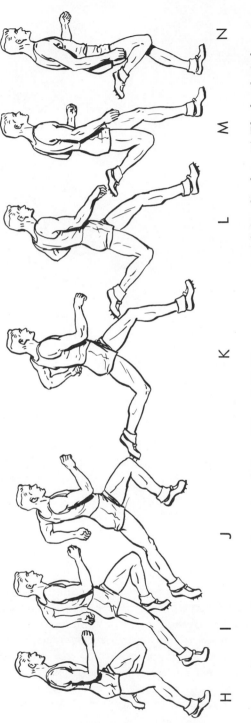

H   I   J   K   L   M   N

FIGURE 2–3 (cont.). Full speed sprinting. (H) and (I) The arms are now carried rather low. (J) The hand of the front arm is not raised above shoulder level. (See also C.) (K) The hips are rolled so that a long stride may be attained. (L), (M), and (N) The relaxed racing stride is seen.

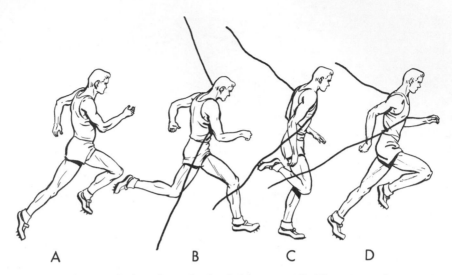

FIGURE 2–4. *Sprinting through the finish tape. (A) The runner is seen approaching the finish tape. (B) Note that the shoulder is thrust forward into the tape. (C) and (D) He carries his drive beyond the finish line.*

220 in high school competition. An older boy frequently has the greater strength and endurance needed to run this distance more effectively. A good 440-yard runner can usually run a good, and sometimes a great, 220-yard sprint race when he has enough speed, because he already has sufficient endurance.

Most of the techniques of performance described earlier in the chapter apply to both the 100 and the 220. Not every good 100-yard sprinter can become good in the 220, but records indicate that, with proper training, more than 80 per cent of the 100-yard sprinters can become effective 220-yard runners.

helpful hints

In addition to the previously mentioned factors, there are others that should be mastered for success in the 220-yard sprint.

1. The distance should be run with maximum speed and minimum tension. This means being able to relax sufficiently to maintain speed as long as possible after accelerating to the maximum. Maximum acceleration is reached in about 6 seconds after leaving the blocks. An inexperienced 220-yard runner will need a pattern to follow in running this distance. Such a pattern may be: (a) Run the first 60 to 70 yards at top speed. (b) Relax and run as fast as possible without trying too

hard for 90 to 100 yards. The running technique employed here is often called the "float." This is actually an erroneous idea, since there should be no conscious effort to slow up. (c) Attempt to run the last remaining 50 to 60 yards faster, with as little tension as possible. Inexperienced 220-yard sprinters need to know how to judge the effort necessary in relation to the distance to be traveled. It is essential that the sprinter know how to pace himself so that he does not expend his effort before the finish of the race.

Many of today's top 220 sprinters accelerate up to about 65 yards, and relax, but run the remaining distance as fast as possible. Occasionally they "pour it on" in the last 20 yards.

2. In running the 220-yard race, the runner should be under control as he approaches the curve. He should run the inside edge of his lane, increase speed on the curve, and maintain speed in a relaxed manner to the finish. A curve can be run most effectively if the stride is not broken and there is no slowing down.

When running indoors on cinder or board tracks, it is imperative that the sprinter accelerate on part of the straightaway, be under control *when coming into the curve,* and speed up on the curve. The runner should lean forward and in toward the inside of the curve, with the outside leg placed wide so that the legs are in a wide stance as the curve is taken. The runner then should push in toward the curve with this outside leg.

3. The 220-yard sprinter should develop enough endurance through repeated 220-yard runs and/or overdistance runs (300-yards) to run this race effectively.

4. He should develop speed by running repeated 50- and 75-yard sprints.

5. In preparation for, and competition in, the sprints in early season, the sprinters should drill on the fundamental skills of performance—starting, proper arm and leg action, relaxation, maximum speed with minimum effort, and gaining endurance. The midseason schedule should include work on skills considered to need most attention. This is the time to perfect form. The late season program should be characterized by reduction in the intensity of practice sessions and concentration on top winning performance in each meet.

training program

Certain training and conditioning principles are recommended for the sprinter: (a) Most endurance running should be done in early season. Overdistances done in midseason or later are usually unnecessary unless the sprinter is to run in the mile relay. (b) Fast starting with a gun should be practiced at least once a week throughout the season. (c) An all-out effort for short distances should be made at every practice session. A vastly superior runner should be handicapped part of the time at the start of the race in order to provide good competition for him and the other sprinters in practice. (d) Movies of each runner should be taken and analyzed early in the season. (e) Starts and short runs should be scheduled at the first part of each practice session. Pulled muscles often occur when a sprinter practices starts *after he has become tired.* (f) Easy workouts in late season are often the most beneficial for the competitive performer. (g) Confidence can be built by having the sprinter win some races (even if against much slower runners).

The sprinter does not need much equipment in order to perform well in his event. While his clothing must not fit snugly and bind his body or limbs, it should not be so loose that it flaps as he runs. The legs of the running trunks should be loose enough to allow free motion of the runner's legs. His shoes should be snug and should adhere closely to the feet. Shoes with some spikes placed near the *front* of the sole have the best leverage position. Short spikes are best for hard surface tracks, including indoor board tracks; long spikes are best for outdoor competition.

Studies on the value of warming up before competing in speed activities have raised some questions as to its worth.[5] It is the belief of the authors that some warm-up is necessary, and that in the past it may have been overdone. It appears that physiological effects similar to those resulting from a warm-up can be secured through excitement, heat, hypnosis, and other means. A runner who is so weak from excitement that he does not feel like running up and down the track prior to a race probably needs very little warming up—and that mostly for relaxation purposes. The main value in the warm-up for speed events is that the runner gets a feel of the track and gains confidence in his own ability as he sees that he can run and is able to move with very little effort.

On a cold day, it is better for a sprinter to keep warm in his sweat suit near a furnace or heater than to go out on the track for a lengthy warm-up session. He should be excited enough about the race that only a minimum of time is spent on the track, to help him prepare for the race.

[5] Peter V. Karpovich and Creighton J. Hale, "Effect of Warming-up Upon Physical Performance," *American Medical Association Journal,* CLXII (November 17, 1956), 1117-19.

Roger Burke, "Relationship between Physical Performance and Warmup Procedures of Varying Intensity and Duration" (Doctoral thesis, University of Southern California, January, 1957).

Exercises for the sprinter during early season should be as follows: (a) Exercises which strengthen his legs and upper torso. (b) Exercises which may help him gain over-all strength. Some weight training should be done. The leg muscles of the upper thigh need especially to be strengthened. (c) Exercises which would help him lengthen his stride as he runs. This is best done by measuring the sprinter's stride and having him increase it by striking white chalk marks on the track, placed a distance apart which seems best for lengthening his stride. Sometimes running low hurdles has the same effect. (d) Those that strengthen the fingers and hands, such as doing 8 to 10 push-up exercises on the fingers, are helpful. (e) Those that increase leg, ankle, and foot speed are needed. Practicing high leg lifts while running in place is a good exercise for developing fast, high, leg action; moving the feet as fast as possible and not bending the knees while in place or traveling very little distance down the track is an excellent exercise for helping increase foot speed. The arms must move rapidly in opposition to the foot movement in the latter exercise.

Other exercises may be used, *but stretching exercises should be used cautiously and sparingly* to avoid. pulling muscles. Additional muscle conditioning may be accomplished in the actual practice workouts.

WORKOUT SCHEDULES

PRESEASON WORKOUT SCHEDULE FOR 100- AND 220-YARD SPRINTERS

Monday
1. Do 15 minutes of stretching exercises.
2. Run the straightaways and walk the curves for 1 mile.
3. Run 3 × 330's at ¾ speed.
4. Rest 7 to 10 minutes.
5. Run 3 × 330's at ⅞ to full speed.
6. Rest 12 to 15 minutes.
7. Repeat number 2.

Tuesday
1. Do 15 minutes of stretching exercises.
2. Run the straightaways and walk the curves for 1 mile.
3. Run 5 × 180's, stressing form and relaxation.
4. Rest 1 to 5 minutes between runs.
5. Jog and walk 1 mile.

Wednesday
1. Do 15 minutes of stretching exercises.
2. Run the straightaways and jog the curves for 1 mile.
3. Run 3 or 4 × 220's at ¾ speed. Increase the speed as the physical condition improves.
4. Rest 10 minutes between runs.

Thursday
1. Do stretching exercises as a warm-up.
2. Run the straightaways and walk the curves for 1 mile.
3. Take 5 starts running 30 yards at ¾ effort.
4. Take 5 starts running 50 yards at ¾ effort.
5. Take 2 starts running 75 yards at ¾ effort.
6. Run 8 to 10 × 110's at ¾ effort.
7. Finish by jogging on the grass.

Friday
1. Do stretching exercises as a warm-up.
2. Run the straightaways and walk the curves for 1 mile.
3. Run 4 × 330's at ¾ speed.
4. Rest 15 minutes between runs.
5. Run 10 to 15 × 110 yards at ¾ speed.
6. Run to finish the workout.

Saturday
1. Do stretching exercises as a warm-up.
2. Jog, walk, and run on the grass for 30 minutes.

MIDSEASON WORKOUT SCHEDULE FOR 100- AND
220-YARD SPRINTERS

Monday
1. Do stretching exercises as a warm-up.
2. Run 1 mile of straightaways and walk the curves for 1 mile.
3. Run in the following manner:

    330 yards at full or ¾ speed.
    220 yards at full speed.
    110 yards at full speed 10 to 15 times.

4. Repeat number 2.

Tuesday
1. Do stretching exercises as a warm-up.
2. Run the straightaways and walk the curves for 1 mile.
3. Take 5 starts running 30 yards at maximum effort.
4. Take 5 starts running 50 yards at maximum effort.
5. Take 2 starts running 75 yards at maximum effort.
6. Repeat number 2.

Wednesday
1. Do stretching exercises as a warm-up.
2. Run the straightaways and walk the curves for 1 mile.
3. Run 3×220's at $\frac{7}{8}$ to full effort.
4. Jog $\frac{1}{2}$ mile.
5. Rest 12 to 15 minutes.
6. Repeat number 3.
7. Repeat number 2.

Thursday
1. Do regular warm-up stretching exercises.
2. Run the straightaways and walk the curves for 1 mile.
3. Take 5 starts running 30 yards.
4. Take 5 starts running 50 yards.
5. Take 2 starts running 75 yards.
6. Repeat number 2.

Friday
1. Do regular warm-up of stretching exercises.
2. Work out on the grass briefly.

Saturday
Participate in meet.

RELAY RACING

Relay racing has been part of man's culture since the dawn of history. However, the distance to be run and the type of exchanges used have varied. Only recently have the distances been standardized and the baton become the usual exchange device.

In some sections of the country and at certain times of the year, relay events are the main attraction on the track schedule. Some of the various types of relays are sprint (440, 880, 1 mile), sprint and distance medleys, 2-mile, 4-mile, and shuttle hurdle. The 440 and 1-mile relays are the events scheduled in most dual meets, and are on the program at the national, international, and Olympic Games levels of competition.

In the 1968 Olympics, the 400-meter relay world record of :38.6 was tied or broken four times prior to the finals. The final race was, without question, the greatest 400-meter relay race ever run, as the first five teams all tied or broke the world record. The United States led the contest with outstanding performances from Charlie Greene, Mel Pender, Ronnie Ray Smith, and Jim Hines in the unbelievable time of :38.2.

They were followed by Cuba in :38.3, France in :38.4, Jamaica in :38.4, and East Germany in :38.6.

The 1968 Olympic team composed of Vince Matthews (:45.0), Ron Freeman (:43.2), Larry James (:43.8), and Lee Evans (:44.4) ran an astounding 2:56.1 in the 1600-meter relay. This was a new Olympic and world record. Kenya's team tied the former Olympic and world record with a most respectable 2:59.0. The United States' team members were never pressed, and ran for the most part 10 to 20 yards in front of the nearest competition, with each team member averaging :44.025 per 400 meters.

Relay racing constitutes a phase of running and/or sprinting. (The sprints include up to the 440-yard dash being run by each runner. For example, the mile relay involves 4 quarter-mile sprinters.) The sprint relays require real baton passing skills, while the distance relays are more dependent upon the running ability of the anchor man.

the sprint relays

The sprint relays are the fastest and *the most dependent on good baton exchange* of all types of relay racing. Fast sprint relay time is made possible by correct baton passing. A relay team composed of good, but not great, sprinters may win a sprint relay race almost solely because of superior ability in baton passing.

The baton must be passed from one sprinter to another within the specified 20-meter passing zone. (There are markers placed 10 meters to either side of the end of each 110 yards of a 440-yard relay; at the end of each 220 of the 880-yard relay; at the end of each 440 of a 1-mile relay; and so on.) In the 440- and 880-yard relays, the outgoing runners may, in addition, start outside of the exchange zone no more than 10 meters (11 yards) as a leadup to the regular passing zone. This starting point must be marked outside of the track. However, the exchange of the baton must take place within the passing zone. In the other relays, the outgoing runner must always start inside the exchange zone, and also complete the pass within the prescribed 20-meter distance.

The sprinters in the 440 and 880 relay races should pass the baton to one another at top speed. This means that the baton is usually passed near the end of the 20-meter zone so that the receiving member may be running his fastest. He will often have been running about 25 to 28 meters when he receives the baton. However, some coaches wish the pass to be made at the end of 10 meters to reduce the possibility of fouling.

The *first* man to run for the sprint relay team is usually the best or second best sprinter on the team. This leadoff man must be fast enough to keep up with the other runners, and should probably be the fastest starter on the team. He starts from the blocks as a sprinter does and holds the baton in his hand in such a manner that he is able to support his weight on his fingers and still keep the baton between his thumb and the fleshy part of the hand supported by the little finger. Some runners prefer to grasp the baton with the two middle fingers and support their weight in the set position with the little finger, forefinger, and thumb. Another method is to hold the baton with the last two fingers and help support the weight with the thumb and first two fingers. The baton should be grasped toward the rear so that over half of it extends beyond the front part of the hand.

The *second* runner is usually the slowest sprinter, but one who has enough speed for the relay team to remain in contention after he finishes his portion of the relay.

The *third* man is the third best sprinter on the team. He should make up any loss that has occurred when the second man ran, or at least not lose any distance, so that the anchor man is not placed at too great a disadvantage.

The *anchor* man is either the best or second best sprinter on the team and the strongest competitor.

In the 440-yard relay, the men's abilities to run the curve may affect the order in which they run, since two or three of them will run on the curves. This is also true in the 880-yard relay. The lane assigned to the team may also become a factor in determining the order of running.

Runners in the 440-yard and 880-yard relays use what is commonly referred to as a *blind* or *nonvisual pass* (baton exchange). The responsibility for the success of this pass falls on both runners, but the major burden lies with the incoming runner. He must hit the target (hand) perfectly the first time. Thus, the four runners must spend hours practicing exchange of the baton with one another. They must come to know each other so well that they become a smooth-running unit. The outgoing runner's responsibility is to present a perfect target, and also to start running at precisely the right moment.

Establishment of the proper takeoff spot for the receiving runner requires that the runners work with one another until an exchange is made with both runners running at top speed. The takeoff spot for the receiver is usually 6 to 10 yards away from the first restraining line. When the incoming runner hits this mark, the outgoing runner, who has assumed a crouched sprinter's start, starts his sprint. The outgoing runner's sole purpose is to accelerate as fast as possible before the incoming runner reaches him. He must sprint, pumping with both arms, for a distance of 10 to 15 yards, then he extends his hand to the rear in order to receive the baton from the incoming runner. If the members of the team have worked together for a considerable time practicing the exchange, the rear hand of the outgoing runner should reach its position just as the baton is placed in it. This, of course, is an ideal situation, but the runners must work toward making a perfect pass.

In the mile relay the same general order of running is used. The 4 quarter-milers, however, finish slower and more tired than do men running in the short sprints. In fact, the importance of the anchor man increases as the distance becomes longer.

Thus, a good anchor man is vital in the distance relays, in which some coaches place the slowest man at the start and move on up to the fastest as anchor man. This idea could be used even in the mile relay if the runners were temperamentally constituted to run their best when behind.

The order of the men running the medley relay is dictated by the distance each man runs. Each man is selected for his ability to run a specific distance. In the sprint medley relay the following distances are run: 220 yards (first or leadoff man), 220 yards (second man), 440 yards (third man), and 880 yards (last or fourth man). In the distance medley relay the distances are: 440 yards (first or leadoff man), 880 yards (second man), 1,320 yards (third man), and 1 mile (anchor man). In the 480 shuttle high hurdle race the men are usually selected to run in the same order as in the sprint relays.

With the advent of the additional 10-meters starting leadup area in the sprint relays, a number of changes came about in the methods used in the exchanging of the baton. Although the old left to right hand exchange is still used in the longer relays and by some coaches, it was not thought fast enough by some world authorities. The changing of the baton from the right hand of the incoming runner to the left hand of the outgoing runner had a tendency to cause other problems which resulted in loss of speed. Now the right to left and left to right method is most commonly used. The leadoff man starts with the baton in his right hand and keeps it there for his portion of the race. As he approaches the second runner, he utilizes his speed to advantage and runs on the inside portion of the curve. The second man starts on the outside of the lane, where he has a less tight curve to run. He receives the baton in his left hand and keeps it there during his leg of the relay. The third man takes the baton in his right hand and keeps it there during his running section. The fourth man takes the baton in his left hand for the same reason as the number 2 runner. It is believed that adoption of the additional runway area caused the teams to develop this different method of exchanging the baton.

While there are many accepted methods of passing the baton, the one recommended for use (in accordance with the above passing method) is illustrated in Figs. 3-1 and 3-2. The exchange is fast, and the baton

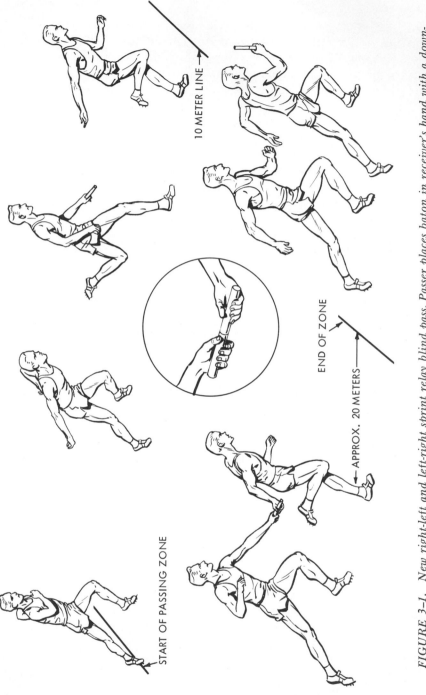

10 METER LINE

END OF ZONE

APPROX. 20 METERS

START OF PASSING ZONE

FIGURE 3–1. New right-left and left-right sprint relay blind pass. Passer places baton in receiver's hand with a downward motion. Receiver extends hand to the rear with the palm up. He (the receiver) passes the baton to the next receiver from the hand with which he received the baton.

10 METER LINE

END OF ZONE

APPROX. 20 METERS

START OF PASSING ZONE

FIGURE 3–2. Old procedure in sprint relay blind pass. Receiver uses an extended receiving hand technique with the fingers pointing downward. This method is still used when the runners have only a short time to work together as a unit. It is a safe method of passing.

is in the proper position for the next exchange to be made without moving it from one hand to the other after it is received.

In the 480-yard shuttle high hurdle race, no baton is exchanged. A restraining line is placed 1 yard in front of the starting line. When the individual who is hurdling crosses this line with any part of his body, his teammate may start running and hurdling his portion of the race.

distance relays

In a relay race run a distance longer than 220 yards, the method used to exchange the baton is somewhat different from that presented for the sprint relays. The type of pass used in these races is referred to as an *open* or *visual pass*. The major responsibility in executing the visual pass rests with the outgoing runner. Here, as in the sprint relays, practice is essential, as the runners must know one another extremely well. The incoming runner concentrates on his running and on getting the baton to the outgoing runner. The outgoing runner, after taking the baton from the incoming runner, starts on his leg of the relay. The method most often used is illustrated in Fig. 3-3. The outgoing runner must gauge the speed as well as the physical condition of the incoming runner. He must be able to recognize any sign of fatigue displayed by the incoming runner in order not to leave too soon or too fast on his leg of the race.

Many distance relay teams are now utilizing a semivisual pass which is very similar to the sprint pass. In this method, the outgoing runner watches the incoming runner very closely. If the latter is running strongly, the receiver will turn and run with his hand back in anticipation of receiving the pass. He does not leave as quickly as he might in the sprint relay race, but he does accelerate at about 3/4 speed. The incoming runner thus must "charge" into the passing zone. Many runners make the mistake of decelerating as they approach the exchange

FIGURE 3–3.   *Most accepted hand style of speed relay passing. This may be used either as a blind or sight exchange.*

zone, thinking that their portion of the race is over. When using this latter method of exchange, deceleration by the incoming runner would be disastrous. (*See* Fig. 3-4.)

summary and further suggestions

1. In sprint relays (including the mile), the speed of the baton exchange is very important.

2. The runners should hold the baton firmly, but not tightly.

3. The baton must be exchanged within a 20-meter zone. A mid-line is placed at 10 meters to enable the runners to judge their location in the zone.

4. In the 440-yard and 880-yard sprint relays, the second, third, and fourth runners may assume a position to begin their portion of the race not more than 10 meters outside of the starting zone.

5. If the incoming runner runs past his receiver after the exchange, the receiver has failed to start running soon enough, and tenths of seconds have been lost. Conversely, the receiver must be careful not to start too soon and run away from his teammate. The incoming runner's speed at the time of the exchange should be equal to that of the outgoing runner.

6. In the sprint relays, excepting the mile, almost the full passing zone should be used, so that the receiver has time to gain speed. A great deal of practice will be necessary in order that the runners know one another's speed and movements well.

7. In the sprint relays, excepting the mile, it is the responsibility of the incoming runner to see that the baton is exchanged accurately and firmly. However, the receiver, after running 10 to 15 yards and then extending his arm to the rear, should not move his arm up and down, thereby making a poor target for the incoming runner.

8. The incoming runner should deliver the baton in the mile relay and longer distances with his left hand to the right hand of the receiver. (In the sprint relays, using the new method, it is right to left, left to right, and right to left.)

9. Runners in the mile relay and long distances should, after receiving the baton with the right hand, shift it immediately to the left hand. This is done in the first two or three strides. However, the anchor man need not shift the baton from his right to left hand.

10. Before taking off, the receiver in the 440-yard sprint relay should let the incoming runner be farther from the restraining line than would the receiver in the 880-yard relay. This spot is usually about

10 METER LINE

END OF ZONE

START OF PASSING ZONE

10 METERS

FIGURE 3-4. *Middle- and long-distance relay passing procedures. The receiver watches incoming runner and judges the speed of his incoming teammate before starting his run.*

44

7½ yards for the 440 and 6½ yards for the 880-yard relay men; the distance generally diminishes as the distance of the relay increases. The speed of the incoming runner helps determine the exact distance, especially in the case of the longer relays.

11. The usual baton exchange method used in sprint relays, excluding the mile, is known as the *nonvisual* or *blind* type. Runners in the mile or longer relay usually use a *visual* type of exchange.

12. The extended hand to the rear (palm up) position appears to be the fastest method of exchange in short sprint relays.

13. In the short sprint relays, the receiver watches the incoming man until he reaches a designated spot, and thereafter must not look back. Many runners have a signal that they use when the incoming man delivers the baton—the incoming runner yells "go" or some similar expression. Many coaches consider this a dangerous habit, especially when there may be many runners yelling commands which could confuse the outgoing runner. Practice on the fundamentals of passing and confidence in one another's abilities will help eliminate the need for the use of commands during the exchange.

14. Almost all sprint relays are run in lanes throughout the entire race. In such a case, the incoming man, after passing the baton, must be careful to jog along only *in his lane.* If he moves out of his lane before all runners have finished their portion of the relay race, he may cause slower runners to spill. As a result, his team would be disqualified.

15. In relay races in which the runner cuts to the pole after a designated distance, a fast starter should almost always be used as lead-off man.

16. The usual order of running in the sprint relays is second fastest runner first, slowest runner second, third fastest third, and fastest runner last or anchor.

17. In the longer distance relays in which lanes are not used for all runners, the position of the receiving runner in the exchange zone is sometimes determined by the position of the passing runner as he comes off the turn into the straightaway. The team in first place gets lane 1, the second place team lane 2, and so on, until all teams are placed.

18. In the sprint medley (220 yards, 440 yards, 880 yards), both nonvisual and visual types of exchanges are often used. To utilize the speed of the shorter distance runners, it is wise to start the 440 and 880 runners at the midpoint of the exchange zone; the runner who is running the longer distance will then run 10 meters less than if he uses the total exchange zone.

19. The type of exchange indicated in 18 can also be utilized to great advantage in the distance medley—440 yards, 880 yards, 1,320 yards, 1 mile. The man running the shorter distance does not make his ex-

change to the outgoing runner until he is in the latter part of the exchange zone.

The training program prescribed for the various relay runners is dictated by the distance they will run in the relay. That is, sprint relay runners will practice sprinting and distance relay runners will practice distance running. (*See* Chapters 2 and 7.)

440-YARD DASH

The quarter-miler, as he was called in former years, was not a specialist. He was usually the type who could compete in and win many races over varying distances. For example, in 1868, E. J. Colbeck, an Englishman, won his country's championship in the 440, took second in the 100-yard dash, and also won the 880 run, setting a new record. Of course the times of such versatile men were slow compared with modern standards. These early all-purpose runners were essentially sprinters. They probably "floated" through many of their running events without being pushed to a great extent, winning on their speed; endurance was not a strong factor in these races.

Some excellent times were recorded for the 440 early in American track history, such as Harvard's Wendell Baker's :47.6 in 1886, Columbia's Maxie Long's :47 in 1900 on a straightaway track, and Pennsylvania's Ted Meredith's :47.4 in 1916.

The concept expressed by both the writers (coaches) and per-formers of that era was that the 440 was merely a shortened 880 race, and the performer should combine these two events in his training and competing program. This meant that the first 220 of the 440 was run at a slow pace, which usually resulted in a rather even pace throughout the race. Time usually was slightly under 25 seconds for the first 220 and just over 25 seconds for the last 220, making 50 seconds flat for the 440 dash the average time of the good performers.

Occasionally a runner traveled the first 220 in under 23 seconds and won the race, as did Eric Liddell of Great Britain in the 1924 Paris Olympic Games. Sprinter Liddell, because of religious scruples about running the 100-meter trials on Sunday, withdrew and entered the 440 instead. Having no preconceived ideas on how to run the race, he ran somewhat the same way he ran the 220. He sprinted all-out during the first part of the race, floated during the middle part, and ran all-out during the last portion. Such exceptions might well have convinced coaches that the 440 should be classified as a sprint rather than a run. However, the 440-880 concept prevailed until the Eastman-Carr duel, which was essentially a race between sprinter Carr and Eastman, the world record holder in both the 880 and 440. Carr set a new record in the 400-meter (:46.2) in the 1932 Olympics, after defeating Eastman in I.C.A.A.A. competition and the N.C.C.A. meet just previous to the Olympics. Carr outsprinted Eastman in a stretch drive in the Olympics in which Eastman led in the first 220 yards, being timed unofficially in 21.4 seconds.

Most of the great quarter-milers from that time forward were trained as sprinters. A great 440 man such as John Woodruff of Pitts-burgh, who was the 1936 Olympic champion in the 880, never became the world record holder in the 440 because he was not primarily a sprinter. The top 440 men of the 1930's and 1940's often ran the first 220 at near maximum speed and tried to maintain as much speed as possible during the last 220. Although the speed of a world record holder in the sprints was not necessary for the 440 man, such national champions as Vic Williams, Harold Smallwood, and Erwin Miller had to develop speed in the 220, just as Ben Eastman did, in order to be successful in the 440. There was often a difference of as much as four or more seconds between the first 220 and the last 220, with the last 220 the slower. This concept prevailed until the 1956 Olympics, when Jim Lea, Lou Jones (:45.9 and :45.8), and others began to train by running many 220's at 22 seconds. (Lea was later injured and ultimately did not compete in the 1956 Olympics.)

Their training programs, translated into a competitive plan, would mean that an even pace of 22 seconds or less for each 220 would enable several runners to run the 440-yard dash in 44 seconds or less. Physiologically, it is considered best to run so that the most exhausting portion of the race is last. This idea is now being explored by many 440 runners, and it appears to be sound from practical and physiological viewpoints. It also becomes much more feasible when one considers that this race is now run in lanes, enabling the runner to establish his own pace and disregard the other competitors.

Present-day 440 men, such as Tommy Smith, Lee Evans, and Ron Freeman, usually run the first 220 slightly faster than the second. Perhaps in the near future a runner will even be able to run the first 220 in 21 seconds and have enough energy left to run the second 220 in 22 seconds for a :43 440-yard run. This almost became a reality when sprint-trained runners, such as Lee Evans and Tommy Smith, were consistent in running under :45. Then Evans set a world record of :43.8 in the 1968 440-meter Olympic race. In the spring of 1968, Larry James of Villanova was clocked in :43.8 in anchoring his team's mile relay at the Penn Relays. There is no question that the younger athletes, such as Wayne Collett of U.C.L.A., Dave Morton of the University of Texas, and others yet unknown, will eventually be running the 440 in :43.0 or less.

characteristics of the 440 man

The variance in body build among 440 men is not quite as great as that among sprinters. Most 440 men tend to be thin and wiry, as mentioned in Chapter 1. They also tend to be smaller and lighter in weight than sprinters. Quarter-milers are sprinters who have good endurance, above average physical strength, and ability to perform at top speed in a relaxed manner. (*See* Chapter 1 for more information.)

correct form

The starting procedures and running form for the 440 are essentially the same as those presented for the sprinter in Chapter 2, with notable exceptions in degree only, especially in the running phase. Some of these differences are:

1. The starting speed off the blocks is not quite as important to the 440-dash man as it is to the 100- and 220-dash man.

2. During the run, the 440 man's leg lift in front and the consequent back kick is not as pronounced.

3. The length of leg stride throughout most of the race is not

quite as long, and the extension of the driving leg against the ground is less.

4. The body is held upright, as is true with the sprinter, except during the acceleration period.

5. The arm action is shorter and more in front of the body.

6. Most coaches agree that greater relaxation is required for the 440 sprinter than for the shorter distance sprinters.

7. The 440 man's movements usually appear to be more rhythmical, and he appears to run under better control than does the sprinter, who uses an accentuated hip swing (*see* Fig. 4-1).

8. Breathing is natural; a breath is taken when needed, except during the beginning and near the end of a race.

factors in competitive racing

The nature of the warm-up prior to a race depends a great deal on the type of runner, his temperament, and how excited he is about his particular race. As stated in Chapter 2, sprinters in the past may have been overdoing the warm-up.

The racing plan the runner should select will depend upon several factors. The 6 most important of these are described below.

1. The kind of opponent against whom the performer is competing must be considered. As stated previously, this event is now run in lanes over the total distance. A runner must practice and establish the pace best suited to his own particular style and ability. He must not be drawn out too fast by a runner who prefers to cover the first part of the race very quickly. (During indoor season, the 440-yards is normally run in lanes around only two turns [or 220 yards] from the start, from which point on it's every man for himself. Under such conditions a runner must be close to the leaders at all times if he is to have a chance at winning.)

Strategy in running, then, plays an important part in how best to utilize one's ability in such a race. A runner must recognize if a competitor is setting too fast a pace. It may be costly in energy output to keep up with him, and might result in trouble in the later stages of the race. He must also be aware of the situation when too slow a pace is set. Some runners will purposely slow down the pace if they have a great finish kick upon which they depend for winning races.

2. The condition of the track is another important factor. With the use of all-weather surfaces becoming prevalent throughout the country, tracks are usually in good running condition in all kinds of weather and help assure that an equal opportunity is available for all

competitors. Where such tracks are not available, some ideas of what to do under certain circumstances may be useful. For example, a wet, heavy track usually means that leg force against the ground should be greater than on a dry track. This same method of extra force in leg running should be applied on a loose surface. On a very hard track, the runner should use short spikes and attempt to run with less leg force against the ground or surface.

3. The number of competitors in the race is a further consideration. Under the official rules, there can only be as many competitors as there are available lanes. This eliminates much of the jockeying for position which is prevalent in longer distance races.

4. The predetermined plan for the race must be heeded. It is usually best for a coach to have a performer run a race in accordance with his own ability and nature; in other words, he must run adhering to a predetermined schedule. If the runner attempts to run a balanced race (the two 220-yard distances negotiated in equal time), then discussion of many of the preceding ideas concerning development of a race plan becomes unnecessary. However, a quarter-miler must still plan to accelerate for the first 60 or 70 yards after leaving the blocks, and in order to reach the desired running speed as quickly as possible. The key to success in this race is to maintain this initial speed throughout the entire distance until the last 110 yards, at which point a definite effort to kick or pick up momentum should begin. Fatigue (lactic acid build-up) will become a factor with which the runner must deal, and he must learn when and how long to stay relaxed and then pour it on so that he won't tie up before reaching the finish line. He must also learn to gauge his energy output so that he won't hold back and have "too much left" when the race is over.

5. The lane position and its effect also enter into the runner's racing plan. The principle of having all runners stay in lanes during a race has many advantages, which have already been discussed. It also has, in the opinion of coaches and athletes, some disadvantages. Lane 1 is often considered a handicap to a runner because of the location of the curb of the track. In all other lanes, a runner may stay extremely close to the inside portion of his lane, but the runner in lane 1 may have a subconscious fear of stepping on the curb and, therefore, runs a little wider than is necessary. Another disadvantage lies in the drawing of the outside lane. Most runners prefer a lane in the middle section of the track, where they will have a few runners behind and a few in front of them. The desire of most runners to have someone in front of them to "run at" makes these lanes the most valued in the draw. However, a coach must convince his athletes that the outside lanes do have an advantage, such as the turns being less severe, and

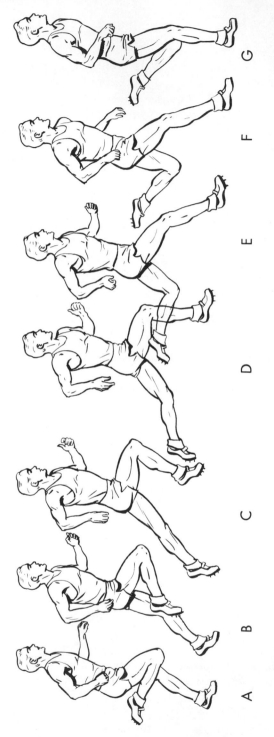

A   B   C   D   E   F   G

FIGURE 4–1. The 440 stride. The runner demonstrates in (A), (B), and (C) good body position, knee lift, and drive off the toe of the left foot. (D), (E), (F), and (G) These show a somewhat exaggerated shoulder swing that is not considered to be good form.

H   I   J   K   L   M   N   O

FIGURE 4–1 (cont.). The 440 stride. (H) through (O) The runner is running with relaxed arms and hands. The trail foot is raised very little above the knee. The lead foot is striking the ground with a ball-heel-toe action.

that they can run them at their own pace without fear of being "drawn out" too fast by a fast starter. A top-notch runner should be placed in the outside lanes at every opportunity in practice and in a dual meet. The experience he gains running in these lanes during the dual meet season will be most profitable if he draws such a lane in the championship meets.

A point to remember regarding lane position is that those runners drawing the inside lanes (since lanes are used for the entire race in most instances) must not be misled in connection with their relative positions. If they are close to the leaders in the outside lanes, then they are apt to be actually in front as they come off the last turn. Those drawing the outside lanes must not be lulled into believing they are far in front because, unless they have a very good lead over the other outside lane runners, they will be behind as they come into the homestretch.

6. The type of runner the individual is will be an additional influence. Quarter-milers are usually classified into two types, sprinters and half-milers. The differences in these two classifications are not clear-cut because many good runners can compete well in races from the sprints up to and including the half mile. The sprinter type possesses good speed and can run a good hundred, a better 200 yards, and come into his own at the quarter-mile distance. This man is invaluable as a relay member, since he can compete successfully in the 440-yards (under the new rules this type of runner has an extra 10 meters in which to accelerate, which may be all he needs to run with the very fast starter), 880-yards, and one mile relays. The half-miler type can run an excellent 440 yards as well as a good half mile. Although these two types of runners are competing in the same event, their workout schedule will be much different. The sprinter will continue to work on his speed and pace, and may never run farther than 330 yards in practice. The half-miler must also work on pace, but he will emphasize speed as well as conditioning for the 880-yards.

training program

There are three schools of thought with reference to training for this event. Some coaches believe in some overdistance work, such as 550- or 660-yard runs, even during the midseason period. Others believe in running overdistance only during early season. Possibly the extreme in the overdistance plan is the program that has the runner do cross-country running from fall until spring, then concentrate on the sprints and occasionally run the 880 during the spring. Most top American 440 men follow the sprinter's program (but more intensely), with some overdistance work interspersed with the sprint work.

On the other hand, some coaches do not believe in having their performers run overdistance at any time. Rather, they want their 440 men to run up to 330 yards in practice, often as fast as possible. The only time the entire distance is run is in a meet. (The authors favor the *underdistance* theory more than the overdistance concept for the performer who runs only the 440, but believe *some of both are necessary*.) The type of runner helps decide on the training and conditioning program selected. A sprinter type will probably work out with the dash men, while the 880 type will work out with the middle-distance runners. However, a runner lacking speed will want to run more of the shorter distances. Conversely, the runner lacking endurance will want to work, at least in the early season, on some overdistance. Regardless of the type of runner, the 440 man must do a good deal more work in practice than a short distance sprinter. The 440 man's run does not demand the explosiveness required of the short distance sprint performer, and he is usually physiologically and psychologically better prepared for endurance training.

WORKOUT SCHEDULES

PRE- TO EARLY-SEASON WORKOUT SCHEDULE FOR 440-YARD DASH

Monday
1. Do stretching exercises.
2. Warm-up by running wind sprints and jogging from 1 to 2 miles.
3. Run 1 × 660 yards or 1 × 550 yards, full effort.
4. Run 1 × 330 yards at pace, running first 220 at 24 to 25 and finishing strong.
5. Run 2 × 220 yards at pace speed, 24 to 25.
6. Run 10 × 110-yard wind sprints (jog 110 between).
7. Jog and walk 2 to 4 laps for cool-down.
8. Interval should be liberal at first, progressively getting shorter as conditioning increases.

Tuesday
1. Do stretching exercises.
2. Warm-up by running wind sprints and jogging from 1 to 2 miles.
3. Run 8 × 220 yards at pace speed, 23 to 25 seconds.

4. Do interval running 2 to 4 minutes, jogging between runs.
5. Run 2 × 220 yards at pace speed, 24 to 25.
6. Run 10 × 110-yard wind sprints (jog 110 between).

Wednesday
1. Do stretching exercises.
2. Warm-up by running wind sprints and jogging from 1 to 2 miles.
3. Run 3 × 330's at full speed.
4. Do interval running 4 to 8 minutes, jogging between runs.
5. Run 2 × 220 yards at pace speed, 24 to 25.
6. Run 10 × 110-yard wind sprints (jog 110 between).

Thursday
1. Do stretching exercises.
2. Warm-up by running wind sprints and jogging from 1 to 2 laps.
3. Run 2 or 3 × (110-220-110) 220's at race pace, interval between sets of 3 minutes and 1 minute.
4. Run 10 × 110's wind sprints.

Friday
Thorough warm-up.

Saturday
Competition.

Sunday
Brief workout, 20 to 30 × 110 yards.

EARLY-SEASON WORKOUT SCHEDULE FOR 440-YARD DASH

Monday
1. Do stretching exercises.
2. Warm-up by running wind sprints and jogging 1 to 2 miles.
3. Run 1 × 660 yards, full effort.
4. Run 1 × 550 yards at pace speed, running the first 440 at 52 seconds.
5. Run 1 × 300 yards at pace speed, running the first 220 at 24 to 25 seconds.
6. Run 10 × 110 yards wind sprints.
7. Jog and walk 2 to 4 laps as cool-down.

Tuesday
1. Do stretching exercises.
2. Warm-up by running wind sprints and jogging from 1 to 2 miles.
3. Run 8 × 220's at pace speed at 23 to 25 seconds.
4. Rest 2 to 4 minutes between runs.
5. Run 10 × 110 yards wind sprints.
6. Jog and walk 2 to 4 laps.

Thursday
1. Do stretching exercises.
2. Warm-up by running wind sprints and jogging 1 to 2 miles.
3. Start with sprinters, concentrating on building up race pace quickly (10 to 20 starts).
4. Run 20 to 30 × 110's wind sprints.
5. Jog and walk 2 to 4 laps for cool-down.

Friday
Thorough warm-up and stretching.

Saturday
Time trials or early season competition.

Sunday
Brief workout, jogging, and 20 to 30 × 110's.

MID-SEASON WORKOUT SCHEDULE FOR 440-YARD DASH

Monday
1. Do stretching exercises.
2. Warm-up by running wind sprints and jogging from 1 to 2 laps.
3. Run 1 × 500 or 3 × 330's at full speed.
4. Rest interval should be 4 to 5 minutes between runs.
5. Run 20 × 110's with 110 jog between.
6. Jog and walk 2 to 4 laps for cool-down.

Tuesday
1. Do stretching exercises.
2. Warm-up by running wind sprints and jogging from 1 to 2 laps.
3. Run 4 to 6 × 220's at full speed.
4. Rest interval should be 4 to 5 minutes between runs.
5. Run 20 × 110's with 110 jog between.
6. Jog and walk 2 to 4 laps for cool-down.

Wednesday
1. Do stretching exercises.
2. Warm-up by running wind sprints and jogging from 1 to 2 laps.
3. Do starts with sprinters (10 to 20).
4. Run 20 to 30 × 110's wind sprints.
5. Jog and walk 2 to 4 laps for cool-down.

or

Wednesday
1. Do stretching exercises.
2. Warm-up by running wind sprints and jogging 1 to 2 miles.
3. Run 3 × 330's at full speed.
4. Rest 4 to 8 minutes between runs.
5. Run 10 × 110 yards wind sprints.
6. Jog and walk 2 to 4 laps.

Thursday
1. Do stretching exercises.
2. Warm-up by running wind sprints and jogging 1 to 2 miles.
3. Run 4 × 100's at full speed.
4. Run 3 × 100's, first 20 yards fast out of blocks, then go into 440 pace.
5. Rest 3 to 5 minutes between runs.
6. Run 10 × 110 yards wind sprints.
7. Jog and walk 2 to 4 laps.

Friday
Warm-up on grass by jogging and stretching.

Saturday
Rest or work out briefly.

Sunday
Brief workout, jogging 20 to 30 × 110 yards.

LATE-SEASON WORKOUT SCHEDULE FOR 440-YARD DASH

Monday
1. Do stretching exercises.
2. Warm-up by running wind sprints and jogging on the grass for 4 laps.
3. Run 3 × 330's at full speed.

4. Rest 5 to 10 minutes between runs.
5. Run 10 to 15 × 110 yards wind sprints.
6. Jog and walk 2 laps.

Tuesday
1. Do stretching exercises.
2. Warm-up by running wind sprints and jogging on grass for 4 laps.
3. Run 4 × 220's at full speed.
4. Rest 5 to 10 minutes between runs.
5. Run 10 to 15 × 110 yards wind sprin's.
6. Jog and walk 2 laps.

Wednesday
1. Do stretching exercises.
2. Warm-up by running wind sprints and jogging on the grass for 4 laps.
3. Run 5 × 150's at full speed.
4. Rest 5 minutes between runs.
5. Run 10 to 15 × 110 yards wind sprints.
6. Jog and walk 2 laps.

Thursday
1. Do stretching exercises.
2. Warm-up with wind sprints on the grass for 4 laps.
3. Run 3 × 100's at full speed.
4. Run 3 × 100's out of blocks, full speed first 20 yards, then go into 440 pace.
5. Run 10 to 15 × 110 yards wind sprints.
6. Jog and walk 2 laps.

Friday
Light workout, thorough warm-up.

Saturday
Participate in meet.

Sunday
Brief workout, jogging 20 to 30 × 110 yards.

It is interesting to note that this system of training may be modified and used for any running event; it is now being used extensively throughout Europe and other parts of the world.

helpful hints

The runner should:

1. Learn to become as good a sprinter as possible while practicing for the 440 dash.

2. Learn to run as fast as possible for 330 yards and still not be straining.

3. Determine whether he is a sprinter or a half-miler type and concentrate on improving endurance or speed respectively during early season workouts.

4. Get into proper condition by running repeat 220's, 330's, and even some 440's, remembering that it takes more stamina to run the 440 than it does to sprint.

5. If not competing in other fall sports, participate in cross-country in the fall.

6. Study running action as seen in personal film. Ask the coach to help point out good and poor motions. Correct any errors.

7. Learn to pace himself by being able to run 220's at predetermined speeds.

8. Learn to run as a sprinter (even though he is the 880 type), but with less arm movement and lower leg lift.

9. Remember there is no such thing as a "float" in this race. Just run as relaxed as possible.

10. Learn to run the curves at full speed. In a race, he should come into the last curve under control and sprint on the curve.

11. If he is a half-miler type in competition, he will need to make the sprinters in the race run fast during the early part (first 220), or else they will sprint him at the finish.

12. Have a racing plan in mind for each race run. Since a race is over so quickly, each runner must be constantly on the alert to keep from being forced into "running another's race."

TWO

RUNS

880-YARD RUN

Just as the "50-second flat" 440 was considered fast in the past, so the "2-minute flat" 880 was likewise a top performance. The method often used in running this event in early American track history involved the good performer jogging a lap to within 220 yards or less of the finish line before he began an all-out sprint that he maintained to the finish.

One of America's earliest and best half-milers was L. E. Meyers, Manhattan Athletic Club, New York City, who ran first as an amateur and later as a professional. He won American titles in the 100, 200, 440, and half-mile. It is evident that he had sprinting ability. In 1885 he ran the 880 in 1:55.4 to establish a new record. He undoubtedly practiced part of the time as a sprinter, and probably ran just to win in most of the longer races.

Another sprinter type, Ted Meredith, University of Pennsylvania, held world records in both the 440 and 880. In 1916 he set the 880 record of 1:52.25 which stood for 10 years.

Some great 880 men attacked Merdith's record. Dr. Otto Peltzer of Germany in 1926 set a new world record of 1:51.6. Douglas G. A. Lane of Cambridge University, England, won the Olympic title in 1928 through having a detailed knowledge of his opponents and being able to capitalize on his own strength and their weaknesses with the surprise of sprinting the last 220 yards of the race. In 1934, Ben Eastman of Stanford University ran the 880 in 1:49.8. In 1939, Rudolph Harbig of Germany, also a good 220 runner and a great 440 (:46.0) man, set the world record in the 800 meters in the unheard-of time of 1:46.6.

After World War II, the Olympic Games were resumed in London in 1948. Among the runners in the 800-meter race were Wint, a Jamaican, who was 6′ 4″ tall (and who had already won the 400-meter race in :46.2); Barten, University of Michigan, a fine 1,500-meter runner and conqueror in an earlier meet of Whitfield, the American champion, who was also in the race; and Hansenne, a Frenchman who had set a new French 800-meter record of 1:48.3 and was also a fine 1,500-meter runner.

Many observers at the Games thought that if Wint, Barten, or Hansenne had been even with Whitfield 200 meters from the finish, they probably would have defeated him because of their strong finishes. Whitfield's strategy was to get a good lead over his opponents and try to win by saving enough energy to maintain pace. In other words, his times of :54.2 and :55.1 for the first and second 400 meters were close to even time for each quarter. On several previous occasions he had won important races by running his races at around even time for each quarter. Probably more important, most of his 220's during the half-mile were close to the same times, being between 26 and 28 seconds. Physiologically, it is sound to attempt near even pace for each quarter. However, it may be even better to concentrate on each 220, and to run the first 440 slightly faster than the second. Whitfield was also able to win the 1952 Olympic 800-meter race, and he ran it in the same time for each quarter as he did in the 1948 race.

In the 1956 Olympic 800-meter race at Melbourne, Thomas Courtney of the United States defeated Derek Johnson of Great Britain in a new Olympic time, 1:47.7. Courtney misjudged the distance he could sprint; he had to relax and let Johnson pass him briefly. He then took up his sprint again and defeated Johnson by inches.

During the early 1960's Peter Snell of New Zealand established himself as the best runner in the middle distances. For a time he held virtually every record from the 600-yard through the 1-mile run. His greatest achievement was winning the 1960 800-meter Olympic race with the time of 1:45.1, setting a new Olympic record, and also winning the 1,500-meter, which he ran in 3:38.1. In the mid-1960's Snell was replaced by Jim Ryun of Kansas University as the top middle runner. He set world records of 1:44.9 in the 880 and 3:51.1 in the mile.

Both of these men possessed great physical strength and were of good size, each being over 6 feet in height and weighing around 175 pounds. They also possessed the ability to sprint the last quarter of the race at top speed. This is an asset to any good middle-distance runner.

The 880 event in the 1968 Olympics was replete with uncontrollable factors that made advance selection of the winner a difficult task. The effect of the altitude, the failure of Jim Ryun to earn a berth because of previous illness, and the injury to Canada's Bill Crothers were the foremost influencing factors. The race ended in a strong duel between Ralph Doubell of Australia, the eventual winner in a new Olympic record of 1:44.3, and Wilson Kiprugut of Kenya, second in a time of 1:44.5. The race was settled in the last 40 to 50 yards, when Doubell outran Kiprugut. Tom Farrell of the United States depended on a brilliant stretch kick to finish third in a personal best of 1:45.4.

Many high school runners have been able to run the 880 yards in under 1 minute and 55 seconds. Better form, greater speed, use of proper pace, greater knowledge about running and opponents, better running tracks, improved training methods, more running experience, and a desire to excel developed through interest in the event are some of the factors that account for increasingly better times.

characteristics of the 880 man

The 880 men are, as a rule, taller and heavier than the quarter-milers. They should be individuals who enjoy running and will run hard enough to get into proper condition. Since this event is the first of the long runs, they should prefer running by themselves to constant participation in team games. However, this situation is not as pronounced as in the longer runs. (*See* Chapter 1 for other comments.) An individual with good speed for a 440 run, enough endurance to run a mile in good time (or ability and desire to gain endurance), knowledge of or willingness to learn pace, determination to practice and perform well in the distance, fierce desire to win, even rhythmic stride, and ability to relax while running at a fast pace should be a good 880-yard runner.

correct form

The running form of the 880 runner differs from that of men in the short and long sprints. However, some of the main points on sprinting in Chapter 2 apply in several respects to running the 880. At the start, the 880 runner does not have to be quite so anxious to beat his opponents off the blocks as the runner in the shorter distances, although every fraction of a second counts. Since the half-miler often starts without the use of starting blocks, some of them consider the start as not particularly important. Six of the elements that go to make up good running form in the 880 follow.

1. *The body is kept relaxed while running.* This is partially accomplished by keeping the mouth open and the lower jaw relaxed. The hands and arms are also carried loose and the wrists relaxed and flexed as the runner moves. The diaphragm (breathing muscle above stomach) is lifted high in order to keep from tensing the abdominal muscles. This movement can be practiced during walking.

2. *The arms are normally carried low* and are not moved very high in front or very far to the rear, but move in the same horizontal plane as the sprinter's, without the high vigorous action to the front and rear. Too vigorous arm action to the rear tends to tense the shoulders (*see* Fig. 5-1).

3. *The body is held upright, with no lean.*

4. *The leg stride is extremely long, with an accentuated hip swing.* The runner appears to be sitting on his hips, and his legs swing back and forth in an arc as he runs. However, this does not mean he should overstride in order to have a good stride. This is one of the pitfalls into which an inexperienced runner may fall. He feels that the longer the stride, the more territory he can cover. However, a long stride takes more enegry than a short stride, and a runner who overstrides may consume so much energy that he is defeated by a runner of less ability and physical condition who avoids overstriding. The actual running stride taken depends upon the leg length of the runner. A short-legged runner should not normally take as long a stride as a long-legged runner. However, the more hip swing (loose, relaxed pelvic and hip region increases the ability to move the legs) the runner can develop, the more he can increase his stride.

5. *The knee action is high enough to enable the runner to extend the foot forward easily* and to permit the hip (pelvis) to swing forward on the side of the swinging leg (*see* Fig. 5-1).

6. *A knowledge of pace and good physical condition* is essential

in the 880. The merit of running a paced race is evident as more and more top milers are able to run the 880 in excellent and even world record time. However, the world's best half-milers are those who have the speed of quarter-milers but decide to concentrate on the 880.

racing strategy

Among the important principles for a performer running the 880 are "know yourself" and "know your opponent." There is no substitute for experience in running if the performer learns during these experiences. Knowledge of a runner's own capabilities and of his opponent's style and ability are gained mainly through awareness of them during competitive situations.

Some of the questions that a runner may ask himself in planning strategy prior to a race are:

1. Am I the type of runner who has above average speed, or must I depend upon stamina alone?

2. Does my opponent have a good "kick" during the last 80 yards?

3. Can my opponent sustain his "kick" for a distance of 220 yards?

4. Is my opponent of such a competitive nature that his desire to win can be dampened by my passing him during the last 50 yards (just as the last curve is completed)?

The answers to such questions should help the runner design an intelligent racing plan.

Some racing tactics which should be considered are:

1. Stay close to the leaders, but do not be fooled by some "rabbit" who goes out too fast at the start or during the middle of the race.

2. Know pace well enough to run each 220 yards near the planned time.

3. Avoid getting "boxed" so that an even pace cannot be maintained, body contact results, and the leaders get too far ahead. It is usually better to run on the outside shoulder of the opponent than to follow him. This position will enable the runner to pass the other runner(s) when he desires to do so.

4. Be convinced that it is possible to defeat anyone entered in the race. An athlete must be fearless and confident. He must know that he can maintain an even, fast pace for the first 660 yards of this race, and that he will finish the last 220 yards with even a little extra left at the finish. The common tendency among many 880 runners is to slow down the pace during the third 220 yards of the race. However, the ambitious runner should make sure that he maintains the same relaxed pace that he used when running the first 440 yards.

A   B   C   D   E   F   G

H   I   J   K   L   M   N

FIGURE 5–1. The 880 stride. A champion 880-yard runner is shown in full stride during the 880-yard race. His knee lift is good. His ankles are relaxed and the drive from the toe of the rear foot is excellent. His arms are carried rather high for an 880 runner. His hands are relaxed. He is getting good hip swing. His kick-up behind is not too high.

WORKOUT SCHEDULES

training program

A workout schedule must be flexible in order to allow for individual differences. The total amount of work done should be about the same for all 880 runners, but the practice lap times may differ to adjust to the athlete's individual ability for the task at hand.

THE WARM-UP USED THROUGHOUT THE SEASON

1. Jog 2 laps slowly, using good form, since this is where both good and bad habits are formed.
2. Do a sequence of limbering and stretching exercises.
3. Again, jog and walk 2 laps.
4. Run wind sprints for 4 laps.
    a. First 2 laps: run the straightaways and walk the curves. When running the straightaways, start slowly and then accelerate.
    b. Second 2 laps: run the straightaways and jog the curves.
5. Walk 2 laps.

PRIOR TO COMPETITIVE MEETS

Monday: combination of distances
1. Run 1 × 1,320 yards at full effort or 2 to 3 × 1,320 yards at a pace that is not too strenuous, interspersed with a walking or jogging interval in which recovery is nearly complete. As training progresses, increase pace and shorten walking or jogging intervals.
2. Run 880 yards at established pace.
3. Jog 880 yards.
4. Run 440 yards at established pace.
5. Jog 440 yards.
6. Run 10 × 110 yards wind sprints.
7. Walk and jog 2 to 3 laps to cool off and to reduce heart rate to near normal.

Tuesday: 440's
1. Run 10 to 12 × 440's, depending on age and strength of performer.
    a. Start at 72 seconds and drop 1 second per week.

b. Run a 440, then walk and/or jog a 440 and repeat until 10 to 12 are completed.
2. Run 10 × 110 yards.
3. Walk and jog 2 to 3 laps and go to showers.

Wednesday: 220's
1. Run 15 to 20 × 220's, depending on age and strength of performer. (This can be increased to 25 for a top performer.)
   a. Start at 32 seconds pace and drop 1 second per week.
   b. Jog a 220.
   c. Run 10 × 110 yards.
   d. Walk and jog 2 to 3 laps and go to showers.

Thursday: 880's
1. Run 6 to 10 × 880's.
   a. Start at 2:20 pace and drop 2 seconds per week.
   b. Run 880, then jog 880, repeat until 3 to 5 are completed.
   c. Run 10 × 110 yards.
2. Walk and jog 2 to 3 laps and go to showers.

Friday: 150's (speed workout)
1. Run 15 to 30 × 150's.
   a. Run at between 17- to 20-second pace, depending on performer's speed.
   b. When running 150's, accelerate slowly up to top floating speed (220 float); this acceleration should occur within 50 to 75 yards from the start. Jog back and repeat until 15 to 30 are completed.
2. It is recommended that the runner use a 150-yard straightaway run on grass, if possible.
3. Walk and jog 2 or 3 laps and go to showers.

Saturday
Time trial or early season competition.

Sunday
Run easy cross-country away from track in the park.

REGULAR SEASON

Monday: combination of distances
1. Run 1 × 990 yards, full effort, with concentration being placed on running first and second 440's. Run relaxed and at an even

pace (within [3 to 5] seconds of maximum 880 effort). Then gradually increase pace over last 110 yards.
2. Jog for 10 minutes.
3. Run and jog 110, 220, 440, 440, 220, 110. The performer must keep moving by running distances at pace speed. Alternate the run and jog at the distance listed.
4. Run 10 × 110 yards.

Tuesday: 220's
1. Run 8 to 10 repeat 220's in 24 to 26 seconds, or run 4 in which speed depends on whether speed or endurance is needed.
2. Run 10 × 110 yards.
3. Walk and jog 2 or 3 laps and go to showers.

Wednesday: 440's
1. Run 10 to 12 repeat 440's at race pace, jogging a 440 between. (Interval of 3 to 4 minutes.)
2. Drop down the 440 time regularly from preseason workout schedule.
3. Run 10 × 110 yards.
4. Walk and jog 2 to 3 laps and go to showers.

Thursday: 150's
1. Run 15 to 20 × 150's sprints.
2. Work on form and relaxation.

Friday
Warm-up thoroughly, but no hard running should be done.

Saturday
Participate in meet.

Sunday
Brief workout: 20 to 40 × 200 yards at slow pace.

summary and additional comments

1. An 880 runner must develop speed in order to become a top performer.
2. Many 880 runners have enough speed to run an acceptable and sometimes even near to a world record 440.
3. A runner in this event should attempt to run his best races at

close to even pace for each 440, with the first 440 run slightly faster than the second.

    4. The 880-yard run is the beginning of the distance runs, and the participant will have to run many practice laps by himself or in the company of a few runners. Conversation will be at a minimum at best.

    5. A knowledge of pace is essential for success. The runner must not be fooled by a "rabbit" in a race.

    6. The running form in the 880 is different from the 440 in that:

      a. The arms are carried lower and their action is not as vigorous.

      b. The body is kept upright with *no lean*. (This is the same in the 440.)

      c. The leg stride is slightly longer, with an accentuated hip swing. However, the runner should not overstride.

      d. The knee action is not as high.

    7. Good racing tactics involve staying close to the leaders, running at an even pace, avoiding getting "boxed," and having confidence.

    8. An 880 runner should run cross-country to develop endurance.

    9. The 880 man should constantly strive for relaxation as he runs. (*See* Chapter 2 on relaxation.)

    10. In his best races, an 880 runner should have expended all his energy and finished the race almost completely exhausted.

    11. An 880 man should run many 220's and 440's to develop speed.

    12. Exercises to loosen up the hip region and to help the shoulders and arms become relaxed are recommended.

    13. Much overdistance running in mid- and late season is not advocated for most of those who run the 880 as their specialty. However, training for the mile doesn't seem to interfere with running the 880, especially at the championship level. Yet it must be remembered that most world 880-yard (800-meter) champions are faster in the 440 and 880 than are most mile champions.

MILE RUN

The mile race is one of today's chief attractions in track and field. It holds this position of recognition partly because it is such an exacting test of speed, stamina, and sound judgment in training and racing. Spectators can pick their favorites and have the time to cheer them as they go around the track 4 times. The layman can see the attempts of various runners to use strategy. For the beginning performer in the mile, there are no absolute mechanical principles that must be followed.

Coaches and physiologists have studied and measured the distribution of effort at different stages of the mile run. Although some of their findings have been used by milers in training and competition, running in the most natural and relaxed manner often proves easiest and most economical. This means that the exact procedure for each runner often becomes an individual matter that can be worked out only after a long period of study, self-observation, and determination, supplemented by the advice and help of the coach. This does not mean that the miler will not be affected by the findings of research and experimentation. Some present training and competitive programs have received their initial stimulus from the laboratory. Concepts have to be subjected to study and either accepted or rejected on the basis of results on the track.

There are, however, certain "musts" that apply to most milers which will be presented in the following pages. The ideal miler usually has an average build, long legs, and a natural, loose-striding running action. Of course, there have been many successful exceptions to this body type. Regardless of body build, the miler must have the will to develop the natural talents he possesses. He must also have a nervous system sufficiently high strung and an oxygen consumption system of top ability to enable him to produce a maximum effort far beyond that of the normal individual.

great performances of the past

Even the general public is aware that distance running times have been lowered with amazing rapidity in recent years. Within the past decade there have been many new world records in the mile run alone. Walter George of England was probably the first great star in the mile and 2-mile distances. In 1882 he set a world mark of 4:21.4 in the mile. As a professional in 1886, he ran a mile in 4:12.8. This mark was not surpassed until 1915, when Norman Taber ran the distance in 4:12.6. Paavo Nurmi, the famous smooth-striding Finn, lowered the record to 4:10.4 in 1923.

The first to break Nurmi's 4-lap time was Jules Ladoumègue, a Frenchman, who ran the distance in 4:09.2 in 1931. Jack Lovelock, the speedy New Zealander with a terrific finish kick, ran the mile in 4:07.6 in 1933. Glenn Cunningham, who had the longest competitive career of any American distance star, set a new mile world record of 4:06.8 in 1934. His record lasted 3 years. Then Sydney Wooderson, a small, slender Englishman, lowered it in 1937 to 4:06.4.

The value of much repeat speed work, used by many milers (especially the Americans), and of the Swedish speed play (*Fartlek*) became evident when two Swedish runners, Arne Andersson and Gunder Hägg, began a fine series of duels that resulted in a new world record by Hägg of 4:06.2 in 1942. Andersson equaled this time a week later, but 2 months later Hägg lowered it again to 4:04.6. The following spring Andersson ran the mile in 4:02.6. The two great runners took turns defeating each other and finally, in July, 1945, running on the fast track at Malmo, Sweden, Hägg lowered the mile record to 4:01.4, defeating Andersson, Rune Persson, and Lennart Strand. Leading all the way, Hägg ran at an almost even pace for the last 3 laps. The prevailing racing concept at that time was that a competitor should run the first quarter of the race faster than the other quarters, then attempt to run the last 3 quarters at even pace.

Andersson and Hägg indicated by their performances that the much sought 4-minute mile was within grasp, but it was not until May 6, 1954, that Roger Bannister, the Great Britain champion, broke the 4-minute barrier with a new world record time of 3:59.4. Then on June 23, 1967, Jim Ryun of Kansas and the U.S. established the present accepted world's record of 3:51.1.

The altitude and a previous illness took much from the efficiency of Ryun during the 1968 Olympics. In one of the finest tactical races ever run in Olympic history, Kipchoge Keino of Kenya ran an unbelievable 3:34.9 for 1,500 meters in establishing a new Olympic record with the second fastest time ever run in this event. Ryun finished second in the excellent time of 3:37.8, well under what he expected to run and, for that matter, what the experts estimated he would need to run to win.

types of milers

There has been a variety of body types among the great milers. Nurmi was a rather short man with a smooth stride who lacked native speed and had to depend on his knowledge of constant pace in order to wear down his opponent. Lovelock, the thin, light-footed New Zealander who followed the pace set by someone else, won with his terrific finish kick. Cunningham, the barrel-chested American who took up running to help rehabilitate legs burned in a childhood accident, ran or walked many miles each day. He was the first American to approach the amount of training work for distance running that is employed by most European runners.

Jim Ryun, who is tall and rather heavy in weight for a miler, is an excellent example of one who displays relaxed smoothness in his running style. He wastes no energy with his arm action, his knee lift is not exaggerated, and he runs with his chest held out. Ryun is blessed with great natural speed, as his explosiveness in the last 220 yards of his races has demonstrated (timed at :26.3 during his world record performance). There seems to be no limit to his ability, and even greater performances can be expected of him within the next few years.

running form

It has been noted that sprinters and quarter-milers strike the ground with the bottom of their toes first, and that half-milers strike the ground with their toes only in the earlier stages of the race. In mile or longer races, it has been found that the ball of the runner's foot will hit first, followed by the heel. The miler performs a rolling motion with his foot against the ground, and does not land flatfooted. A runner who lands flatfooted will tire rapidly because of the consequent pounding action, which is very fatiguing to the legs.

Naturalness in running is one of the most important acquisitions for the miler. He should use a freely moving leg action and have a stride of medium length, making no conscious effort to lengthen or shorten the natural stride. A good front knee lift is important, especially when the runner starts his final kick. The feet are not lifted in the rear action much higher than the level of the knee. The ankles must be relaxed when the foot strikes the ground. The body is held erect, with no body lean. The chest should be thrust out and the shoulders held back but relaxed. This position will allow the runner good chest expansion while running.

The arms are used mostly for balance purposes in distance running. It is important to remember that the shoulders are relaxed, with the forearms carried parallel to the ground. The elbows of the runner are moved back and forth naturally as he runs, but must not restrict the movement of the chest cavity or interfere with the natural swing of the shoulders. An easy, relaxed arm action synchronized with the action of the legs is the goal of the mile runner. Vigorous arm action will fatigue the arms and shoulders and slow the runner.

Each runner has a natural running style which is best suited to his size and build. This principle applies especially to the action of the arms. It would be foolish to say that all milers must have the same style of running. However, from watching champions in action and studying slow motion pictures of their running forms, the athlete may pick up hints that might improve his own style of running. There are certain principles of movement that apply to mile running which may be used by all mile aspirants. These involve pacing, arm and leg action, no body lean, relaxing, and so on, as mentioned in previous discussions (*see* Fig. 6-1).

training program

There are some differences of opinion on the type of training program best suited for accomplishing the desired results for the

A   B   C   D   E   F

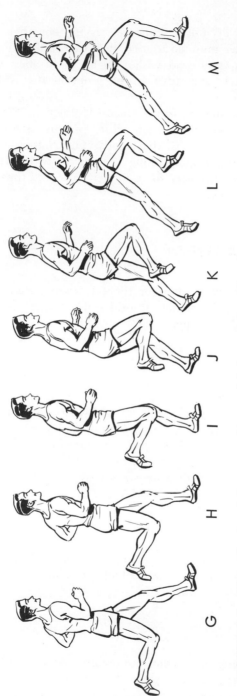

G H I J K L M

FIGURE 6-1. The mile run. A former world record holder for the mile run is shown here. Note the constant erect body position that he maintains by keeping the head, neck, trunk, and driving leg in alignment with each other. The front leg is relaxed and slightly flexed when landing. The rear foot is not raised above knee level. His chest is thrust out, his arms are carried rather high, and his hands are relaxed. In fact, the wrist is so relaxed that the hand can be seen to drop as he runs. There is no excessive swinging of the shoulder.

greatest number of milers. However, it is generally agreed that, primarily, the runner must do a great deal of running over a long period of time. The aspirant who wishes to be at his best during the competitive season must start his training program at least 6 months before the season opens.

The great distance coach, Gosta Holmer of Sweden, originated the *Fartlek* method of training, which means "speed play." This is usually done on grass or in the woods. The runner sets his own pace, running fast or just jogging along as suits his whim. It is thought that he will gradually run faster for a longer period of time as he continues this type of training.

WORKOUT SCHEDULES

A typical workout plan for the fall season, suggested by Holmer, is presented here. The athlete should train from 1 to 2 hours each day, according to this schedule.

FALL SEASON

1. Easy running on the grass for 5 to 10 minutes (as a warm-up).
2. Steady, hard speed work for a distance of ⅝ to 1¼ miles.
3. Rapid walking for about 5 minutes.
4. Easy running, interspersed by running wind sprints from 55 yards to 65 yards distance, and repeated until runner feels tired.
5. Easy running with 3 or 4 swift steps taken now and then.
6. Full speed runs uphill (165 to 220 yards).
7. Fast pace running for one minute following the uphill running mentioned in 6.

This training plan may be repeated many times, but the runner should remember that he must feel stimulated, not tired, after the daily workout.

MIDSEASON

The following is a typical midseason training schedule as recommended by coaches in the past. This is a so-called *Fartlek* workout, which not all coaches utilize except during early season. See schedule shown later for another type.

Monday
1. Do *Fartlek* for 45 minutes.
2. Run the first 40 yards of a race at competitive speed.
3. Repeat 1, 2, or 3 times. Do easy running for 5 minutes between these runs.
4. Walk and run easy to complete a 2-hour workout.

Tuesday
1. Do *Fartlek* for 20 minutes.
2. Run 880 yards on the track, 2 seconds per lap slower than time in a competitive race.
3. Repeat 1 and 2 until an hour has elapsed. Run easy on grass between and after each run.

Wednesday
Walk in the woods for 2 hours.

Thursday
Follow same schedule as Monday's, but run uphill 2 to 9 × 150 yards each time during the *Fartlek* portion.

Friday
Follow same schedule as Tuesday's, but run 4 × 440-yard laps instead of 2 × 880 yards. Run each lap one second slower than racing speed.

Saturday
Rest.

Sunday
Warm-up and run a mile. Run the first 440 yards and the last 100 yards of the distance at racing speed. Run each lap of the middle of the race 2 seconds slower than racing pace.

Racing workouts are done at the individual athlete's own pace. Work out at the competitive distance once every 10 days.

These schedules are not to be followed as blueprints. Each athlete must use initiative in planning his workouts with the help of his coach.

Other ideas. In a further interpretation and development of *Fartlek,* the runners practice *Fartlek* twice each week during early training, and once each week during competitive periods over the countryside or on a grass sports field. Speed is added by 220-yard bursts being done on the track 2 or 3 times each week. The runner does a series of such bursts at a speed faster than the average speed of his race. For instance, a 4:24 miler runs each 220 yards in 28 seconds. He runs 220 yards, walks back to the starting point and repeats, doing this until he begins to feel weary. The training is then finished off with about 30 minutes of easy running on the grass.

The training has been classified into 4 separate periods of progressive activity.

1. Conditioning period: January to mid-March. Walking, easy running, and indoor gymnastic exercises.

2. Preseason: Mid-March to mid-April. Running work and *Fartlek* with some speed training.

3. Early competitive season: Mid-April to early June. Training progress is same as that of the preseason, except there is one competitive run each week.

4. Competitive season: Early April to late June. The amount of training corresponds to the number of competitive races in which the runner participates. Usually the training is much like that of the preseason except that much less time is spent.

Interval training. Frank Stamptfl, who is now coaching in Australia and has developed some very fine distance competitors in England and Australia, has a theory on training somewhat different from those mentioned above. Two of the sub-4-minute milers he has coached are Merv Lincoln and former world record holder John Landy. Stamptfl strongly believes that the best way to develop stamina is through the "interval training" method. This simply means that the runners run 440 yards, jog 440 yards, and repeat this procedure as many as 20 times in one workout session. These repeat 440's are run at paced time for the distance of the race for which the athlete is training. When the athlete's physical condition is such that he can follow this procedure easily, he then runs repeat 440's with jogs of only 220 yards between.

The authors believe that this interval training plan helps develop some stamina and good judgment of pace, but it does not adequately develop two important phases of conditioning for the mile run—*speed* and *top endurance*. Some sub-4-minute milers are not endowed with a great deal of natural speed, but by practicing sprints at distances of 100 to 220 yards at full effort, running with fast leg action and good knee lift, they are able to develop the extra speed and endurance needed in running the mile.

The workload undertaken by today's distance runners is staggering. Every great runner from the mile on up trains on a 12 months basis, and usually twice per day. With high school runners running sub-4-minute miles and sub-9-minute two miles, there is no question that they are following the same vigorous schedule as are the older runners. The normal morning workout consists of from 4 to 10 miles of running, which varies in intensity depending on the level of competition, time of season, and day of the week.

The type of training schedule recommended by the authors is as follows:

PRESEASON WORKOUT FOR MILE RUN

Mornings

6 to 10 miles; do not run to the point of exhaustion. You should feel exhilarated as well as a little tired.

Monday: 440-yard runs

1. Start running 440-yard runs at 70-second pace and drop 1 second each week.
2. Run 440's 10 to 14 times, depending on age and strength.
3. Run 440, then jog 440, and repeat (2 minutes for the 440 jog).
4. Run 10 × 110's.
5. Walk and jog 2 to 3 laps and go to showers.

Tuesday: 220-yard runs

1. Start running 220's at 32- to 35-second pace and drop 1 second each week.
2. Run 20 yards 12 to 16 times.
3. Run 220, then jog 220 and repeat.
4. Run 10 × 110's.
5. Walk and jog 2 to 3 laps and go to showers.

Wednesday: 880-yard runs

1. Start running 880's at 2.20 pace and drop 2 seconds each week.
2. Run 880 yards 6 to 8 times.
3. Run 880 and jog 880 in about 5 minutes, and repeat.
4. Run 10 × 110's.
5. Walk and jog 2 to 3 laps and go to showers.

Thursday: 1,320-yard runs

1. Start running 1,320's at 3.35 pace and drop 2 to 3 seconds per week.
2. Run 1,320 yards 3 or 4 times.
3. Run 1,320 and then jog 1,320 (about 8 minutes), and repeat.

4. Run 10 × 110's.

5. Walk and jog 2 or 3 laps and go to showers.

Friday: combination of distances (breakdown)

1. Run 1 mile, first 3 laps at 72- to 76-second pace, accelerate on fourth lap, trying for a 60-second last lap.

2. Jog 1 mile.

3. Run 1,320, first 2 laps at 68- to 72-second pace, accelerate on third lap, trying for 65 seconds.

4. Jog 1,320.

5. Run 880, first lap in upper 60's, and accelerate on second lap, trying for 65 seconds.

6. Jog 880.

7. Run 440, first 220 in 35 seconds, and accelerate on second 220, trying for a 26- to 28-second 220.

8. Run 10 × 110's.

9 Jog 2 to 3 laps and go to showers.

Saturday

Time trial or early season competition.

Sunday

Cross-country workout away from the track, running 6 to 8 miles.

REGULAR SEASON WORKOUT FOR MILE RUN

Monday

1. Run 1 × 1,320 yards, full effort, or 2 to 3 × 1,320 yards at race pace, with 5 minute rest intervals in between.

2. Run 220, 440, 880, 440, 220. Performer keeps moving as he runs distance at race speed, then jogs distance.

3. Run 10 × 110's.

4. Jog 2 to 3 laps for cooling down.

Tuesday

1. Run 10 to 12 × 440's at 1 to 2 seconds below race pace.

2. Jog 440 between, not to exceed 70 seconds.

3. Run 10 × 110's.

4. Jog 2 or 3 laps to cool down.

Wednesday

1. Run 6 to 8 × 880's at race pace or slightly below.

2. Jog 880 between, not to exceed 2 minutes.

3. Run 10 × 110's.
4. Jog 2 or 3 laps to cool down.

Thursday
1. Run 15 to 20 × 220's at 2 or 3 seconds below race pace.
2. Jog 220 between, not to exceed 60 seconds.
3. Run 10 × 110's.
4. Jog 2 or 3 laps to cool down.

Friday
Light workout, but do a thorough warm-up.

Saturday
Competition day.

Sunday
Do sprint work, running 20 to 40 × 200's, or run 5 to 8 miles on cross-country course.

To help combat monotony involved with the standard workouts, certain combinations can be used:
4 × (110—220—110)
3 × (220—440—220)
2 × (440—880—440)
These are run as sets, with the jogging intervals between runs brief, and with additional time intervals established between sets.

It has also been found that placing the miler in an 880-yard race will occasionally help develop speed. Some of the better milers have run on the mile relay team with recorded times of *48 seconds* or less for their lap in the relay.

In summary, it might be said that there are 3 major goals for which the miler must train: (1) *endurance* acquired through the use of *Fartlek* activities and a lot of running; (2) *pace judgment* acquired through doing repeated quarter- and half-miles; and (3) *speed* acquired through participation in wind sprints and repeated 220's.

strategy and pace

There has been much discussion in the past regarding the ideal pace to set for running the mile in the time of 4 minutes or less. It is generally agreed that each of the 4 quarters should be run at nearly equal time, with the last half-mile possibly a little faster than the first half. Physiologists tell us that running the first quarter at near the athlete's maximum speed will build up a large oxygen debt which is impossible to overcome. The first quarter should usually be run about 1 to 2 seconds faster than the second quarter, because during the first 50 yards of the race the milers are running for the lead or a position near the leaders.

When Jim Ryun ran his record setting 3:51.1 mile at Bakersfield, California, in 1967, his lap times were :59 for the first quarter, :59.8 for the second, :58.5 for the third quarter, and :53.7 for the fourth quarter. His first half-mile was run in 1:58.9 and his second half in 1:52.2. The preceding year, at Berkeley, California, Ryun had established the previous world record of 3:51.3. His lap times on this occasion were :57.9 for the first quarter, :57.6 for the second, :59.8 for the third quarter, and :56.0 for the fourth quarter. His first half was 1:55.5 and his second half 1:55.8. This falls somewhat more in line with the recommended balanced pace idea, but, for strict accordance with the concept, his last half-mile should have been run slightly faster than the first.

There are several things that should be considered in planning the strategy for a race.

1. Many races are won by knowing the characteristics of the competing runner. Does he have a good "kick"? How far can he maintain this "kick"? Does he have the ability to sprint at the end of the mile? If it is known that an opponent has a good "kick" during the last 100 yards of the race, then a runner must set a fast pace during the early part in order to build up a lead, or to make his opponent run so fast to keep close that he has no kick left.

2. If the opponent is a strong runner but has no finishing kick, an opposing runner should let him set the pace and then outsprint him in the last 100 yards.

3. It is important that a runner attempt to keep his stride even throughout the race.

4. A runner should avoid running on the pole if there is danger he might be boxed in by the other runners. It is much better for him to run, in this case, on the outside of other competitors, and to try to avoid the congestion that may cause him to lose ground and force him to change his pace too often.

Physiological and psychological aspects. There have been many explanations offered as to what causes an athlete to get his "second wind" during the third lap of the mile run, but tolerance to the body stresses involved in running is thought by many to explain why experienced runners seldom seem to get the so-called "second wind."

It is the opinion of the authors that this phenomenon is more psychological than physical. For example, an athlete who has run the first lap reasonably fast thinks, "Can I keep up this pace for two more laps?" Most of the time he will run his last lap at a fast pace because he knows by this time that he can run it fast. The third-lap "tired feeling" he experiences must be disregarded; he must run as if he were just starting the race on this third lap. He must convince himself that the others in the race are just as tired as he is, and that his workout schedule has been sufficiently strenuous to train him to run the entire race as well as they. Runners have been able to overcome a "stitch in the side" by simply ignoring it and running as if they had no such pain. Soon they were able to tolerate this "trouble" and run a normal race. Actually, most top runners state that they do not experience this feeling.

The competitive season in the United States is very long and strenuous. Meets begin in early January and continue through June or later. Many runners are required to compete in races almost every Friday or Saturday. The workout schedule should be planned so that the runners will reach their peak of condition at the time of the more important meets in May and June. Acquiring the right mental attitude for these "big" meets is very important. A runner must mentally condition himself in advance for each race but must especially concentrate on winning the big meets.

The workouts should be varied enough to insure that no mental staleness occurs. There must be a feeling of joy and exhilaration in the running during the workouts, and a realization of accomplishment after the competition. Any runner who does not enjoy competing will usually not be a consistent winner.

helpful hints

The runner should:

1. Run "his own race," and not be misled by some runner who runs "all-out" early in the race. However, he should stay close enough to the leaders to be able to overtake them at the finish.

2. Be careful not to pick up the running rhythm of an opponent that is entirely unsuited to him. Again it should be said: Run at your own speed and pace.

3. Practice long hours in order to be successful. Enough time must be provided for the runner to condition himself properly before competition begins.

4. Remember that it is usually best to run on the pole in a race, especially in long-distance races.

5. Run most of the year in order to be "good" at distance run-

ning. Boys who compete in other sports should not forget to do some distance running each week.

6. Plan each particular race with his coach so that he will have in mind exactly what he must do; be flexible enough to modify plans to meet the situation.

7. Know his liabilities as well as his assets, and plan his training program and racing strategy accordingly.

8. Remember that mile runners have various body builds, and that unless he is extremely large he will have a chance. However, the moderately tall and average weight individuals are usually the most successful in this event.

9. Learn to relax when running by consciously relaxing the wrists and ankles. (*See* Chapter 2 on relaxation.)

10. Not do a great deal of jockeying back and forth when attempting to pass an opponent in a race. Pass him quickly, and, if possible, unexpectedly.

11. Attempt to make it costly in energy for an opponent to pass him, but should not expend too much energy in thwarting his move.

LONG-
DISTANCE
RUNNING

7

Long-distance races are usually considered as those of 2 miles and over. Proper techniques of training for distance running have undergone great changes in the last 10 years. However, *Fartlek,* interval running, and walking given distances were also part of the training used by most of the great runners of years ago. Nurmi, the Finn, one of the great distance men of all time, did repeat runs of from 200 to 1,500 meters while training. When the Swedish runners made their world records from 1930 to 1940, the method of repeat running was organized into *Fartlek.* The great Finnish runners, Salminen, Iso-Hollo, Askola, Hockert, and Lehtenen, who dominated the 5,000- and 10,000-meters in the 1936 Olympics used the interval training method. The fabulous Zatopek, who won the 5,000, 10,000, and Marathon events in the 1952 Olympic Games, used a combination of *Fartlek* and interval running in preparing for these races.

Kuts of Russia, Thomas of Australia, and Chataway of Great Britain improved their distance running by using training procedures composed of a combination of interval running and *Fartlek*. Recently, Clarke of Australia, Keino of Kenya, and Lindgren of the United States used *Fartlek* early in the season, followed by interval training, and climaxed by the use of the "logging miles" technique (simply running a given number of miles in one outing). However, Ron Clarke, the great runner from Australia, reverted to the overdistance or marathon principle of training, and at various times held virtually every record from the 2-mile through the 20,000-meters. In 1968, he simultaneously held world records in the 3-miles (12:52.4), 6-miles (26:47.0), 10-miles (47:12.8), 10,000-meters (27:39.4), 20,000-meters (59:22.8), and the distance covered in the 1-hour run.

On the other hand, Kipchoge Keino of Kenya has developed into a world class distance runner, holding world records in 3,000-meters and 5,000-meters in 13:24.2, while using a system of training completely different from Clarke's. By utilizing some of each method above, he incorporated various systems into one, to serve him as a miler as well as a distance runner. (He proved that he was a miler by winning the 1968 Olympic 1,500-meter run.)

The United States enjoyed its greatest day in distance running at the 1964 Olympics in Tokyo, when Bob Shul won the 5,000-meter in 13:48.8, with Bill Dellinger finishing third. In the 10,000-meter run, unheralded Billy Mills of the United States stunned the track world with a brilliant 28:24.4, a new Olympic record. Gerry Lindgren finished an excellent ninth in 29:20.6.

The United States did not fare as well in the 1968 Olympics, as no United States runner placed high in these events. But it is hoped that the future of distance running in the United States will be on the upgrade, as young men such as Gerry Lindgren of Washington State and Van Nelson of St. Cloud State still have many years of competitive running ahead of them.

characteristics of the long-distance runner

The ideal distance runner is short and tends to be light in weight, although he may be somewhat stocky. He has a slow pulse rate and likes activities that require endurance. He doesn't object to continuous practice of the same thing, and enjoys running by himself for hours. What is sheer monotony to others (running for long distances) is fun to him (*see also* Chapter 1). Boys with these characteristics should be successful at distance running. The essentials of good distance running are knowledge of pace, knowing how to conserve energy, knowing how to relax, and willingness to work very hard to achieve endurance.

running form

Emil Zatopek, the Czech, demonstrated good leg action and proper "stride length" in the three races (5,000-meters, 10,000-meters, and Marathon) he won in the 1952 Olympic Games. It was observed that he ran the 5,000-meters with a normal, relaxed, "short" stride, with no effort to lengthen or shorten it as he ran. However, in the 10,000-meters he cut down the length of his stride by dropping the lead foot to the ground sooner through having less knee lift. In the marathon race he used even *less* knee lift, and thus got a still shorter stride.

The foot in distance running should strike the ground almost directly under the body's center of gravity. If the foot hits the ground too far in front of the center of gravity, it will act as a "brake" on the runner's movement, tending to make his body react in the opposite direction. The foot should first strike the ground on the ball or sole, drop lightly down to the heel, then back to the ball of the foot, and from there to the big toe. The rear foot in the "pickup action" should not be raised higher than the knee of that leg as it comes up off the ground after the push-off. The contact of the foot with the ground is very brief, as is the time the leg is in the air. The knee of the front leg is not raised very high during the run, but is gently thrust forward to help keep the center of gravity over the lead foot.

The body should be held rather erect, with the chest pushed out during each stride. The body should be directly above the center of gravity as the foot contacts the ground.

The arms should be carried up high and across the chest in a relaxed position. They should move in a short circular action across the body. No undue swinging of the shoulders or rolling of the head should be allowed. However, the head and neck should be relaxed; the head may even flop a bit as the runner moves, especially in very long-distance runs. The goal of the runner should be *to try to conserve as much energy as possible,* and this would mean no extra use of the arms and shoulders. The arms are used for balance, moving in coordination with the legs, and the action may differ a little with each individual. *Relaxation while running* must be one of the distance runner's major physical and mental concerns. Learning to pace himself properly for the entire distance and adjusting to the physiological stress by tolerance are other musts (*see* Fig. 7-1).

training program

Among the things that have been learned about training for distance running is that *hard running over a long period of time* is

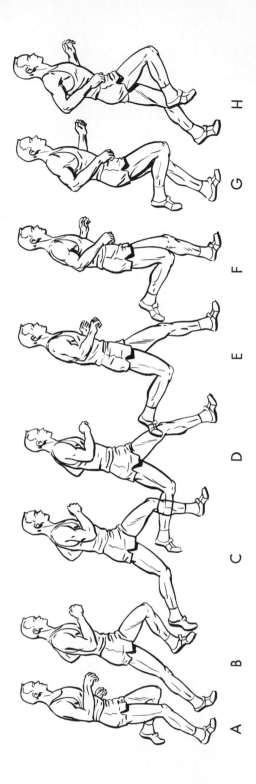

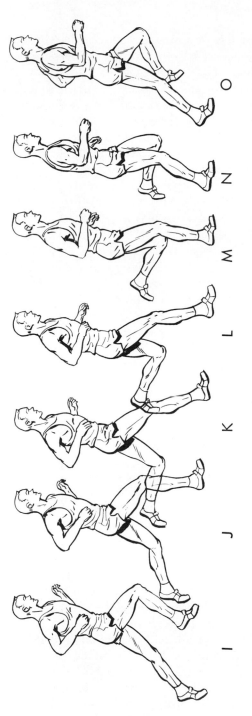

I   J   K   L   M   N   O

FIGURE 7-1.   Long-distance running. A former American record holder in the 2-mile and NCAA cross-country champion. He runs with his body upright, as seen in (F). The head is erect and the chest is out. The arms are carried high, with the hands relaxed. The hips swing freely. The knee is not raised too high and is slightly flexed when the ball of the foot strikes the ground. The rear foot is not raised above knee level. The stride is relatively short.

necessary for success. Training must be carried on throughout the entire year. The body must be conditioned to perform at close to its peak much of the time. Training must be increased and intensified *gradually* from early season to late season. An aspirant should not be led to believe that he can follow a champion's workout schedule for three months and hope to break the record. It will take time and hard work over many years for a good runner to emerge as a champion. In fact, most good distance runners currently work out twice a day in order to develop proper endurance.

There seems to be no single training schedule that will insure success for all performers. However, continuous running at a fast pace for long distances appears to be the best final endurance developer.

Training must not be too exhausting or wearisome. Schedules should be changed from time to time. The performer should usually run with others, and train at different places to get a change of scenery. He should run on grass whenever possible—a golf course is an ideal place to train. The performer should take the trouble to *develop the entire body*. The arms and upper torso of the runner can be developed with weights and by working on the parallel and horizontal bars. The legs can be developed with weights and by running up hills. Running up and down flights of stairs in a stadium is also a good training procedure for distance runners. Running in sand, in shallow water, and as previously mentioned, up hills, helps in the conditioning process.

WORK-TRAINING SCHEDULE

DURING OFF-SEASON—USING WEIGHTS

1. *Warm-up:* 1 set of 10 repeats using 100 pounds.
2. *Curls:* 2 sets of 10 repeats; start with 75 pounds.
3. *Leg lunges:* 2 sets of 10 repeats with barbell on shoulders; start with 100 pounds.
4. *Pull overs* (on bench): 2 sets of 10 repeats; start with 75 pounds.
5. *The raises:* 2 sets of 10 repeats with toes on 3-inch blocks; start with 100 pounds on shoulders.
6. *Knee bends:* 2 sets of 10 repeats; start with 100 pounds.
7. *Step test:* Step up on 12-inch bench with 20-pound dumbbell in each hand; continue 3 to 5 minutes.

Initial training each year for the long-distance races to be run from January through July should start the previous September. Cross-country running during the first 3 months in the fall can be used to build strength and endurance for distance running in the winter and spring. (*See* Chapter 8.)

With the advent of a much expanded indoor track season, which includes many highly publicized television meets, conditioning for speed and pace must become part of the workout schedule from the very first week of the cross-country season. The 4 to 8 weeks that may fall between the completion of cross-country and the start of the indoor season can be used to establish race pace and increase the speed intensity of the workouts.

It is imperative that long-distance runners get plenty of rest and sleep and eat well-balanced meals in order to be able to follow these workout schedules. Some men will require more sleep than others, but usually all runners should get at least 8 hours of sleep each night.

There will be some days when the performer does not feel like following his specific training schedule. A day's rest or a change in routine will not affect him adversely as long as he does not deviate from his schedule too often.

WORKOUT SCHEDULES

A typical weekly training schedule for the 3- and 6-mile runner during the month prior to the season's opening meet is as follows:

Monday
  1. Run 3 to 5 × 1 mile starting at 5 minutes and gradually lowering time.
  2. Jog 7 to 10 minute intervals in between distances run, gradually decreasing interval time as strength and endurance increase.
  3. Run 15 to 20 × 110's.
  4. Jog 3 to 5 laps to cool down.

Tuesday
  1. Run 20 to 25 × 440's at slightly below Monday's workout pace.
  2. Jog 440 yards in between each 440 at a time not to exceed 90 seconds.
  3. Run 15 to 20 × 110's.
  4. Jog 3 to 5 laps to cool down.

Wednesday
  1. Run 12 to 16 × 880's at pace established at Monday's workout.
  2. Jog 880 yards in between, at a time not to exceed 2½ minutes.

3. Run 15 to 20 × 110's.
4. Jog 3 to 5 laps to cool down.

Thursday
1. Run 30 to 40 × 220's at slightly faster pace than that established on Monday.
2. Jog 220 yards in between at a time not to exceed 70 seconds.
3. Run 15 to 20 × 110's.
4. Jog 3 to 5 laps to cool down.

Friday
Warm-up thoroughly, then go to showers.

Saturday
Participate in time trials or in early season competitive workouts.

Sunday
Run 10 to 12 miles on cross-country course.

The statement following the end of the 1-mile workouts section in Chapter 6 is of even greater significance here. The distance workout combinations are organized in sets, and if performed as such they are considered to be a great deterrent to the development of mental fatigue. Success in running is proportionate to the amount of work done. However, the workload must not become drudgery, which begets mental staleness.

PRESEASON: 2-MILE PREPARATION

Monday
1. Run 2 to 3 × 1 mile, starting at 5 minutes and gradually lowering time.
2. Jog a 7 to 10 minute interval between each distance, gradually decreasing time as strength and endurance increase.
3. Run 10 to 15 × 110's.
4. Jog 3 to 4 laps to cool down.

Tuesday
1. Run 15 to 20 × 440's at slightly below pace used in Monday's workout.
2. Jog 440 yards in between, not to exceed 90 seconds.
3. Run 10 to 15 × 110's.
4. Jog 3 to 4 laps to cool down.

Wednesday
   1. Run 10 to 12 × 880's at pace established at Monday's workout.
   2. Jog 880 yards in between, not to exceed 2½ minutes.
   3. Run 10 to 15 × 110's.
   4. Jog 3 to 4 laps to cool down.

Thursday
   1. Run 20 to 30 × 220's at slightly below established pace.
   2. Jog 220 yards in between, but at a time not to exceed 70 seconds.
   3. Run 10 to 15 × 110's.
   4. Jog 3 to 4 laps to cool down.

Friday
   Warm-up thoroughly and go to showers.

Saturday
   Run in time trials or take part in early season workouts as prescribed.

Sunday
   Run 8 to 10 miles over cross-country course.

racing strategy

Participation in a warm-up program before a distance race is very important. Twenty to thirty minutes should be spent in limbering up and preparing the muscles and circulatory and lymphatic systems for the race. A procedure of jogging 3 to 6 laps, interspersed with a few short running bursts, then resting and trying to relax for 15 minutes before the race, is recommended by most coaches.

Judgment of pace can be learned by doing repeat runs during the training period. An experienced runner is not often misled by an opponent who goes out too fast or too slow at the start of the race. The distance races should be run at as even a pace as possible, with the times for the various 440's about identical. However, during a given 440 the runner may wish to speed up or slow down a little to relieve fatigue in the arms and legs. Each runner must run his own race; he must run within his own capacity.

It is much easier to follow than lead in running the long-distance races. If possible, and if the pace is right, a runner should follow one of the other runners until he is ready to make his move for the lead.

However, he should not follow a slow pace too long or he will not be able to recover in time. Success in the instant when a runner makes his move to sprint for the finish depends on his ability to outsprint the opposition.

A race cannot usually be won by plodding along. A runner should at some stage of the race try to "break" the opposition. If he can maintain a faster tempo than his opponents for half a lap or much longer, some runners may become discouraged. If he does not have the ability to sprint at the end of the race, he must make his move early and try to build up a commanding lead, or take the finish kick out of the opposition by increasing the tempo over a longer period.

A runner should try to avoid running with a group if he is apt to get boxed or bumped in such a way that he will have to change his natural relaxed stride. He should run his own race and stay near the pole on the turns most of the time in order to run the shortest distance possible.

After the race is finished, it is best to keep walking and jogging for 10 to 15 minutes to allow the circulatory system to settle down gradually to normal functioning. The distance runner does not lie down or stand still unless sickness results from the hard running.

summary

1. Distance runners have a slow pulse rate and usually like activities that demand endurance.

2. Distance runners usually enjoy running alone for hours.

3. These runners easily develop tolerance to the stress of running.

4. Pace is probably the most important factor in this event. This is learned by running many repeat 440's.

5. The runners use a short, easy, quick stride.

6. The longer the race, the shorter the stride, and the lower the knee lift of the leg.

7. In running, the foot should strike the ground almost directly under the center of gravity of the body.

8. The foot should strike the ground first on the ball or sole, then drop lightly down to the heel, then back to the ball of the foot, and thence to the big toe.

9. The backward motion of the rear foot should not be higher than the knee of the opposite leg.

10. The body should be held rather erect, with the chest pushed out during each stride.

11. The arms should be carried high and across the chest in a

relaxed manner. They should move in a short to-and-fro motion across the body.

12. The head may be so relaxed that it hangs loosely from the body as the runner progresses down the track.

13. Complete relaxation while running is necessary for success.

14. Hard running over a long period of time is necessary in order to be successful at distance running.

CROSS-COUNTRY

Cross-country, the sport involving the running of long distances over open terrain, is considered the foundation of successful distance running programs. This activity has enjoyed great popularity for many years in Europe. In England, for example, cross-country is truly run across the country. Races are run from town to town, with the runners obliged to find their own directions. In a sense, the races are run as if there were obstacle courses laid out between the towns.

Cross-country did not gain much prominence in the United States until the late 1930's. On November 28, 1938, the first annual National Collegiate Cross-Country Meet was held at Michigan State University. Since this date, except for the war year of 1943, when it was not held, the number of participants who enter this meet has grown every year. More and more schools have formed teams which run this race competitively. Cross-country is now recognized as an essential part of the over-all track program in most high schools, colleges and universities in the United States.

The administration of cross-country as an event is included as an integral part of this chapter, even though such an approach is not used in the other chapters. Many cross-country coaches are given this duty as an extra assignment, especially at the high school level, and need help in administering this program. In addition, performers in this event depend on endurance and knowledge of procedures, rather than on speed per se, to gain excellence. Therefore, in order to give them the opportunity they deserve, the meets must be conducted as effectively as possible and in accordance with established rules and regulations.

scoring

Cross-country is scored similarly to the game of golf. This means that the team with the low score wins. A team in championship meets is composed of 7 men—5 scorers and 2 so-called pushers. (In less formal meets, more men can be used as possible scorers.) The positions of the first 5 runners determine the final score made by a team, with 15 points being a perfect low score. The sixth and seventh men, though they do not affect their own team's score, can influence the score made by the opponents if both finish in front of any of the other team's first 5 men. Therefore, a perfect score would be 15-50, with the winning team's pushers placing sixth and seventh, in front of all of the members of the opposing team. This possibility is a definite inducement for every runner to turn in his top performance.

Collegiate level competition involves the runner traversing any distance from 3 to 6 miles. The NCAA championships are run over a 6-mile distance, while many collegiate conferences set the length of their courses at a distance of 5 miles. At the high school level, 2 miles is the most popular distance, with a few courses being 3 miles in length.

Most races are run over a university- or city-owned golf course (*see* Fig. 8-1). Municipal parks are often made available to city schools which don't have their own facilities. The distance of each course will vary according to its terrain, which may be composed in some cases of flat ground, or a combination of both hills and flat surfaces.

special training and techniques

The coach faces a difficult assignment in designing a workout program to help acquaint his team with the various courses over which they will run during the season. If their home course is hilly and they

FIGURE 8-1. Cross-country runners in action. Note the type of terrain, which is typical of that often used for a cross-country course.

are to run a race on a flat course, part of the prior week's workouts must be run on a flat surface emphasizing speed. On the other hand, a team used to running on a flat, fast course must get in some hill or grade work during the week's practice before competition on the latter type of course.

Certain special techniques must be used in running over hills. Adequate information about and practice of these techniques help a runner become more effective in running up and down hills, and therefore lessen the psychological tensions which hills may effect in many runners. There are some conflicting opinions as to which are the most effective hill running techniques. A discussion of the different opinions is presented here.

In downhill running, the most important point is that the runner should take advantage of the momentum he can gain from use of the pull of gravity. The conflicting opinions involve the following points of view: (1) the runner should sprint downhill in order to utilize hill slope and downward pull of gravity to the greatest advantage for picking up speed; (2) the athlete should use controlled free running downhill in order to utilize gravity and hill slope properly; very little effort should be made to run any faster than the pull of gravity requires.

The *first technique* is very effective in picking up distance on the other runners, but involves some difficulty in controlling foot placement. Therefore, its use is more apt to cause injuries. The *second technique,* the controlled, relaxed running, has many advantages for the runner, but is not as fast. By letting gravity and hill slope pull the body, the runner can conserve energy, and possibilities of injuries and heel jars are lessened.

The runners should shorten stride as they run downhill. The steeper the incline, the shorter the stride that must be used. In this manner, the body's center of gravity is kept as nearly as possible over the feet.

When approaching a hill, a runner must adjust his stride if he is to navigate such an obstacle effectively. The adjustments a runner must make are as follows: (1) lengthen stride slightly; (2) have some body lean; and (3) increase pace going uphill. The runner should make these adjustments just prior to starting up the hill, so that he is mechanically correct in his running form and prepared to start up the hill. Upon reaching the top, the runner should return to his race pace.

Analysis of cross-country runners' styles of running reveals that many of them do not use the above techniques. They frequently sprint downhill, using long strides, and prepare for running uphill by using short strides. Because they have superior ability, some runners have succeeded in spite of their using the above wrong techniques.

team strategy

A coach should encourage his team members to stay close together during a race. This does not mean that the front runners should wait for those who are falling behind, but that the back runners be encouraged to stay up with the lead runners. A team whose members run together and have balanced scoring will often upset teams with a few superior front runners.

For effective team running, a small time gap should exist between the first and fifth members. Nevertheless, team members should be encouraged to work together and stay close together. If one of the team members starts to fall off the pace, the others should encourage him to stay up with the group.

Each team member should establish, with the aid of his coach, the pace at which he is going to run a given race. Of course, pace will vary according to the type of course being run. The ideal procedure is to have the runners spread their energy out to last over the entire distance of the race. Some coaches, however, disregard individual pace assignments completely in favor of the establishment of an over-all team pace. Many coaches will also have the members of their team run the first ½ or ¾ of the race together, enabling the back runners to use the team lead runners as pace setters. After this distance has been covered, the principle of "every man for himself" is adhered to for the rest of the race.

However, a team staying close together can have a dispiriting psychological effect on the opponents. It is very discouraging to see all the members of an opposing team together and at or near the front of the race.

other racing comments

Some runners have the tendency to "fall asleep" during a race; they are simply not as alert as they should be to what is going on in the race. They start the race, establish a pace, and never change it. Every runner should be aware of his position in comparison with members of the other team. If a runner falls into this inattentive state of mind, the coach should instruct him to "check out" (that is, run fast) for 5 or 10 yards every quarter of a mile or so, and then settle back into his race pace. This should "awaken" the runner.

During a race, the runners usually split into competitive groups.

A given runner must strive to maintain contact with a group of runners or a single runner of similar ability. Once a runner drifts off from a group, it is extremely difficult for him to regain his contact.

Every member of a team should take the time, with the coach present, to study a strange course prior to participation in the competition. The coach should point out steep hills, loose surface, holes, sharp turns, and any other hazards that could be a potential problem. Obviously, team and pace strategy must be planned around the type of course that is to be the scene of the race.

All athletes have a certain amount of reserve energy which they can call upon near the end of the race to help them increase their speed. Since the amount each has in reserve varies, the coach must help each athlete to determine at what point in the race his drive for the finish must begin.

Cross-country races are run in all kinds of weather (sun, rain, sleet, or snow). Consequently, lightweight protective uniforms must be a part of every runner's standard equipment. The running shirt and shorts are the basic equipment. Lightweight long shirts and pants may be worn under this running gear in the event of cold weather. Gloves and stocking caps may also be utilized by the runner in cold and snowy weather.

meet preparations

A coach should make every effort to insure that home meets are conducted in an orderly, accurate, and fair manner. Hosting a meet necessitates some very careful preparations by the coach; a checklist of things that should be done follows.

Program. A simple, informative, single-sheet program can be developed and mimeographed for distribution to spectators and competitors. (*See* Fig. 8-2.)

Course. Each visiting coach should be provided with a layout of the course prior to his arrival for the meet. His team members should also be permitted to jog over the course prior to competition. If possible, a long, reasonably flat stretch should start and finish the race, so as to eliminate any unnecessary congestion and give the competitors every opportunity to perform without hindrance. The course should be marked off in accordance with existing regulations. Every runner should be able to run the course without fear of getting lost or taking a wrong turn.

Some suggested methods of marking off the course include the following: (a) a continuous line, painted or limed, should be visible

INDIANA UNIVERSITY
CROSS COUNTRY

I. U. Golf Course - Bloomington, Indiana
September 23, 1967 at 10:30 a.m.

Course Record - 20:24.3 - Dick Sharkey
of Michigan State University - October 1, 1966
Course Record, I. U. Varsity - 20:32.5 - Mark Gibbens - October 8, 1966
I. U. Varsity Record - 19:28 - Mark Gibbens - November 12, 1966

No.	Indiana	Place	Time	No.	Indiana State	Place	Time
05	Atkinson, Dave			53	Andrews, Larry		
06	Brown, Jay			58	Busby, Dave		
07	Crask, Don			59	Christensen, Dick		
10	Desper, Dave			60	Clark, Tom		
11	Gibbens, Mark			61	King, John		
14	Kennedy, Bob			63	McKinney, Don		
16	Killingbeck, Dave			67	Spurgeon, Tom		
17	LeMar, Bruce			68	Stewart, Mick		
18	Mann, Hans						
19	Pidhirny, Bill						
21	Rehmer, Jim						
22	Rowe, John						
25	Russell, Charles						
27	Stout, Mike						
28	Stucker, Rick						
32	Wells, Bill						

Scoring

Indiana   Indiana State

Places _____   Places _____
        _____   _____   _____   _____
        _____   _____   _____   _____
        _____   _____
        _____   _____

Total   _____   Total   _____

Next Home Meet

Varsity - October 14 - vs. Iowa and Ohio State - 10:30 a.m.
Freshmen - November 4 - vs. Indiana State and Purdue -
                                          10:30 a.m.

FIGURE 8–2. Single-sheet cross-country program.

along a side of the course; (b) posts should be painted with arrows pointing in the direction the race is to be run; and (c) indication flags should be located at regular intervals and around turns in the following manner: *red* means left turn; *yellow* means right turn; *blue* means straight ahead.

A combination of these methods is considered the most effective. When a line is used in combination with flags, placement of the flags is very important. Runners are usually allowed to run within 5 yards of the white line, with the flag placed directly on the line. In the "flagging" of the turns, all runners are instructed to go around the flags. Since this is confusing, double "flagging" is recommended around the turns, with 1 set on the line and 1 set used as the curb. During the heat of competition, it is quite possible for a competitor to cut inside of a flag, especially if it is placed on the line. Such an error would make him subject to disqualification, so the use of two flags is recommended to avoid this misjudgment.

Timing.   Most athletes are usually interested in the time in which they are running a given distance, whether in practice or during competition. Intermediate and total times should be taken and recorded during practice. This will enable the athlete and the coach to keep a continuous check on progression or change from week to week as various workout distances are run.

In meets, the intermediate times (e.g., 1 mile, 2 miles) should be called out loud and clear by the head timer, in such a manner that every runner is given his own time. In addition, four men may work in two separate groups. One member of one set of partners calls out the time of every runner, and his partner records the individual time of each runner at every distance, as well as the final time. The other set of partners work so that one man calls out the rank order of each man at each distance and the final order of finishing while the other records this finish order in relation to the time called out by the head timer.

The recording of intermediate and final times can be simplified through the use of time charts (*see* Fig. 8-3). To assure proper recording, 2 men familiar with cross-country times who are quick, alert, and not easily flustered should be selected for this task. One man records as the other reads the times, with no effort made to determine places. The timer simply reads the times as the runners pass the designated places and the finish line; the recorder places a mark at the time indicated by his partner. The time recorded in the chart is later combined with the rank order at which the runners passed the intermediate distances, as well as the order of the finish.

Judging the finish in dual meets is relatively simple. A number

CROSS COUNTRY TIME SHEET

19:30	20:20	21:10	22:00	22:50	23:40
31	21	11	01	51	41
32	22	12	02	52	42
33	23	13	03	53	43
34	24	14	04	54	44
35	25	15	05	55	45
36	26	16	06	56	46
37	27	17	07	57	47
38	28	18	08	58	48
39	29	19	09	59	49
19:40	20:30	21:20	22:10	23:00	23:50
41	31	21	11	01	51
42	32	22	12	02	52
43	33	23	13	03	53
44	34	24	14	04	54
45	35	25	15	05	55
46	36	26	16	06	56
47	37	27	17	07	57
48	38	28	18	08	58
49	39	29	19	09	59
19:50	20:40	21:30	22:20	23:10	24:00
51	41	31	21	11	01
52	42	32	22	12	02
53	43	33	23	13	03
54	44	34	24	14	04
55	45	35	25	15	05
56	46	36	26	16	06
57	47	37	27	17	07
58	48	38	28	18	08
59	49	39	29	19	09
20:00	20:50	21:40	22:30	23:20	24:10
01	51	41	31	21	11
02	52	42	32	22	12
03	53	43	33	23	13
04	54	44	34	24	14
05	55	45	35	25	15
06	56	46	36	26	16
07	57	47	37	27	17
08	58	48	38	28	18
09	59	49	39	29	19
20:10	21:00	21:50	22:40	23:30	24:20
11	01	51	41	31	21
12	02	52	42	32	22
13	03	52	43	33	23
14	04	54	44	34	24
15	05	55	45	35	25
16	06	56	46	36	26
17	07	57	47	37	27
18	08	58	48	38	28
19	09	59	49	39	29

FIGURE 8–3. Cross-country time sheet.

is assigned to each competitor and pinned on the front of his shirt. The numbers are read and recorded in order of finish. Two men used for judging and two men used for recording the finish positions can perform their tasks very efficiently.

In larger meets, where more control is required over the competitors as they finish, a quick, effective method of determining scores is essential. The most popular method used to control the competitors is referred to as the finish chute method (*see* Fig. 8-4). The chute can be made of various available equipment, such as park benches, hurdles, narrow fencing, hockey fencing, posts, and flagged rope. It does not have to be elaborate in design, as its main purpose is for control of the finishers.

If there are a large number of competitors, a jam-up may occur in the chute. To avoid confusion in this connection, various methods are utilized to assure accurate results and a fair chance for every athlete to be placed as he finishes. One way is to enlarge the chute in width so that it can be divided into 2 sections. When one section fills up, the rest of the incoming runners can be funnelled into the other section. Another method is the utilization of ropes attached to the base of the funnel of the chute. If a jam-up occurs in the chute, the runners are backed up into the funnel; the ropes guide the front line of competitors to the side of the funnel. If the jam-up is large, the next line of

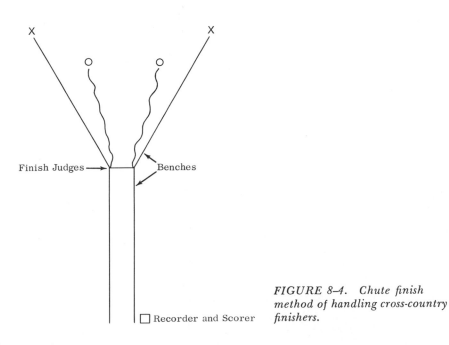

Finish Judges →

Benches

☐ Recorder and Scorer

FIGURE 8–4.   Chute finish method of handling cross-country finishers.

competitors can be guided to the other side of the funnel. As the competitors proceed through and out the end of the chute, their number, name, and school are recorded on the score sheet by the recorder and scorer.

A much quicker scoring method than described above is utilized in many larger meets. As the competitor passes the recorder, he is handed a card with his finish place written on it. He turns this over to his coach, who writes his name and school on the back of the card. On the front of a scoring envelope, the coach places the runner's number, his name, and his place of finish, and totals his score (*see* Fig. 8-5). Use of this method will help in the accumulation of a quick unofficial team score, and may also serve as a double check on the recorder's official placement of the finishers and the results determined by the scorer. There are many similar methods in use which are quick and effective in helping to determine the winners. Those mentioned here are not the only ones known to be effective, but are considered more than adequate for the administration of cross-country meets.

FIGURE 8–5. Cross-country unofficial quick score envelope.

3,000-METER STEEPLECHASE

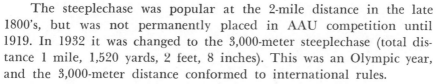

The steeplechase was popular at the 2-mile distance in the late 1800's, but was not permanently placed in AAU competition until 1919. In 1932 it was changed to the 3,000-meter steeplechase (total distance 1 mile, 1,520 yards, 2 feet, 8 inches). This was an Olympic year, and the 3,000-meter distance conformed to international rules.

In 1948 it became one of the events scheduled every 4 years in the NCAA championship meets, when they were held during an Olympic year. In 1959, it became a permanent part of the NCAA meet schedule. The first NCAA record holder was Pat Traynor, Villanova, whose time of 8:48.6 was set in 1962.

In world class competition, Horace Ashenfelter won the 1952 Olympic Games race in Helsinki, Finland, with a time of 8:45.4. Since this date, the United States has not fared too well. Gaston Roelants of Belgium dominated this event during the mid- and late 1960's, winning the 1964 Olympic Games. The present world record holder is Jouko Kuha of Finland, who ran this distance in the outstanding time of

8:24.2. George Young, the top United States prospect and fifth in the 1964 Games, set an American record of 8:30.6 during the pre-Olympic training session. Young ran an exceptional race in the 1968 Mexico City Olympics, placing third in this event.

In recent years, the 3,000-meter steeplechase has become a very popular track event in this country. In fact, it is now an integral part of several intercollegiate conferences and dual and championship meets. Many excellent distance runners perform well in this event. It is a very demanding physical experience, as the performer must clear 4 wooden barriers (3 feet high) and 1 water jump (from a 3-foot barrier) that is 12 feet long. This is done every one of the 7 complete laps of the 400-meter track which is run in this race (a total of 28 jumps over the hurdle and 7 over the water hazard).

The steeplechaser's training program must be two-fold, embracing both distance running and hurdling. The training needed for proficiency as a hurdler is the less exacting. The 3-foot barriers are not much of an obstacle, yet the steeplechaser must display good hurdling form, utilizing the same mechanics of movements used by the intermediate hurdler. One key to successful hurdling of the barriers is for the steeplechaser to "charge" the hurdle (*see* Fig. 9-1); hesitation causes problems. Failure to clear the hurdle through jumping rather than hurdling will temporarily slow or stop all forward momentum. The idea is to get over the barrier and return to a running stride as quickly as possible without loss of forward momentum. This means that the

FIGURE 9–1.   *Steeplechaser hurdling 3-foot barrier.*

steeplechaser must hurdle rather than jump the barriers. (*See* Chapter 10 for hurdling techniques.)

On the other hand, clearing the water barrier does take a lot of practice, as there are definite techniques to be used in the effective accomplishment of this task. The length of the water hazard jump (12 feet) makes it necessary for the steeplechaser to jump to the top of the 3-foot barrier placed immediately prior to it (*see* Fig. 9-2). He then pushes off from the barrier with his feet in order to clear or go over as much of the water hazard as possible. The steeplechaser's intent should be to clear the hurdle barrier and the water jump area without any appreciable loss of his forward momentum. (He lands on one foot in a stride position.)

The steeplechaser is also a long-distance runner, and so will follow a suitable endurance program. Suggested training programs for long-distance runners are to be found in Chapter 7.

hurdle practice

The steeplechaser should practice his hurdling form at every practice session, during either the warming-up or "warming-down" running periods. Regular hurdles set at the height of 3 feet should be placed on the track at the official locations; as the steeplechaser runs his laps he also hurdles these barriers. Use of proper hurdling form in

FIGURE 9–2. Steeplechaser mounting wooden barrier and jumping water hazard.

these practice sessions is essential to the development of proper hurdling mechanics needed in a competitive race. In most instances, the hurdle should be taken with the dominant leg. That is, if the steeplechaser is right-handed, he would normally lead with his right leg, and therefore take off from the ground with his left foot (rear leg).

water jump technique

The water jump, as can be imagined, is the most difficult part of the race. Fortunately, it only occurs once during each lap of the race. The reason for its difficulty is that the steeplechaser must clear the 3-foot wooden barrier as well as the 12-foot water jump. As has been stated, continuous momentum is essential for successful clearance of all of the barriers. To insure attainment of sufficient distance in the jump, and in order to maintain continuous momentum, the steeplechaser should spring to the top of the hurdle and jump the water barrier in one motion. If he is right-handed, he should probably plan to land on the top of the hurdle with his left foot, as does the long-jumper on the takeoff board. This will put him in position to use the so-called "springing leg" for jumping the 12-foot distance, and to keep the strong (dominant) leg available for landing purposes.

In practice, a marker placed a few strides from the hurdle for foot striking purposes will enable the runner to adjust his stride in order to assure proper foot placement up to and on top of the hurdle. If these last few steps and the move up to the top of the hurdle are taken smoothly, and executed rapidly, the runner can push off the top of the barrier with confidence that he has the strength and momentum to clear much or all of the water hazard. Most steeplechasers attempt to land at approximately the 11-foot mark. Some top performers land beyond the water hazard. Since the landing position of the runner is important for proper subsequent action, it is necessary that he land and reach with the opposite leg for the next step in one continuous movement. Consequently, he should not land with a stiff leg, but with one which is slightly bent and ready for a quick extension. If the runner lands in a straight, stiff-legged position, he will tend to "brake" his momentum and disturb the rhythm. Therefore, mastery of the technique of negotiating the water jump is of paramount importance.

A water jump can be simulated by placing one of the hurdles near the long jump area. The stride patterns could be marked off and the 12-foot water jump measured out, using the long jump pit as part of the area. The runner can run, hit his stride pattern, jump onto the hurdle, push off, and land in the sand. This is the safest procedure, and also makes use of much drier material than is contained in the regulation water jump.

Confidence in every phase of the water jump technique can be gained through practice in this type of simulated area. Ability to hurdle the barriers, clear the water hazard, and run the 3,000-meter distance with assurance characterizes the champion steeplechaser.

training program

As has been stated, the steeplechaser must first be a distance runner. The training program that he should follow would be almost identical to that designed for a 2-miler (*see* Chapter 7). In addition, he must also be a hurdler; hurdling techiques are described in Chapter 10.

THREE

HURDLES

HIGH
HURDLES

some performances of the past

There is disagreement as to whether the Egyptians or the Greeks were the first hurdlers. In any event, the first hurdles were probably "sheep hurdles" (fences) or solid jagged barriers staked out in a meadow. The main objective was to get over the barriers alive.

Later came the barrier placed across a running track. If the lead runner knocked the barrier down, the other runners had no hurdle to jump. This led to the practice of constructing the individual hurdle in sawbuck fashion, heavy and hazardous on contact. In time much lighter hurdles were made, and hurdlers began to run through them rather than over them. Naturally this resulted in the adoption of a universal rule (agreed to by all governing bodies) to restore the *essential* skill of hurdling: If 3 or more hurdles were knocked over, the hurdler was disqualified. The "L" hurdle brought about a change in this rule.

It is believed that hurdling as a competitive track event began in

1837. The first 120-yard high hurdle event was recorded at an 1864 meet between Oxford and Cambridge, when A. W. T. Daniel ran it in 17¾ seconds.

The earliest hurdling form known is that of the athlete clearing the hurdle in an upright sitting position. Change from this form came about through attempts to maintain momentum by jumping the hurdle and landing on the lead foot. However, the lead leg was kept bent at the knee and the trail leg was not flattened; consequently, the action over the hurdle was more like broad jumping than hurdling. This form did not help much in saving time over the hurdle. Many national championships before 1860 were won in 19 seconds, which means that it took 5 seconds to go through the air over the hurdles, compared with the 2 seconds or less needed by hurdlers of today to perform the same act.

The major credit for development of the hurdling form using a straight lead leg and a forward trunk lunge is in some dispute. However, in the United States Al Kraenzlein of Pennsylvania is given credit as the innovator. His time in 1898 was :15.2. Fred Kelly of the University of Southern California ran the high hurdles in 15 seconds flat in 1913, Earl Thompson of Southern California and Dartmouth in :14.8 in 1916, and Robert Simpson of Missouri in :14.6 in the same year. Thompson set a new record of :14.4 in 1920. In 1931, Percy Beard of Alabama Polytechnic College ran them in :14.2. George Saling of Iowa, 1932 Olympic high hurdle champion, ran them in :14.1, but was not given official credit for this performance.

Until 1935 the inverted "T" type of hurdle had been used, but it was found that it would rise several inches when hit, causing many hurdlers to fall during a race. The "L" type of hurdle, with weights at the base to meet the newly established requirements of the 8-pound overturning force, was then adopted. This change helped the hurdler to relax while going over the hurdle, and allowed him to run without fear of injury.

The performance improvement evidenced by the faster times recorded was due to such factors as: (1) an attempt to keep good sprinting action, that is, elimination of the "stagger" as the hurdler landed; the shouders and hips were not twisted; (2) definite forward body lean as the hurdler went over the hurdle; (3) the semi-straight lead leg; (4) the flattened trail leg and its delayed action; and (5) a conscious effort to keep the feet on the ground and running as much as possible.

Forrest Towns from Georgia, employing what many thought was perfect form, lowered the world record to :13.7 in 1937. Fred Wolcott of Rice Institute, one of the first real sprinter-hurdlers (:9.5 100-yard dash man), then entered hurdling competition. Practically all of the great hurdles until Wolcott's time ranged in height from 6'2" to 6'5". Wolcott, not quite 6' tall, ran the high hurdles in :13.7 in 1941. Harrison Dillard, a still shorter man (5'10") and a great sprinter (1948 Olympic sprint champion), lowered the record to :13.6.

The sprinters all jumped farther over the hurdle with a faster-moving trail leg. Because of their great speed and leg drive, they were able to make up for the greater time spent in the air.

The trend to such short sprinters as Wolcott, Dillard, and Allan Tolmich of Wayne caused some coaches to wonder if speed would offset hurdling skill. Then Dick Attlesey of Southern California ran the race in 13.5 seconds in May, 1950, at the Fresno relays, and restored the concept that it takes a tall man to be a great hurdler. He was 6'3½" tall and weighed 178 pounds. Attlesey used what is considered near-perfect form: He had a good forward lean with a modified two-arm forward thrust, a delayed trail leg which he snapped down quickly, and a relaxed lead leg, which he also snapped down quickly as he descended after clearing the hurdle. His hurdle clearance time was 2 seconds for the 10 hurdles, as compared to Dillard's time of 2.3 seconds.

Jack Davis of Southern California, the so-called· "hard-luck kid" of 2 Olympiads (he finished second in the 1952 and 1956 Olympics, both in photo-finish races), climaxed a brilliant career by running the race in 13.3 seconds at Bendigo, Australia, just prior to the 1956 Olympic games, for a new world record. Davis was 6'3" tall and weighed 178 pounds.

In the 1968 Olympics, the United States finished one-two, with Willie Davenport winning in :13.3, thus tying the Olympic record established by Irv Hall in the semi-finals. Hall placed second in the finals, in :13.4. Earl McCulloch was another great hurdler who ran :13.3, but chose not to compete in the Olympics. If a hurdler comes along who can sprint 120 yards in 11 seconds and clear the 10 hurdles in 01.8 seconds, the world record will probabbly drop to 13 seconds flat or less.

characteristics of the high hurdler

Most high hurdlers are tall boys, or at least have long legs. They should have good flexibility in the rear of the pelvis. Since high school hurdles are shorter (39 inches) than college hurdles (42 inches), shorter boys may be successful in high school—to the discomfort of college coaches, who find that they are often unable to become college hurdlers because of the added hurdle height. Speed is necessary, but hurdling skill is just as important (with some notable exceptions) for success in the high hurdles.

If a boy is not afraid to smash through a hurdle and will not let a fall discourage him, and he has the other requirements mentioned above, he should become a good hurdler (*see* Chapter 1).

modern hurdling form

Correct hurdling form should first be thought of as correct sprinting form. Next, the action to and over the hurdle must be smooth and relaxed. In order to get proper speed, the performer must be on the ground as long as possible, maintain proper balance over the hurdle, and land with a good forward lean. This means maintaining continuous leg action from takeoff to landing when going over the hurdle. The knee of the lead leg must not be locked, and the trail leg should be delayed to make the action smooth and continuous. The rapid cutdown of the lead leg and the forward pull of the trail leg are phases of a single action, just as in sprinting, and are essential moves.

As the runner approaches the hurdle, he must have his eyes focused on its top. To go over the hurdle, he should: (1) take off from 6'10" to 7'2" from the hurdle; (2) drive his lead knee forward much as in a sprinting stride (the lower leg and foot are then raised to straighten the leg for hurdle clearance; the knee is not locked, but a relaxed, slightly flexed lead leg is used); (3) thrust the opposite arm forward (not above eye level) to keep the shoulders straight and to insure body lean and balance; (4) use the other arm for balance—like the arm action used in sprinting; (5) bend the upper body at the hips so that, when going over the hurdle, the head is never raised much higher than in proper sprinting; (6) drive the trail knee forward as in sprinting (as the trail leg comes up it is flattened out, so that when the thigh is parallel with the hurdle it forms a right angle with the body); (7) snap the lead leg down so that the heel of the foot will land from 3'6" to 4'2" from the hurdle; (8) snap the trail leg forward and down after a slight delay (the foot of the trail leg must be kept flat over the hurdle with the toes turned slightly up to avoid striking the hurdle; the knee must not be raised too high when coming down over the hurdle); and (9) maintain a forward lean so that the lead foot hits the ground with the weight on the toe and ball of the foot.

To summarize the action over the hurdle (*see* Fig. 10-1):

1. Maintenance of proper body lean, accomplished by proper lead arm action, and proper position of the head and shoulders is para-

mount. Some hurdlers use a distinct dip of the head while clearing the hurdle to help obtain good forward lean.

2. Delayed action of the trail leg insures the accomplishment of a full leg split, and also enables the performer to have a forward lean at the takeoff. A trail leg horizontal (flat) as it comes off the hurdle will aid the hurdler in keeping a continual forward lean and full leg stride beyond the hurdle.

3. A relaxed trail leg with an accompanying rapid pull-through will help in performing a downward snap of the lead leg. A quick, hard cut-down of the lead leg will bring the lead foot down not more than 4 feet from the hurdle, which will get the hurdler on the ground faster and help him in maintaining proper body lean for the next step.

The start and steps to the first hurdle. This is the area in which many hurdle races are won or lost, and much time and practice must be spent on this phase. Momentum must be gained as quickly as possible, but confidence and proper balance over the hurdle are necessary.

The starting position of the hurdler is like that of the sprinter, but the body is straightened up a little sooner during the first 3 strides from the blocks, and the strides must be adjusted in order to accomplish the best approach to the hurdle.

Most hurdlers take 8 strides to the first hurdle, in which case the same foot that the hurdler will use to lead with over the hurdle will be placed in the back block. However, some taller men use only 7 strides, and therefore place the lead foot on the front block. Any chopping of stride necessary to insure that the hurdler has a proper takeoff must be done in the first 4 strides, so that the hurdler may run with confidence. If his steps are off only a very small amount to the first hurdle, this can be corrected by shifting the blocks a few inches closer or farther apart.

It is very important to make the takeoff from the exact and proper spot each time. If the hurdler is too close to the hurdle, it will take him 3 or 4 hurdles to regain his smooth hurdling form, and by then the opposition will be much nearer the finish tape.

Steps between hurdles. Leading hurdlers today take 3 strides between the hurdles. These strides should be approximately the same length each time to eliminate the tendency to "gallop" between hurdles. A typical stride pattern between hurdles would be: first stride, 6'3"; second, 6'5"; third 6'4".

Length of the hurdle stride. The length of the hurdle stride (distance over hurdle) has varied from 13' (8' + 5') to 10'2" (5'9" + 4'5"). One top hurdler took an 11'6" (7'1" + 4'5") stride, while another used an 11' (7'2" + 3'10") stride.

The takeoff spot first used by a beginner should be approximately

A   B   C   D   E

FIGURE 10–1. *High hurdle form. A former world record holder. (A) Starting form is the same as for the sprinter. However, the high hurdler comes up to an upright position sooner, as seen here. (B), (C), and (D) The forward and upward thrust of the lead leg (not upward and forward) is shown. (E) The lead leg is relaxed (not locked). The eyes are focused on the next hurdle throughout the race.*

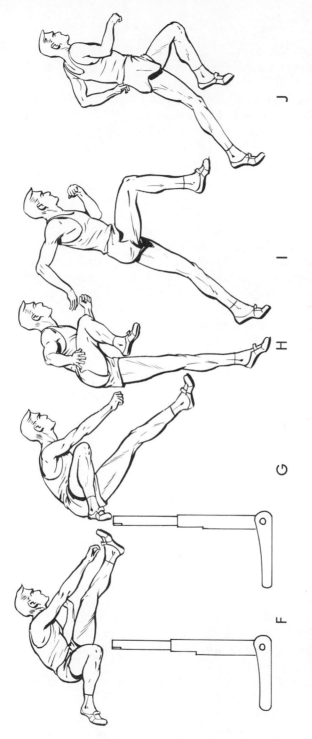

F   G   H   I   J

FIGURE 10–1 (cont.). High hurdle form. (F) Proper forward lean and the correct position of the flat trail leg is demonstrated. (G) He is landing on the toe of the lead foot. (H) Note the high knee position of the trail leg, which will enable him to make a fast recovery. (I) and (J) He returns to good sprinting form before attempting to clear the next hurdle.

7 feet from the hurdle. This distance should be adjusted after the coach observes the hurdler and determines what takeoff distance will be best for him to maintain proper body angle and hurdle clearance.

The most important point in connection with hurdle stride is that if the takeoff spot is too close to the hurdle, the hurdler will be forced to throw his lead leg up straight to clear the hurdle, which, in turn, will straighten up his body and eliminate any chance of his attaining a proper lean (*see* Fig. 10-2).

training program

The potential champion will work 9 or more months a year to develop speed, endurance, flexibility, and hurdling skills.

The fall months should be spent running on the grass (using *Fartlek*) to develop stamina and endurance. Stretching exercises which include the "hurdle exercise" while sitting should be used. The hurdler should stand to the side of the hurdle many times each day, lay one leg on top of the hurdle, and touch the toe of the other foot with the fingers of both hands. All exercises that will stretch the hamstring muscles and loosen the hips should be used. However, these exercises should be done easily at first to avoid straining these muscles.

Since most of the high hurdlers also run the intermediate hurdles, it is good practice for them to do intensive training work with the 440 men during both preseason and seasonal practice. Low hurdler competitions are primarily outdoors (180 yards) in high school, and at 60 or 70 yards indoors in both high schools and in a relatively few collegiate conferences.

WORKOUT SCHEDULES

FOUR WEEKS PRIOR ΓO COMPETITION

Monday
1. Jog ¼ mile.
2. Work vigorously 15 minutes on stretching exercises.
3. Run ½ mile of wind sprints by running the straightaways and walking the turns.
4. Work 10 minutes hurdling over first 3 hurdles.
5. Run 8 flights over practice hurdles at full effort 3 to 5 times.
6. Run out of the blocks over the first 3 hurdles 5 times.
7. Run 220 yards at ⅔ speed.

8. Run 10 × 110 yards wind sprints.
9. Jog and walk 2 to 3 laps as cool-down.

Tuesday
1. Jog ¼ mile.
2. Do stretching exercises for 15 minutes.
3. Run ½ mile of wind sprints (same as for Monday).
4. Run 3 flights of low hurdles, starting from the blocks 5 times.
5. Run out of the block and over the first 3 high hurdles 5 times.
6. Take 6 starts with the sprinters, running 50 yards 3 times and 75 yards 3 times.
7. Run 220 yards twice. Run the first 50 yards at full speed, then the next 120 yards at ⅔ speed, and the last 50 yards at full speed.
8. Run 10 × 110 yards.
9. Jog 2 to 3 laps as cool-down.

Wednesday
1. Jog ¼ mile.
2. Do stretching exercises for 15 minutes.
3. Run ½ mile of wind sprints.
4. Work for 10 minutes going over one hurdle.
5. Run 3 flights of high hurdles from out of blocks at full effort 5 times.
6. Run 5 flights of high hurdles from out of blocks at full effort 3 times. The hurdle stride distance over the hurdles should be checked carefully, as well as distance of strides between hurdles. Work also on cutting down time over the hurdle.
7. Run 3 × 220 yards at ¾ to ⅞ speed.
8. Run 10 × 110 yards.
9. Jog 2 to 3 laps as cool-down.

Thursday
1. Jog ¼ mile.
2. Do stretching exercises for 15 minutes.
3. Run ½ mile of wind sprints.
4. Run out of the blocks and over the first 3 high hurdles 5 times.
5. Run 5 flights of low hurdles from the blocks 3 times.
6. Take 10 starts with the sprinters running a distance of 50 yards.
7. Run 2 × 330 yards—the first 50 yards at full speed, the next 230 yards with a relaxed stride at ⅔ speed, and the last 50 yards at full effort.
8. Run 10 × 110 yards.
9. Jog 2 to 3 laps as cool-down.

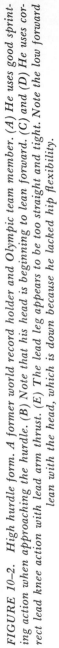

A   B   C   D   E

FIGURE 10–2. High hurdle form. A former world record holder and Olympic team member. (A) He uses good sprinting action when approaching the hurdle. (B) Note that his head is beginning to lean forward. (C) and (D) He uses correct lead knee action with lead arm thrust. (E) The lead leg appears to be too straight and tight. Note the low forward lean with the head, which is down because he lacked hip flexibility.

128

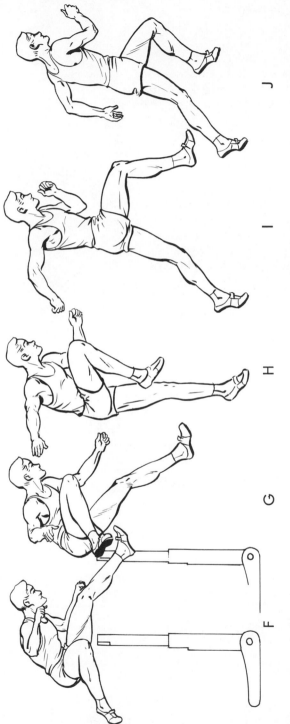

F   G   H   I   J

FIGURE 10-2 (cont.). High hurdle form. (F) Proper clearance with the flat trail leg is made. (G) He has snapped his lead leg down and has a good trail leg lift. (H) The right arm is swept wide to help maintain balance. This is done because of the tightness in the hips. (I) A good long stride is taken. (J) Sprinting form is maintained.

Friday

1. Jog ¼ mile.
2. Do stretching exercises for 15 minutes.
3. Run ½ mile of wind sprints.
4. Work over first 3 hurdles for 10 minutes.
5. Run 3 flights of high hurdles 3 times.
6. Run 10 × 110 yards.
7. Jog ¼ mile on the grass as cool-down.

Saturday

Time trial or early season competition.

Sunday

1. Do ½ hour of stretching and hurdle exercises.
2. Run 20 to 30 × 110 yards.

AFTER MEETS START

Monday

1. Jog ¼ mile.
2. Do stretching exercises for 15 minutes.
3. Run ½ mile of wind sprints.
4. Work over 1 to 3 hurdles for from 5 to 10 minutes.
5. Run 3 flights of high hurdles from out of the blocks 5 times.
6. Run 5 flights of high hurdles from out of the blocks 3 to 5 times.
7. Run 220 yards at ¾ speed.
8. Run 10 × 110 yards.
9. Jog 2 or 3 laps as cool-down.

Tuesday

1. Jog ¼ mile.
2. Do stretching exercises for 15 minutes.
3. Run ½ mile of wind sprints.
4. Run 5 flights of low hurdles 3 times.
5. Take 8 starts with sprinters, running 50 yards 4 of the times and 75 yards 4 times.
6. Run 330 yards at ⅔ speed.
7. Run 10 × 110 yards.
8. Jog 2 or 3 laps as cool-down.

Wednesday

1. Jog ¼ mile.
2. Do stretching exercises for 15 minutes.

3. Run ½ mile of wind sprints.
4. Work over 1 to 3 hurdles for 5 minutes.
5. Run 3 flights of high hurdles from out of the blocks 5 times.
6. Run 2 full flights of high hurdles from out of the blocks.
7. Jog ¼ mile on grass.
8. Run 10 × 110 yards.
9. Jog 2 or 3 laps as cool-down.

Thursday

1. Jog ¼ mile.
2. Do stretching exercises for 15 minutes.
3. Run ½ mile of wind sprints.
4. Run out of the blocks and over 1 to 3 high hurdles 5 times.
5. Run 3 flights of low hurdles from out of the blocks 5 times.
6. Run 5 flights of high hurdles from out of the blocks 2 or 3 times.
7. Jog ¼ mile on the grass.
8. Run 10 × 110 yards.
9. Jog 2 or 3 laps as cool-down.

Friday

Do a thorough warm-up followed by some stretching exercises.

Saturday

Day of meet. Be sure to warm-up properly and slowly by doing stretching exercises and wind sprints. Work over first 3 hurdles out of the blocks before race starts.

Sunday

Do ½ hour of stretching and hurdle exercises, then run 15 to 30 × 150's.

A single workout schedule should be considered only as a guide, and should be altered to fit individual differences and abilities. For example, a thin, wiry hurdler will probably need less overdistance work than a larger, heavier one.

helpful hints

1. Work with the sprinters at least twice a week to attain speed.
2. Exercise to loosen the hips and leg muscles almost every day for 2 months prior to season's opening meet in order to obtain flexibility.

3. Help avoid injury by using flip board on hurdle (3-inch strip of wood hinged to the top of the hurdle that will flip down when hit) during early season practice.

4. Work often over 1 hurdle to help perfect the step to the first hurdle and to gain speed of leg action.

5. Avoid using 5 steps between hurdles during practice except on occasions when running at ½ speed. Bad habits of taking off too close to the hurdle and using an improper body lean may be developed from this procedure.

6. Work over 3 hurdles at near top speed. This can be done many times without fatigue.

7. Be sure the takeoff is not too close to the hurdle.

8. Have no fear of the hurdle; be tough.

9. Maintain the action of the legs, arms, shoulders, and hips in a straight forward direction, as in sprinting.

10. Lead the movement into the hurdle with a full forward lean of the upper trunk. The head during the race should maintain the same level as when sprinting.

11. Be sure to lead with the knee when approaching the hurdle. The leg is straightened out about 2 feet away from the hurdle.

12. Do not hurry the action of the trail leg until on top of the hurdle.

13. Do not lock the knee of the lead leg.

14. The action of the lead arm must not come back so far as to make the shoulders turn to one side.

440-YARD HURDLES AND LOW HURDLES

11

It is believed that hurdling as a separate event was developed in America and adopted by other countries; it was part of the AAU program as early as 1888. Possibly, in the past, obstacles set up as in the steeplechase were used to test men in a combination of jumping and endurance running, as mentioned in Chapter 9. The 400-meter (or 440-yard) hurdles are an event in the collegiate, AAU, and Olympic programs. Low hurdles of 180-yard distance are run outdoors by high school performers. Colleges often include an indoor 70-yard low hurdle race in a dual meet.

the 440-yard hurdles

The 440-yard intermediate hurdle event has recently been added to the dual and championship meets of the schools and conferences in the country. For many years the value of adding this event to the collegiate schedule was under discussion. The coaches finally realized that a great quarter-miler with hurdle experience could compete in the Olympic Games, but that the 220-yard low hurdler could compete only in the United States. Thus, the 220-yard low hurdles were eliminated from the program.

Great 440-yard hurdlers of the past, such as 1952 Olympic champ Charlie Moore of Cornell, Glen Davis of Ohio State in 1956, and Bob Steele of Michigan State, 1956-1957 NCAA champion, were all established quarter-milers as well as being top intermediate and high hurdlers.

Dave Hemery of Great Britain and Boston University stunned the track world in setting a new Olympic and world record in the 1968 Olympics with a :48.1 performance. He was off the blocks very quickly, and ran at an unheard of speed of :23 for the first 200 meters. Hemery ended United States domination in this event by defeating all premeet favorites—Ron Whitney (U.S.), who set a new Olympic record of :49.0 in the trials, and Geoff Vanderstock (U.S.), who took fourth in :49.0. The field was fast, demonstrated by the fact that the second through fourth runners all tied the Olympic record of :49.0 established earlier by Whitney.

The training for this event includes some of the "interval training" used by most middle-distance men. The training in sprints used by quarter-milers and sprinters must also be part of the program.

techniques of good form

Most 440-yard hurdlers take off about 7½ feet from the hurdle and land about 4½ feet beyond. The normal number of strides to the first hurdle will be 23, with 15 strides used between hurdles. (*See* Fig. 11-1.) These strides must be accomplished in a smooth and relaxed manner, using good hip swing. (*See* Fig. 11-2.) Unless the athlete is very tall and has a naturally long stride, he will find it almost impossible to use 13 strides between the hurdles (yet champions use 13 strides part of the distance).

Knowledge and judgment of pace is very important in the 440-yard hurdle race, much as it is in the 440-yard dash. This knowledge is gained by having times checked at the 100-meter, 200-meter, and 300-meter marks to see at what pace a runner is capable of running these distances, and how closely he is able to determine his speed. He must learn to run at the predetermined pace.

The 440-yard hurdles is a tough race. Endurance is absolutely necessary. Many races are lost by the runner's striking the last few hurdles because his legs have tied up and he is unable to get over the

Start	H1	H2	H3	H4	H5	H6	H7	H8	H9	H10, Final
8 strides 15 yards	3 strides 10 yards	3 strides 10 yards	3 strides 10 yards	3 strides 10 yards	3 strides 10 yards	3 strides 10 yards	3 strides 10 yards	3 strides 10 yards	3 strides 10 yards	Sprint 15 yards

Recommended number of strides for 120-yard high hurdles: college, 42" high; high school, 39" high.

Start	H1	H2	H3	H4	H5	H6	H7	H8, Final
10 strides 20 yards	7 strides 20 yards	7 strides 20 yards	7 strides 20 yards	7 strides 20 yards	7 strides 20 yards	7 strides 20 yards	7 strides 20 yards	Sprint 20 yards

Recommended number of strides for 180-yard low hurdles: high school, 30" high.

Start	H1	H2	H3	H4	H5	H6	H7	H8	H9	H10, Final
22–24 strides 45 meters	15 strides 35 meters	15 strides 35 meters	15 strides 35 meters	15 strides 35 meters	15 strides 35 meters	15 strides 35 meters	15 strides 35 meters	15 strides 35 meters	15 strides 35 meters	Sprint 40 meters

Recommended number of strides for 400-meter hurdles; college, 36" high; high school, 36" high.

FIGURE 11–1. Stride plan.

FIGURE 11–2.   Intermediate hurdle form. Note body lean and flexed right leg as the hurdler is on top of the hurdle.

barriers. Thus, training to be both a quarter-miler and hurdler is necessary.

training program

Many of the same general training comments that have been made previously about quarter-milers apply here (*see* Chapter 4).

WORKOUT SCHEDULES

440-Yard Intermediate Hurdles: Preseason

Monday
1. Warm-up by running and jogging 1 mile.
2. Work vigorously 15 minutes on stretching and hurdle exercises.
3. Run ½ mile of wind sprints and first 3 hurdles.
4. Run 1 × 550 at pace speed, running first 440 at 52 seconds.
5. 10 to 15 minute rest interval.
6. Run 1 × 660 at pace speed, running first 440 at 53 seconds and finishing strong.
7. Run 10 × 110 yards.
8. Jog 2 to 4 laps as cool-down.

Tuesday
  1, 2, 3. Same as Monday.
  4. Run 3 × 220's at pace speed, 23 to 25 seconds.
  5. 4 minute interval.
  6. Run 10 × 110 yards.
  7. Jog 2 to 4 laps as cool-down.

Wednesday
  1, 2, 3. Same as Monday.
  4. Run 3 × 330's at full speed.
  5. 5 to 8 minute interval.
  6. Run 10 × 110 yards.
  7. Jog 2 to 4 laps as cool-down.

Thursday
  1, 2, 3. Same as Monday.
  4. Run 5 to 8 hurdles 4 to 6 times.
  5. 3 to 5 minute interval.
  6. Run 10 × 110 yards.
  7. Jog 2 to 4 laps as cool-down.

Friday
  1, 2, 3. Same as Monday.

Saturday
  Run time trials or participate in early season competition.
  1, 2, 3, 4. Same as Monday.
  5. Run 20 to 30 × 200 yards.

440-Yard Intermediate Hurdles: Midseason

Monday
  1. Warm-up by running and jogging one mile.
  2. Work vigorously 15 minutes by doing stretching and hurdle exercises.
  3. Run ½ mile of wind sprints. Run over just 3 hurdles several times.
  4. Run 3 × 330's at full speed.
  5. 5 to 7 minute interval.
  6. Run 10 × 110 yards.
  7. Jog 2 to 4 laps as cool-down.
    (110's listed in 6 may be modified by placing hurdles on track

and running over them as the 10 × 110 distance is covered. This is of special benefit when you are tired.)

Tuesday
1, 2, 3. Same as Monday.
4. .Run 3 × 5 to 8 intermediate hurdles at 23 to 25 pace for 220 yards.
5. 5 to 7 minute interval.
6. Run 10 × 110 yards.
7. Jog 2 to 4 laps as cool-down.

Wednesday
1, 2, 3. Same as Monday.
4. Run 220-330-220 full speed.
5. 5 to 7 minute interval.
6. Run 10 × 110 yards or modify by use of hurdles.
7. Jog 2 to 4 laps as cool-down.

Thursday
1, 2, 3. Same as Monday.
4. Run 5 to 8 × gun starts and first 3 hurdles.
5. Run 3 × (110-220-110) at race pace.
6. Run 5 × 110 yards or modify by using hurdles.
7. Jog 2 to 4 laps as cool-down.

Friday
1, 2, 3. Same as Monday.
4. Jog 10 to 15 minutes.

Saturday
Competition.

Sunday
1, 2, 3. Same as Monday.
4. Run 15 to 20 × 150 yards on grass.

low hurdle form

Form in the low hurdles should be as similar to sprinting as possible. There is no need for the runner to change the sprinting position when the hurdle is taken. The head should be maintained at the same height, the arms should swing in the same manner, and it is not necessary to settle down over the hurdle just to make a close clearance. The only change is that the foot of the lead leg is lifted to clear the hurdle and the trail knee and foot are flattened out slightly as they go over the hurdle. Usually, in clearing the hurdle, the trail leg is carried much farther forward and more under the runner's body than is true in high hurdling.

Good low hurdle form is characterized by uninterrupted smoothness and quickness of movement as the hurdle is taken. There must be no sense of sailing or of a break in the continuity of leg and arm action. (*See* Fig. 11-3.)

Length of stride over the hurdle. The length of the stride over the hurdle may vary from 10 to 13 feet, depending upon the leg length of the hurdler. The taller hurdler often has trouble cutting down his strides between hurdles in order to avoid getting too close for a proper takeoff for the next hurdle. In such cases it is important that he make an effort to land not more than $3\frac{1}{2}$ feet beyond the hurdle.

The start and steps to the first hurdle. The start of the low hurdles should be exactly like that of the sprints. Most hurdlers take 10 strides to the first hurdle in the 180-yard event. It may be necessary to alter the length of the first 4 strides in order to insure a proper takeoff. Some men may want to change the position of their feet in the blocks so that what would customarily be the front foot is the rear foot. This will enable them to go over the first hurdle using the preferred takeoff foot. They then would take either 9 or 11 steps to the first hurdle. (*See* Fig. 11-1.)

Steps between hurdles. All of the outstanding low hurdlers use 7 strides between hurdles. (*See* Fig. 11-1.) The short-legged hurdler may have difficulty getting close enough to the hurdle to go over it in good sprinting form. It may then be necessary to work on increasing stride length by having more vigorous arm action, lifting the knee higher, swinging the hips more, and increasing the landing position of each foot by 2 or 3 inches.

On the other hand, the taller man may have the difficulty of overrunning the hurdles. He must get the lead foot on the ground as near the hurdle as possible after clearing it. Each stride may be shortened 2 or 3 inches by constant practice.

training program

The low hurdler in high school who also runs the high hurdles should practice running over from 3 to 5 low hurdles 4 to 6 times once

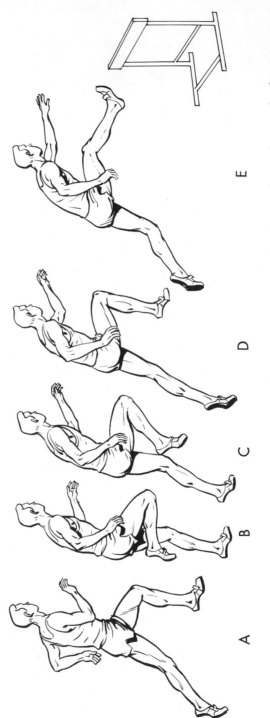

A   B   C   D   E

FIGURE 11–3. Low hurdle form. A top performer. (A) through (D) Note the fine sprint action used when ap-proaching the hurdle. (E) The lead arm is placed forward to help maintain proper balance.

F   G   H   I   J

FIGURE 11–3 (cont.). Low hurdle form. (F) As near as possible, sprinting form is maintained even in the air. (G) The trail knee is raised just high enough to clear the hurdle. (H) and (I) The lead foot is snapped down quickly. (J) The knee action is used to maintain proper stride and balance.

141

a week. He should also follow a workout schedule that combines some parts of the sprinter's and high hurdler's training programs.

The low hurdler who also runs the sprints should add 2 days per week practice over the low hurdles to the sprinter's schedule, in order to perfect form and gain confidence in approaching and running between the hurdles.

WORKOUT SCHEDULES

LOW HURDLES: PRESEASON

Monday
1. Warm-up by running and jogging 1 mile.
2. Work vigorously 15 minutes on stretching and hurdle exercises.
3. Run ½ mile of wind sprints and run over the first 3 low hurdles.
4. Run 3 × 220 yards, ¾ speed. Increase speed as conditioning improves.
5. 5 to 7 minute interval.
6. Run 10 × 150-yard sprints.
7. Jog 2 to 4 laps as cool-down.

Tuesday
1, 2, 3. Same as Monday.
4. Take 8 to 10 starts and run over first 3 hurdles.
5. Take 2 to 3 starts and 5 to 8 hurdles (depending on whether indoors or outdoors).
6. Run 10 × 150-yard sprints.
7. Jog 2 to 4 laps as cool-down.

Wednesday
1, 2, 3. Same as Monday.
4. Run 20 × 150-yard sprints, concentrating on form and relaxation.
5. 2 to 4 minute interval.
6. Jog 2 to 4 laps as cool-down.

Thursday
1, 2, 3. Same as Monday.
4. Take 3 to 5 preliminary starts for warm-up.
5. Take 4 starts, concentrating on first 15 yards.
6. Take 4 starts, concentrating on first 30 to 50 yards.

7. Run 10 × 150-yard sprints.
8. Jog 2 to 4 laps as cool-down.

Friday

1, 2, 3. Same as Monday.

Saturday

Participate in time trials or early season competition.

Sunday

1, 2, 3. Same as Monday.
4. Run 20 to 25 × 200 yards.

Low Hurdles: Midseason

Monday

1. Warm-up by running and jogging 1 mile.
2. Work vigorously 15 minutes on stretching and hurdle exercises.
3. Run ½ mile of wind sprints and first 3 low hurdles.
4. Run 3 × 220 yards full speed.
5. 5 to 7 minute interval.
6. Run 10 × 150-yard sprints. (May be modified by placing 2 or 3 hurdles on track and running over them when tired.)
7. Jog 2 to 4 laps as cool-down.

Tuesday

1, 2, 3. Same as Monday.
4. Take 5 to 8 starts and run over first 3 hurdles.
5. Take 2 or 3 starts and 5 to 8 hurdles (depending on whether indoors or outdoors).
6. Run 10 × 100-yard sprints.
7. Jog 2 to 4 laps as cool-down.

Wednesday

1, 2, 3. Same as Monday.
4. Run 1 × 330 yards, full speed.
5. 7 to 10 minute interval.
6. Run 1 × 220 yards, full speed.
7. Run 10 × 150-yard sprints.
8. Jog 2 to 4 laps as cool-down.

Thursday

1, 2, 3. Same as Monday.

4. Run 3 to 5 preliminary starts for warm-up.
5. Take 4 starts, concentrating on first 15 to 20 yards.
6. Take 4 starts, concentrating on first 60 to 100 yards (progression from 50 to 100 yards).
7. Run 10 × 110-yard sprints.
8. Jog 2 to 4 laps as cool-down.

Friday

1, 2, 3. Same as Monday.
4. Jog 10 to 15 minutes.

Saturday

Take part in competition.

Sunday

1, 2, 3. Same as Monday.
4. Run 15 to 20 × 150 yards on grass.

helpful hints

1. In addition to speed and flexibility, the 180-yard low hurdler must have endurance. The 70-yard hurdler needs speed and rhythm. If he is to specialize in low hurdles, he must run repeat 200's and an occasional 300-yard dash as part of his workout schedule.

2. The low hurdler must learn to *sprint through the entire 180 yards.* This event is not a hurdle-jumping contest.

3. He should be sure to keep the shoulders square and maintain proper balance when coming off the hurdle.

4. Best form in low hurdling is attained by running at full effort during practice. Competitive runs with teammates over 5 flights of hurdles are good practice.

5. The hurdler should practice taking off without being too close to the hurdle.

6. He should learn to *run over* the hurdle, not to jump or float over it.

7. He should keep a smooth, relaxed sprinting stride throughout the race. He should not gallop.

FOUR

JUMPS

LONG JUMP AND TRIPLE JUMP

historical performances

The long jump seems to be one of the oldest events in track and field. The Greeks carried weights in the hands and used a short run; thus they were able to jump almost as far as our best jumpers of today.

The earliest United States records reveal that a leap of 17'4" won the first AAU national championship. Ellery H. Clark of the United States won the 1896 Olympic title in Athens with a leap of 20'9¾". Chronologically, the following men are among those who have helped to improve performance in this event: Alvin Kraenzlein, Pennsylvania; Myer Prinstein, Syracuse; Ed Gourdin, Harvard; Robert Legendre, Georgetown; DeHart Hubbard, Michigan; Edward Hamm, Georgia Tech; Jesse Owens, Ohio State; Eulace Peacock, Temple; Robert Long, Southern California; Lorenzo Wright, Wayne State University; Willie Steele, San Diego State; Jerome Biffle, Colorado; George Brown, UCLA; John Bennett, U.S. Army; Greg Bell, Indiana University; Peter O'Connor, Ireland; Sylvio Cator, Haiti; and Chuhei Nambu, Japan.

A particularly outstanding performance occurred on May 28, 1935, when Jesse Owens set a world record of 26′8¼″. His greatest asset was probably his then world record speed of 9.4 seconds for the 100 yards. He jumped with great ease, and his speed was so great that, according to a film of his action, he did not seem to kick up his lead leg as high or attain as great an altitude as some of our jumpers do today. He often used the "float" style while he was in the air. Of course, he had good landing position.

Many early jumpers used some of the same styles of jumping used today, although the distance of the run has increased through the years from 90 or 100 feet to a minimum of 120 feet. It is thought that pits in the early period were very poor, and a takeoff board was not used until 1886. Undoubtedly, more impressive records would have been made in these earlier attempts if the facilities had been better.

Greg Bell of Indiana, the 1956 Olympic long jump winner, combined what some coaches believe are the ideal essentials for correct long jumping. He had a relaxed run to the takeoff, good lead leg swing, arched back with chest and head up to assure proper hip swing, and good landing position.

Recently, Ralph Boston, Lynn Davies of Great Britain, and Igor Ter-Ovanesyan have dominated this event, all being able to project themselves beyond 27′. However, probably one of the greatest feats in track history was the 29′2½″ distance jumped by Bob Beamon of the United States in the 1968 Olympics. (It has been calculated mathematically that man could long jump 35′.) Beamon approached the board at near maximum speed. His center of body mass was behind his takeoff foot. His takeoff foot was on the board long enough to generate force and give him upward thrust at a reasonably high angle. He arched his back in flight and extended his legs as far as possible. The 1968 Olympics revealed the greatest collection of long jumpers ever assembled as the results show:

finals (Oct. 18.   * = OR)

1. Bob Beamon (United States)						29′2½″	WR, OR, AR
29′2½″ *	26′4½″	P		P	P	P	
2. Klaus Beer (East Germany)						26′10½″	
26′1¾″	26′10½″	F		25′0″	F	F	
3. Ralph Boston (United States)						26′9½″	
26′9½″	26′5″	25′11½″	F		F	26′1½″	
4. Igor Ter-Ovanesyan (Soviet Union)						26′7¾″	
26′7¾″	26′6½″	F		F	26′7″	26′6¼″	

5. TONU LEFIK (Soviet Union)   26'6½"
   25'8"   26'6½"   25'1½"   24'1¾"   25'8¾"   25'5¼"

6. ALLEN CRAWLEY (Australia)   26'3¾"
   F   26'3½"   F   25'7"   F   26'3¾"

7. JACQUES PAN (France)   26'1¾"
   26'½"   26'1¾"   25'2¾"   24'10½"   24'11¾"   F

8. ANDRZEJ STALMACH (Poland)   26'½"
   25'3½"   26'½"   25'10¾"   25'5¼"   25'5¼"   25'8¾"

9. LYNN DAVIES (Great Britain)   26'½"
   25'1¼"   26'½"   F   —   —   —

10. HIROOMI YAMADA (Japan)   26'¼"
    F   26'¼"   F   —   —   —

11. LEONID BARKOVSKIY (Soviet Union)   25'11"
    25'11"   25'8"   F   —   —   —

12. REINHOLD BOSCHERT (West Germany)   25'10¾"
    F   24'9"   25'10¾"   —   —   —

13. MICHAEL AHEY (Ghana)   25'3½"
    25'3½"   24'10"   24'3¼"   —   —   —

14. LARS-OLOF HOOK (Sweden)   25'1½"
    25'1½"   F   F   —   —   —

15. VIC BROOKS (Jamaica)   24'7¾"
    F   F   24'7¾"   —   —   —

16. GERARD UGOLINI (France)   24'5"
    24'5"   23'1½"   F   —   —   —

— CHARLIE MAYS (United States)
    F   F   F   —   —   —

characteristics of a long jumper

The characteristics of a long jumper are the same as those of a sprinter, low hurdler, and quarter-miler, but he may possess more spring in his legs than the average competitor in these events (*see* Chapter 1).

long jumping form

The long jumper should be concerned with 5 factors: (1) a run long enough to gain optimum speed; (2) a good lift off the board to gain height; (3) a forceful kick or swing by the lead leg at the takeoff to project the body upward; (4) a good balanced position in the air to insure proper landing position; and (5) a full leg-extended position upon landing.

The run. The length of the run depends on the distance it will take the individual to gain maximum speed. A run of about 135 feet is the average used by most jumpers today, although a 160-foot run might be ideal. It is most important for the jumper to use a consistent stride during the run. He must also be able to run under control. This means he is running at not quite full speed, but in a fast, relaxed manner.

In order to insure a legal or fair jump each time, it is necessary for the performer to use at least 2 check marks. The following method of securing these marks is suggested: (1) Measure off approximately 130 feet (or more) on a smooth portion of the running track. (2) Start with both feet on the first mark, and, stepping forward with the takeoff foot, attempt to run in a relaxed manner down the runway. (3) At the midpoint of the run, or about 65 feet, the coach should check the spot where the takeoff foot hits as the run is continued through the entire 130 or more feet. (4) After a second runthrough is made to verify this check mark (65′), the coach should check the spot made by the takeoff foot near the end of the runway distance. (5) Measure the distance of these check marks from the start of the practice runway and transfer these measurement points to the site of the long jump runway. As the jumper runs through, the takeoff foot should land a few inches beyond the board to allow for the few shortened strides that occur when many men actually jump. However, it is best not to shorten the last few strides.

Usually the jumper strides to the first check mark, tries to reach near maximum speed by the time he reaches the second check mark, and then runs under control, but at near top speed, to the takeoff board in order to prepare for the "gather."

It is important that the jumper hit the second check mark with the toe of the takeoff foot. The runthrough must be practiced continuously so that the jumper will be able to hit the board accurately without "eyeing" it. He must concentrate on the path of his flight and the place in the pit at which he will land, rather than keep his eyes and head down looking at the board. He usually looks at a spot some distance away, observing this possible landing point through peripheral vision.

The takeoff. This part of the jump is probably the most important in determining the distance attained. The jumper is trying to transfer his forward momentum to *upward and forward* momentum.

During the last 3 or 4 strides before takeoff, the runner "settles" into a relaxed, controlled run. For average to good jumpers, the last stride to the toe-board is usually from 4 to 8 inches shorter (only 2 to 4 inches shorter for top jumpers) than the preceding one. This shorter stride helps the jumper to place his weight over the takeoff foot, and prevents him from having too much backward lean at the takeoff. The latter would cause him to lose some forward momentum. The great sprinter could probably use a longer last stride if he had gained enough forward momentum to carry his body to beyond his foot at the takeoff. (The body would be behind the takeoff foot as it is placed on the board.) This would enable him to keep his foot longer on the board, and therefore exert more force with it. Most 26- and 27-foot jumpers have good speed and use a relatively long last stride.

As the takeoff foot strikes the board in a heel-ball-toe motion, the eyes, head, and chest are held in an erect position. The lead leg is swung vigorously forward and up, with the knee flexed as much as in a running stride. The back is arched to enable the jumper to use a hip swing. The takeoff leg then comes up and the body assumes a sitting position in preparation for the landing. The arms are raised at the takeoff to aid in elevating the body, and thereafter used for balance (*see* Fig. 12-1).

Action in the air. One of the most important things to have in mind at the takeoff is to get height in the jump. Any action done by the jumper in the air will not add distance to the jump, except that the spot where the feet land determines the distance attained. To assist in getting the feet in the best landing position, the jumper will need to put his legs out in front as far as feasible just before landing. Many of the best jumpers today take one full stride while in the air so that their legs can be in an extended position upon landing. The 2 most commonly used kinds of movements in the air are the "hitch-kick," or "running in air action," and the "hip swing," or "hang." The running in air form is accomplished by driving the lead leg forward and upward, and then back in a clawing movement. The takeoff leg is simultaneously brought forward in a running action and extended forward into a horizontal position for a proper landing. The lead leg is then brought forward and extended horizontally alongside the takeoff leg in preparation for a landing.

The hang style is accomplished by dropping the lead leg after the takeoff so that both legs appear to drag in the air. At the same time the back is extended and the chest thrust forward. At the top of the arc, the legs and feet are violently swung forward and outward in an attempt to touch the now extended arms and hands. It becomes difficult to hold the legs in any one position while in the air, so several moves in midair are used by jumpers.

The landing. An effective landing is accomplished by holding

FIGURE 12-1. Long jumping form. A former Olympic champion. (A) The heel-ball-toe foot plant is used. (B) Note the slightly flexed knee of the takeoff leg. (C) He has thrust the lead knee up and out, with the head and chest held up high. (D) The extended stride in the air is executed. (E) The trail leg is coming toward the lead leg.

152

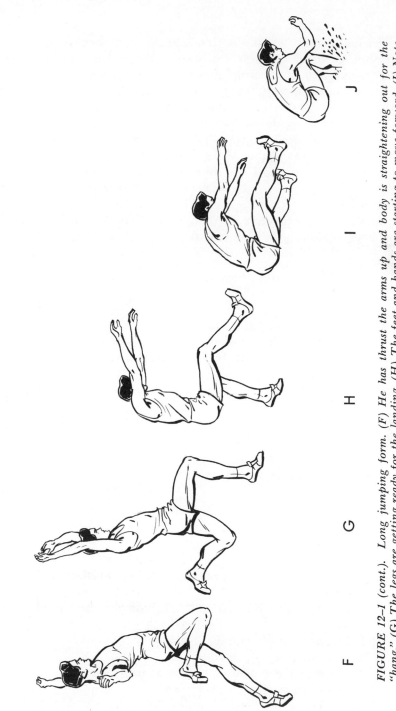

F   G   H   I   J

FIGURE 12-1 (cont.). Long jumping form. (F) He has thrust the arms up and body is straightening out for the "hang." (G) The legs are getting ready for the landing. (H) The feet and hands are starting to move forward. (I) Note the extended position of the legs, with the arms thrust forward. (J) The knees are relaxed upon landing to allow for the body "roll" over the feet.

the feet high as the landing begins. The legs are kept extended as far as possible until the buttocks nearly strike the ground. Then the head, chest, and shoulders are thrust forward and the knees are relaxed just as the heels touch the pit. The jumper should fall directly forward into a compact tuck position and onto his hands and knees. Keeping the feet high is very difficult and will take strong abdominal muscle action. The jumper will need a great deal of practice on this phase of the jump, which can consist of doing short runs jumping into a pit of foam rubber or other shock-absorbing material. Another type of landing used by some jumpers is to relax one knee upon landing and then stiffen the other after the heels have hit, causing the jumper to fall off to one side as the landing is completed. This style is not quite as popular as the one previously mentioned (*see* Fig. 12-2).

training program

Since speed is very important to the long jumper, it is essential that he practice sprinting constantly. The abdominal and back muscles must be strengthened to act in the air and upon landing. The following schedule assumes that 2 months of practice that included back and abdominal exercises and sprinting have previously been completed.

WORKOUT SCHEDULES

Four Weeks Prior to Meets

Monday
1. Jog ¼ mile.
2. Do stretching exercises:
    a. Hurdle exercises from sitting position.
    b. Touching the toes from a standing position, keeping the knees stiff.
    c. Situps, raising the feet and touching the toes in a jackknife action.
    d. Inverted bicycle riding.
3. Run wind sprints ½ mile.
4. Go through the "run-up" 5 times at full speed.
5. Take 10 jumps, using a short run.
6. Run 3 flights of 70-yard hurdles.
7. Do horizontal bar-leg raises for 10 minutes.

Tuesday
1. Jog ¼ mile.
2. Do stretching exercises.
3. Run ½ mile of wind sprints.
4. Take 5 jumps, using a short run from on the field position, not from the runway (called "pop-up").
5. Run 3 flights of 70-yard low hurdles.
6. Take 5 starts from the blocks, running 50 yards each time.

Wednesday
1. Jog ¼ mile.
2. Do stretching exercises.
3. Run ½ mile of wind sprints.
4. Take 5 jumps, using a short run (pop-ups).
5. Take 10 jumps using full run—5 jumps at half speed and 5 jumps at ¾ speed.
6. Do horizontal bar-leg raises for 10 minutes.

Thursday
1. Jog ¼ mile.
2. Do stretching exercises.
3. Run ½ mile of wind sprints.
4. Take 6 starts from the blocks, running 50 yards each time.
5. Run 3 flights of 70-yard low hurdles.

Friday
1. Jog ¼ mile.
2. Do stretching exercises.
3. Run ½ mile of wind sprints.
4. Run through a full run, checking accuracy of the stride with the check marks 3 times.
5. Take 10 jumps using a full run—5 at half speed, 5 full speed.

AFTER MEETS START

This schedule is made to account for Saturday meets. If meets are held on Friday, the schedule should be altered accordingly.

Monday
1. Jog ¼ mile.
2. Do stretching exercises.
3. Run ½ mile of wind sprints.

A   B   C   D   E

FIGURE 12-2. Long jumping form. A top performer in action. (A) He appears to hit the board first with the ball of the foot. (B) The body weight is directly over the takeoff foot when the lift begins. (C) This shows good knee lift and upward thrust of the right arm. (D) The stride in the air is very long. (E) He has straightened up the entire body in preparation for the hip swing.

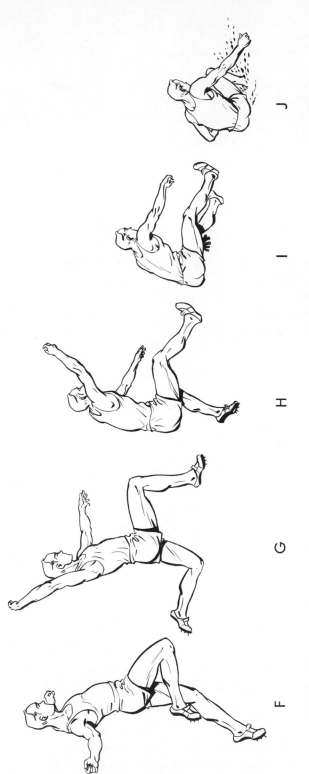

F   G   H   I   J

FIGURE 12-2 (cont.). Long jumping form. (F) The body is extending for the "hang" in the air. (G) The arms are held at different positions to help maintain balance and to begin to move them forward and down. (H) The legs have started to move together for the landing. (I) Note the full extension of the legs and forward thrust of the arms. (J) The right knee has relaxed, allowing him to swing to the right side of the pit.

157

  4. Go through the full run 5 times at full speed.
  5. Do 5 to 10 pop-ups.
  6. Take 5 jumps using the full run at ¾ speed; work on "gather" for the takeoff and on lifting off the board.

Tuesday

  1. Jog ¼ mile.
  2. Do stretching exercises.
  3. Run ½ mile of wind sprints.
  4. Run 3 flights of low hurdles 70 yards.
  5. Take 3 starts from the blocks, running 50 yards each time.
  6. Do horizontal bar-leg raises for 10 minutes.

Wednesday

  1. Jog ¼ mile.
  2. Do stretching exercises.
  3. Run ½ mile of wind sprints.
  4. Do 5 to 10 pop-ups.
  5. Take 5 jumps, using full run at full speed each time.

Thursday

  1. Jog ¼ mile.
  2. Do stretching exercises.
  3. Run ½ mile of wind sprints.
  4. Take 5 starts from the blocks, running 50 yards each time.
  5. Do horizontal bar-leg raises for 10 minutes.
  6. Go through the "run-up" 3 times.

Friday

Rest, and study movies of previous jumps made in practice and in meets.

WEIGHT-TRAINING PROGRAM (THE FOLLOWING IS TO BE USED AT BEGINNING OF ALL WEIGHT PROGRAMS)

Use 1 to 4 sets of 5 to 15 repetitions with near maximum weight that can be handled. It is best to start with about 75 pounds and work up to the athletic maximum over a period of 3 weeks to a month.

  1. Do partial squats and heel raises, jumping off floor.
  2. Do 2-arm military press.
  3. Do leg lunges with barbell on shoulders.
  4. Do toe raises with barbell on shoulders.
  5. Do situps with the knees flexed. Start with 25, progress to 200.

6. Do leg raises slowly. Progress from 10 to 100.

7. Run and hop up stairs with and without weighted vest.

helpful hints

1. Be sure to get into proper physical condition before starting to practice jumping.

2. Work consistently on the run to gain confidence and to help minimize fouling.

3. Prevent heel bruises by wearing proper shoes and using heel cups.

4. Practice good form in jumping by using pop-ups at the takeoff.

5. Be sure that the surface behind the board is not below the level of the board. This condition could cause heel bruises.

6. Practice some full runthroughs. It is necessary on occasion to jump using a full run in order to get the proper timing for taking off.

7. Concentrate on jumping *off* the board. It is not necessary to emphasize a hard "foot stamp," but an effective jump will mean that a forceful jumping action was used.

8. Concentrate on the lift off the board with the lead leg swung up, the chest kept high, and the spring being made from the big toe.

9. Hold the feet up high for as long as possible.

10. Check carefully the measurements for the run, the type of runway, and wind conditions before competing.

the triple jump

The triple jump was on the program from the very beginning of the modern Olympics. The triple jump, composed of a hop, step, and jump, is one of the most complex and highly coordinated events in track and field. It begins with a full run and a takeoff such as is used in the long jump, but the landing is made on the same foot executing the takeoff. This is called the "hop" phase. A so-called second jump, one "step," is made immediately and in sequence by the performer's landing on the foot opposite from the takeoff foot. From that point, he completes the final "jump" by taking another jumping step and landing on both feet, as in the long jump.

It has been stated that the triple jump originated in Ireland, and men of Irish birth and ancestry dominated this event in its early history. However, during the first three Olympics, Americans won this event. J. B. Connolly was the first Olympic winner in 1896 at Athens, Greece, with a "jump" of 45 feet. Myer Prinstein won the event in 1900 and 1904 with a best "jump" of 47 feet 4½ inches. In 1911 Dan Ahearne of the Irish-American Athletic Club of New York set a world's record of 50 feet 11 inches. This remained the American record until 1941, when Billy Brown of Louisiana State University "jumped" 50 feet 11½ inches.

No one country consistently provided top performances for the event through the years. During its early history (1896-1928), Europeans dominated the event. From 1928 to 1940 Japanese performers set many records and won the Olympic hop, step, and jump (now called the triple jump).

The distances achieved in this event fell off after World War II until the 1950's, when A. F. da Silva of Brazil began setting new records. He was the first competitor to jump over 54 feet and was Olympic champion in 1952 and 1956. Certainly da Silva has done more than any single person in recent years to perfect the form and to create world-wide interest in the event. One of the authors had an opportunity to watch him perform and to talk with him during some practice sessions held in the United States. A study of his form was included in the preparation for writing this material.

characteristics of a triple jumper

The characteristics of a triple jumper are about the same as those of a long jumper. He must possess good speed, strong legs (especially strong knees and ankles), and have good spring. He is usually of average height and slim in build. He must be highly coordinated in leg and foot action and possess good rhythm in jumping and hopping movements.

triple jump form

The triple jump performer should be concerned with five basic factors: (1) a run long enough to insure good speed; (2) a proper takeoff to secure maximum distance in the hop with as little loss of forward momentum as possible; (3) a long, unhurried step; (4) a good balanced position in the air to help in making a proper final landing; (5) as much relaxation as possible while executing the hop, step, and jump movement.

The run. The length of the run depends upon the distance it takes the individual to gain near maximum speed. A distance of about 130 to 150 feet is used by most jumpers today. It is most important that the jumper maintain a consistent stride throughout the run. He must run under control. This means he is not running at quite full speed as he approaches the takeoff board.

The method used for securing the proper run is the same as that used by long jumpers (see early part of this chapter).

The takeoff. The accomplishment of proper takeoff is basic. It insures making a good long hop and maintaining proper balance and momentum for the step. In long jumping, when there is only one explosive effort to be made, the distance a man travels through the air is determined by his takeoff velocity and angle of projection. He should strive to obtain maximum speed and takeoff from the board at an angle as great as possible (25 degrees or more, depending upon the speed of the jumper at the takeoff). However, in the triple jump there are other things to be considered. A takeoff angle of 20 degrees or even less will cause much lower loss of velocity, which is very important to the execution of the remaining actions.

There must be a definite effort to obtain distance on the hop, but not so much that the step and the distance of the jump are shortened, causing a decrease in total distance. Therefore, the jumper strives to take off at a relatively low angle of projection. He also shifts his body weight over his takeoff foot during the last stride before striking the board (as does the long jumper).

At the instant of pushoff from the board, perfect balance is essential. If the jumper is off balance his leg may collapse at the end of the hop. To insure proper balance, the jumper should keep his line of vision straight ahead by looking at a spot beyond the pit. He must not look up or down as he jumps, for this will upset his balance. The arms aid in maintaining good balance and forward velocity. The arms should be thrust forward and upward at the takeoff.

Upon landing after the hop, the jumper prepares himself immediately for the "step" portion of the event. He must absorb the shock of the landing and in turn be prepared to take the step. The performer must keep under control during his hop, and never allow his takeoff foot to get very far in front of his body. In landing from the hop, the body's center of gravity must be only slightly behind the landing foot, but it moves in front of the body before the preparation for the step is complete. The body is held erect, but the leg "gives" during the landing. If there is conscious effort to extend the leg, balance will be lost.

The step. Proper action in the step is very important, for this is the portion of the event in which most inexperienced jumpers have difficulty. Most poor jumpers take a quick, short step, which partly accounts for their inability to get good over-all distance. Balance and momentum are also important in the step. The performer coming down to the ground from the hop may be in good position for the step, but he must make a maximum driving effort with the landing foot in order to make a good step. After the jumper has made a forceful spring off his landing or hop foot, his "step" leg must swing up vigorously, with the bent knee raised waist-high and the upper leg held parallel to the ground. This must be an unhurried action coordinated with the arms in order to help maintain balance and get good body lift upward.

The body should be leaning slightly forward at the waist. The jumper must get as much distance as possible without overextending the lead leg. If the lead leg is overextended forward, the jumper will find that his center of gravity is far back of his jumping takeoff foot, and he is then in a poor position from which to execute the jump. The step may be described as a floating motion that is done slowly and very deliberately.

The jump. The techniques employed and the form used in the "jump" portion of the event should be the same as those used in the regular long jump. The performer shoud endeavor to obtain as much height as possible by driving the arms upward and swinging the lead leg forward and upward. The chest is raised and held high, and the head thrown backward. The feet should be held at the highest possible level until the last moment before landing.

One of the most important things to try to achieve in the triple jump is an even, rhythmic movement throughout the entire event. Each portion must be considered separately, but the 3 parts must be coordinated into a smoothly integrated performance. Each action should be deliberate and rhythmical. (*See* Fig. 12-3.)

It is generally agreed that the ratio of the hop to the step to the jump shoud be 6 to 5 to 6; in other words, in a total jump of 51 feet the hop would be 18 feet, the step 15 feet, and the jump 18 feet. This relationship is not a strict rule, but it gives an indication of what many better performers try to achieve.

training program

Since speed and leg strength are so vital to the triple jumper, it is essential that he practice sprinting and low hurdling frequently and constantly. The abdominal and back muscles must also be strengthened in order to accomplish the action in the air and land properly. The following schedule assumes that 3 months have been spent in a weight-training program and leg strengthening exercises. Hopping on alternate legs on the grass as the performer circles the field is considered an essential exercise to be done every week. This can also be done with light weights strapped on the shoulders.

WORKOUT SCHEDULES

FOUR WEEKS PRIOR TO MEETS

Monday
1. Jog ¼ mile.
2. Do stretching exercises:
   a. Hurdle exercises from sitting position.
   b. Touching the toes from a standing position, keeping the knees stiff.
   c. Situps, raising the feet and touching the toes in a jackknife action.
   d. Inverted bicycle riding.
3. Run ½ mile of wind sprints.
4. Go through the run-up 5 times at full speed.
5. Take 10 triple jumps, using a short run.
6. Run 3 flights of 70-yard low hurdles.
7. Do horizontal bar-leg raises for 10 minutes.

Tuesday
1. Jog ¼ mile.
2. Do stretching exercises.
3. Run ½ mile of wind sprints.
4. Take 5 triple jumps, using a short run each time.
5. Run 3 flights of 70-yard low hurdles.
6. Take 5 starts from the blocks, running 50 yards each time.

Wednesday
1. Jog ¼ mile.
2. Do stretching exercises.
3. Run ½ mile of wind sprints.
4. Take 5 triple jumps, using a short run each time.
5. Take 10 triple jumps, using a full run—5 at half speed, 5 at ¾ speed.
6. Do horizontal bar-leg raises for 10 minutes.

Thursday
1. Jog ¼ mile.
2. Do stretching exercises.

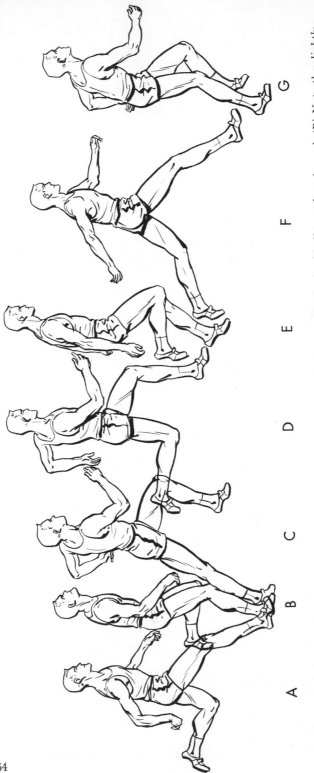

FIGURE 12–3. Triple jump form. A former world record holder is shown. (A) The heel-ball-toe plant is used. (B) Note the slightly bent knee of the takeoff leg. (C) He has thrust the lead leg up and out, with the head and chest held high. (D) The extended stride in the air has been executed. Note use of arms for balance. (E) The trail leg is coming toward the lead leg. (F) The takeoff leg is extended forward (but not too far) in preparation for the landing, with the trail leg being held far to the rear. (G) The landing has been completed but the step, in the process of being made by the lead leg, is delayed.

A   B   C   D   E   F   G

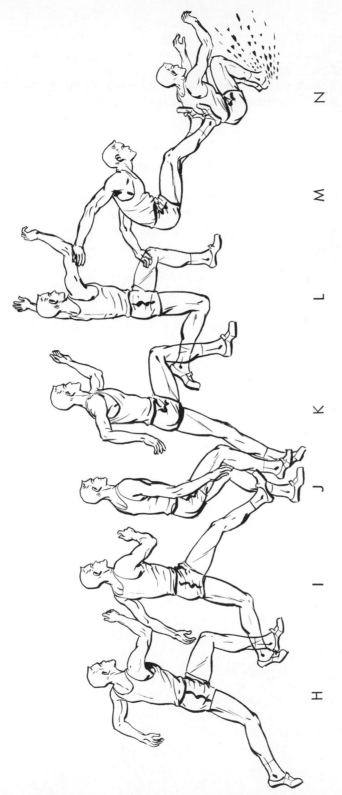

H   I   J   K   L   M   N

FIGURE 12–3 (cont.). Triple jump form. (H) The lead leg is now moving toward extension. (I) The lead leg is extended in preparation for the landing. (J) The heel-ball-toe plant is again used. Also, note the slightly bent knee of the takeoff leg. (K) He has thrust the lead leg up and out with a vigorous action. His head and chest are held high. (L) The trail leg is coming toward the lead leg. Note the upward thrust of both arms to help gain lift. (M) Note the extended position of the legs, with the arms thrust to the rear. (N) The knees are relaxed upon landing to allow for the body "roll" over the feet to be accomplished.

3. Run ½ mile of wind sprints.
4. Take 6 starts from the blocks, running 50 yards each time.
5. Run 3 flights of 70-yard low hurdles.

Friday

1. Jog ¼ mile.
2. Do stretching exercises.
3. Run ½ mile of wind sprints.
4. Run through the full distance to the takeoff, checking accuracy of the stride with the check marks 3 times.
5. Take 10 triple jumps, using a full run—5 at half speed, 5 at full speed.

AFTER MEETS START

This schedule is made to account for Saturday meets. If meets are held on Friday, the schedule should be altered accordingly.

Monday

1. Jog ¼ mile.
2. Do stretching exercises.
3. Run ½ mile of wind sprints.
4. Go through the full run 5 times at full speed.
5. Take 5 triple jumps, using a short run.
6. Take 5 triple jumps, using the full run at ¾ speed, work on gather for the takeoff, and be sure to take a long, unhurried step before the final jump.

Tuesday

1. Jog ¼ mile.
2. Do stretching exercises.
3. Run ½ mile of wind sprints.
4. Run 3 flights of 70-yard low hurdles.
5. Take 3 starts from the blocks, running 50 yards each time.
6. Do horizontal bar-leg raises for 10 minutes.

Wednesday

1. Jog ¼ mile.
2. Do stretching exercises.
3. Run ½ mile of wind sprints.
4. Take 5 triple jumps with a short run—work on a long "step" and on proper landing.
5. Take 5 triple jumps, using full run at full speed each time.

Thursday

1. Jog ¼ mile.
2. Do stretching exercises.
3. Run ½ mile of wind sprints.
4. Take 5 starts from the blocks, running 50 yards each time.
5. Do horizontal bar-leg raises for 10 minutes.
6. Go through the full distance to the takeoff 3 times.

Friday

Rest and study movies of previous action made in practice and in meets.

WEIGHT-TRAINING PROGRAM

This is the same as that used in the long jump.

helpful hints

1. Be sure to get into proper physical condition before starting to practice jumping.

2. Work consistently on the run to gain confidence and to help minimize fouling.

3. Prevent heel bruises by wearing proper shoes and by using heel cups.

4. Practice good form in jumping, spending much time on rhythm and attempting to get proper step distance.

5. Be sure the surface back of the board is not below the level of the board.

6. Be sure that the runway is smooth and firm enough to help prevent sprained ankles and knees.

7. Practice on the grass to help prevent shin splints and heel bruises.

8. Work on maintaining proper ratio of the hop, step, and jump —approximately 6 to 5 to 6.

9. Check arm action in the air, as seen by film, to insure maintenance of proper balance.

10. Check carefully the measurements for the run, the type of runway, and the wind conditions before competing.

11. Run and triple jump in a relaxed manner.

HIGH JUMP

13

There have been 4 basic high jumping forms used in the past. First came the *scissors,* used by most athletes up to 1895. This form required the jumper to concentrate on the run and takeoff, with very little thought of the clearance or "lay-out" over the bar. He went over the bar in a sitting position. The jumper could transfer the speed of the run to a vertical lift quite effectively, as proven by the record of 6'4" established in 1887 by W. Byrd Page (who must have used some type of backward "lay-out" as he cleared the bar).

The *eastern* form, thought to have been initiated by Michael Sweeney in 1895, was a type of scissors jump, but a definite "lay-out" over the bar was added. Sweeney's record of 6'5⅝" proved that the position over the bar was an important factor. This form was used in the United States with a few variations until 1930, and by most foreign performers until 1948. Using this style, John Winter of Australia jumped 6'6" to win the high jump in the 1948 Olympic Games. However, since he used almost a 60° approach, as compared to most other

168

jumpers' approach of 45° or less, he had the advantage. The takeoff place was wet and muddy during this competition, and the more a spot was used the worse it became. He was one of the very few who utilized a takeoff spot not previously used.

The *western roll* was introduced by George Horine of Stanford University in 1912. He jumped 6'7" with this style. A description of this style by Horine seems to demonstrate that he jumped in the same manner as modern jumpers.

This method of clearance was an improvement over the 2 previous forms of jumping. The body was placed flat over the bar, horizontal to the ground, and on the side. Walt Davis of Texas established a new world record of 6'11⅝" in 1953 using this form.

The *straddle* or *belly-roll* form was first used successfully in competition by Jim Stewart of the University of Southern California in 1930. The advantage of this straddle style lies in the fact that the body is in prone "lay-out" position over the bar, and only the *thickness* of the body must rise above the bar (in contrast to the *width* that must be above the bar in the western roll).

Most top high jumpers today use this form or a variation of it which involves the addition of a dive to the straddle roll (Valery Brumel, the present world record holder, used this variation). However, for several years track scientists have predicted that the high jumper must also be able to tumble in order to gain greater height. Dick Fosbury, United States 1968 Olympic champion, uses a backward layout tumble over the bar from a scissors takeoff style to corroborate this prediction.

The straddle dive and western roll styles of high jumping will be described more fully later. The Fosbury "flop" is analyzed briefly in Fig. 13-1.

characteristics of a high jumper

Tall boys with long legs often make the best high jumpers. A certain amount of "spring" is necessary for success. Good hip flexibility is another important attribute. Confidence in ability to jump also helps the performer (*see also* Chapter 1). Ability to tumble may be necessary in the future.

high jumping form

The straddle form of high jumping seems to be the best method, not only because of the records obtained, but because of the economy

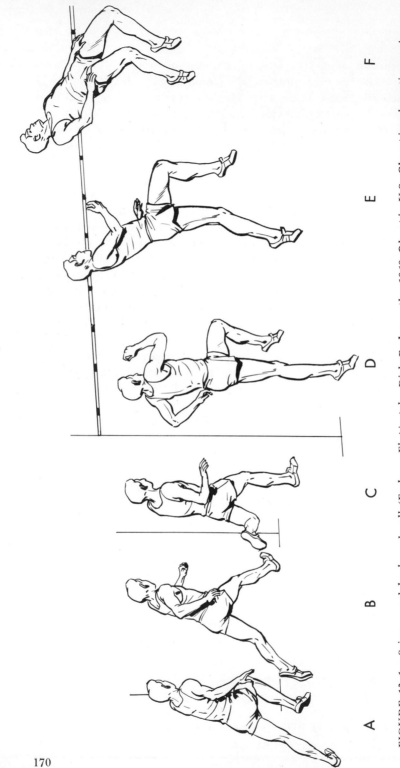

A   B   C   D   E   F

FIGURE 13–1. Scissors and backward roll (Fosbury Flop) style. Dick Fosbury, the 1968 Olympic U.S. Champion in action, using the "Fosbury Flop." (A) and (B) Fosbury is seen approaching at a point facing the front of the bar. He ends up on the left side of the bar, as in a scissors jump. (C) He is planting his right foot for the takeoff. (D) The "lift" is commenced. Note the high left knee position accompanied by elevated right flexed arm. (E) He is beginning his turn from his scissors jump. (F) The backward tumbling action is seen.

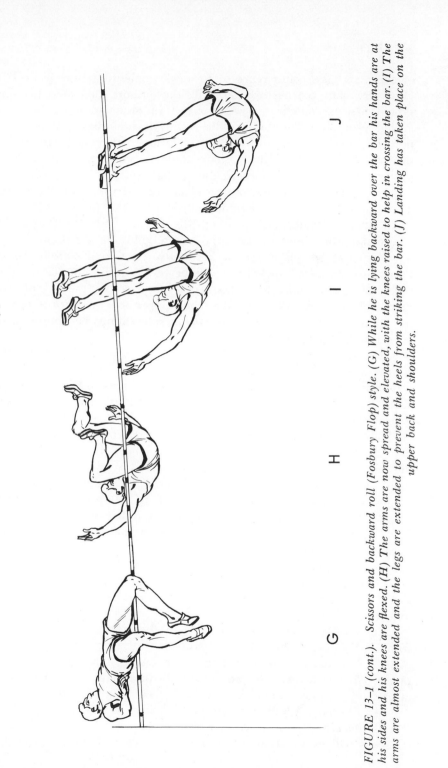

G   H   I   J

FIGURE 13-1 (cont.). Scissors and backward roll (Fosbury Flop) style. (G) While he is lying backward over the bar his hands are at his sides and his knees are flexed. (H) The arms are now spread and elevated, with the knees raised to help in crossing the bar. (I) The arms are almost extended and the legs are extended to prevent the heels from striking the bar. (J) Landing has taken place on the upper back and shoulders.

of effort and the transference of forward momentum into vertical lift. However, many coaches believe, as do the authors, that most beginners should first be taught the western roll in order to establish correct takeoff procedures for the straddle roll. The foot plant in the takeoff must be in the direction of the run in order to prevent "leaning" into the bar and dropping the inside shoulder before the lift is accomplished. This is *best learned* in the western roll.

The run. The length and speed of the run vary with the jumper. The run should be of sufficient duration for the jumper to gain an even, relaxed stride and for a settling of the body, or "gather," to take place. Most jumpers use approximately 40′ for the approach run. There should be one check mark slightly less than 25′ from the bar. From this distance onward the jumper concentrates on clearing the bar, and should not worry about the location of the takeoff spot. Practicing the run will insure that the jumper uses the proper distance for taking off from the bar. The takeoff spot should be approximately 1 yard or less from the bar.

The run should be started with a slow, relaxed trot for the first 3 or 4 steps. Some coaches now advocate a much faster run-up than was formerly used. This would mean greater horizontal speed. A decided backward lean or tumbling-like motion at takeoff is necessary to convert this horizontal velocity into vertical thrust. The steps are gradually accelerated up to the last 3 steps, which are much faster than the others. These last 3 strides are also longer than the others, with the next to last step the longest and the last stride the fastest. This rapid speed-up tends to produce a lowering of the center of gravity of the body. A backward lean and a bracing action of the takeoff leg helps stop forward momentum and convert it upward.

The takeoff. Some important points to consider just before and during the takeoff are:

1. The jumper's eyes should be focused on the bar during the last 20 feet before taking off. The head should be held up straight, and if the bar is at a low height the eyes should be focused on a height somewhat above it.

2. The last 3 steps are faster than the others. The next to last stride is the longest and the last stride is the fastest.

3. The body is lowered during the last 2 steps, and the *heel* is planted firmly against the ground on the last step. The knee of the takeoff leg is flexed slightly as the heel strikes the ground.

4. The body should be leaning back and well behind the takeoff foot as the last step is made. The distance of the takeoff spot from the cross bar will be different for each jumper and style of jumping. It is

usually from 30″ to 36″ for the straddle jumper and 36″ to 48″ for the western-roll jumper.

5. The jumper should concentrate on getting as much height as he can from the takeoff, not on how he will "lay-out" over the bar.

6. The lead leg should be swung up to as close to full extension as possible. By keeping this lead leg straight, and with a forceful swing upward, the jumper gets a terrific lift from the toe of the takeoff foot. The timing of the leg swing and push-off with the jumping foot at the takeoff are *very* important elements. The jumper should be leaving the ground from the big toe of the takeoff foot just as the lead leg reaches its highest point on the swing upward. The lead leg is then bent after the takeoff and extended again as the jumper gets on top of the bar.

7. The inside shoulder should be hunched vigorously to the opposite side and upward, with no leaning in toward the bar. This left shoulder (or inside shoulder) lean-in is a common fault of straddle jumpers as well as western rollers.

8. The takeoff foot must be placed on the ground in the direction of the run. The angle of the run-up varies from 20° to 45°. The low angle (20° to 25°) of approach is theoretically ideal because the jumper moves along the long axis of the cross bar, which allows more time for him to clear the trailing leg and also prevents direct body contact with the cross-bar. A higher angle allows less clearance time for the jumper and a more direct body contact with the cross-bar.

9. The right arm (for a left-footed jumper) is thrown up vigorously in a natural and coordinated fashion for body control and better clearance. The left arm is also thrown up to prevent left shoulder lean-in at the takeoff, and is then dropped to the chest in a relaxed manner when the jumper is in the air (*see* Fig. 13-2).

Landing is important enough to warrant a few comments. Many jumpers land on the side; some land on the back. Western-roll jumpers (left foot takeoff) land with their left hand and left foot touching the pit first. Straddle rollers (left foot takeoff) land on their right hand and foot first. Those using a dive fall on their backs. The straddle-dive roller should be looking at the sky when he lands so that he is sure he did a turn or twist in going over the bar.

THE WESTERN-ROLL FORM

The western roll is easier for most jumpers to learn; therefore, it may be taught more effectively to beginners and to certain individuals who are very tall and not very quick in their movements. Clearance

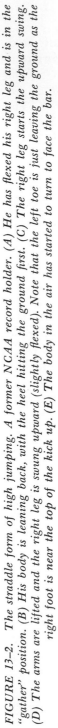

A   B   C   D   E

FIGURE 13–2. The straddle form of high jumping. A former NCAA record holder. (A) He has flexed his right leg and is in the "gather" position. (B) His body is leaning back, with the heel hitting the ground first. (C) The right leg starts the upward swing. (D) The arms are lifted and the right leg is swung upward (slightly flexed). Note that the left toe is just leaving the ground as the right foot is near the top of the kick up. (E) The body in the air has started to turn to face the bar.

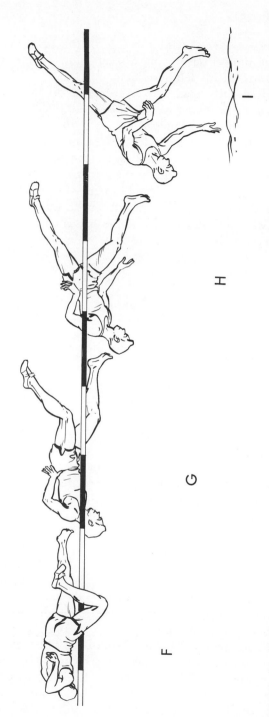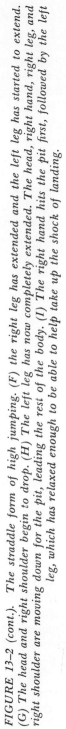

F   G   H   I

FIGURE 13-2 (cont.). The straddle form of high jumping. (F) the right leg has extended and the left leg has started to extend. (G) The head and right shoulder begin to drop. (H) The left leg has now completely extended. The head, right hand, right leg, and right shoulder are moving down for the pit, leading the rest of the body. (I) The right hand hits the pit first, followed by the left leg, which has relaxed enough to be able to help take up the shock of landing.

of the bar is accomplished with the side of the body next to the bar. The left-footed jumper clears on his left side by approaching from the left. He lands on his left foot first.

The run is usually made from an angle of 45°. However, some jumpers use an angle closer to 60°. The takeoff foot is planted in the direction of the run and the lead leg is vigorously thrown up straight. The inside shoulder is lifted vertically at the time of the takeoff. The head is held vertically to prevent inward body lean before the takeoff. The takeoff foot is then tucked in close to the lead leg in a bent position as the jumper moves up in the air to clear the bar. After the takeoff, the head is dropped quickly forward and sideward toward the bar. The left arm is also thrust forward and downward as the bar is cleared. This will help lift the hips over the bar (*see* Fig. 13-3).

THE STRADDLE FORM

The straddle form of high jumping, until the recent tumbling action used by Fosbury, has been the best form devised for bar clearance. However, the jumper must practice continually to avoid making the common errors that occur when using this form. Suggestions to help left-foot jumpers overcome these errors on takeoff include: (1) avoid leaning in toward the bar and dropping the left shoulder; (2) plant the takeoff foot in the direction of the run; (3) strike the ground with the heel first in the takeoff in order to get the proper "rock-up" action; and (4) do not bend the lead leg in the kick-up. In other words, think in terms of jumping high before considering the "lay-out" over the bar.

The takeoff and clearance of the bar are important factors in good high jumping. The last 3 steps before the foot plant is made in the straddle form are longer and faster than the others. The jumper assumes a backward lean as these steps are made. The shoulders are kept level and the head is erect. The heel of the takeoff foot strikes the ground first, then the straight lead leg is swung vigorously up at a point above the crossbar, if possible, and between the standard and the point of clearance. The lead arm is swung up over the head to aid in the lift and maintain proper body position in the air. As the lead leg reaches its highest point, the spring is made from the big toe of the takeoff foot. The speed of the run and leg swing and spring shoud take the jumper to the top of the bar. The right shoulder and the head are then quickly dropped to accomplish the turn over the bar. The hips, knee, and foot of the trail leg turn out in a relaxed manner to complete the turn around the bar. Many straddle jumpers find that they knock the bar off with the trail leg. Sequence drawings of a straddle roller show that the trail leg is first bent, and by the movement of the head and shoulder and twisting of the hips the trail leg is then turned *out* in a relaxed position to avoid striking the bar (*see* Fig. 13-4).

The straddle-diver (Brumel) seen in Fig. 13-5 has improved on the standard straddle by partially tumbling over the bar, bending and straightening the takeoff leg to decrease the leg lever, and twisting the body over the bar so as to land on his side or back. The left arm is placed across the chest to prevent the occurrence of a counterforce to the twist.

training program

The proper training program for high jumpers is difficult to determine. Some jumpers work very hard, jumping every day until the meets start, and then they jump Monday, Tuesday, and Wednesday of the week prior to each meet. Some actually jump very little in practice, being content to run hurdles, do some sprinting, and work for many hours on stretching exercises. However, those who do not work on their steps and the timing of their lead leg kick-up with the takeoff push find it difficult to jump their best. A happy medium between the 2 extremes of training programs might be best for the majority of jumpers, at least until they find one better suited to their individual requirements. The top jumpers participate in a weight-training program while in a body position simulating the leg action used in jumping.

WORKOUT SCHEDULES

Four Weeks Prior to Meets

Monday
1. Jog ¼ mile.
2. Run wind sprints for ½ mile.
3. Do stretching exercises that include:
   a. Touching the toes from standing position with knees straight.
   b. Situps, raising feet and touching toes in a jackknife position.
   c. Hurdle exercises from sitting position.
   d. Standing with feet spread, knees straight, alternately touching right toe with left hand and left toe with right hand.
   e. Inverted bicycle riding.
   f. High kicking with straight leg. Be sure to hold on to something for balance. Start easy and gradually kick higher.

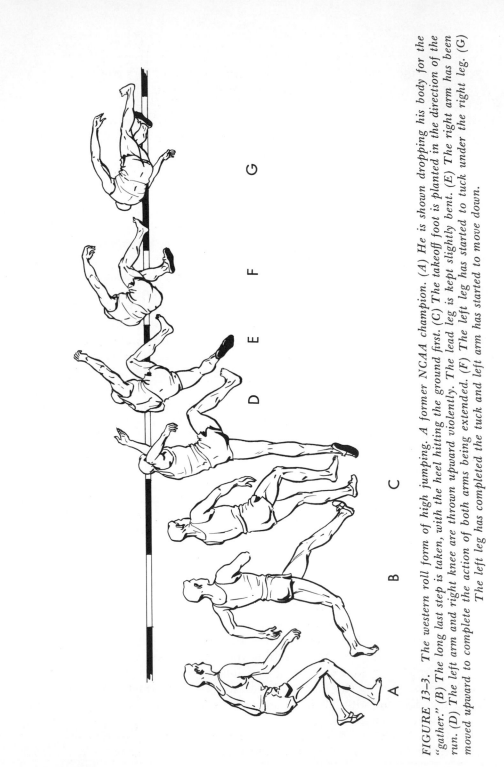

FIGURE 13–3. The western roll form of high jumping. A former NCAA champion. (A) He is shown dropping his body for the "gather." (B) The long last step is taken, with the heel hitting the ground first. (C) The takeoff foot is planted in the direction of the run. (D) The left arm and right knee are thrown upward violently. The lead leg is kept slightly bent. (E) The right arm has been moved upward to complete the action of both arms being extended. (F) The left leg has started to tuck under the right leg. (G) The left leg has completed the tuck and left arm has started to move down.

FIGURE 13–3 (cont.). The western roll form of high jumping. (H, (I), and (J) The left arm and shoulder drop to help lift the hips over the bar. (K) The right leg straightens out and the left leg remains tucked under the right leg. (L) The hands reach for the pit to help raise the hips and ease the shock in landing.

F   E   D   C   B   A

FIGURE 13–4. The standard straddle form of high jumping. A former Olympic champion and world record holder. (A) He is dropping his body for the "gather." (B) The relatively long last step is shown with the body leaning backward and the heel hitting the ground first. (C) the right leg starts the upward swing as the weight of the body moves over the left foot. (D) The left foot is pointed in the direction of the run. The right leg, fully extended, swings up. (E) The arms are swung up as the toe of the jumping foot leaves the ground. Note the tremendous height attained by the right foot as the takeoff foot is leaving the ground. (F) The body has started to turn to face the bar.

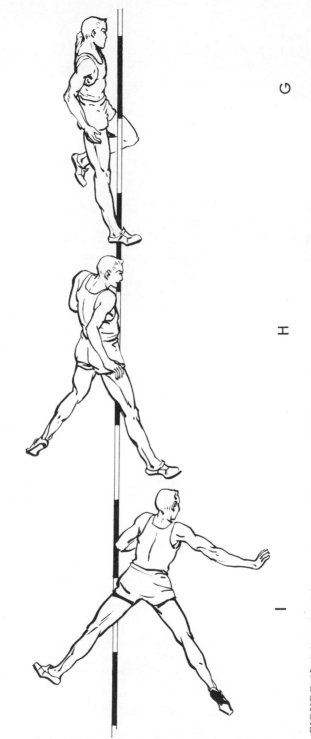

G

H

I

FIGURE 13–4 (cont.). The standard straddle form of high jumping. (G) He has an almost perfect lay-out on top of the bar. The hands are kept at the sides. The left leg has started to extend into a relaxed position. (H) The head and right shoulder have started to drop. The left leg still remains slightly flexed. (I) The body has completed the turn and is preparing for the landing.

182

A   B   C   D   E

FIGURE 13–5. The straddle roll with a dive. Note the backward lean in (C) and the full extended swing up leg in (D).

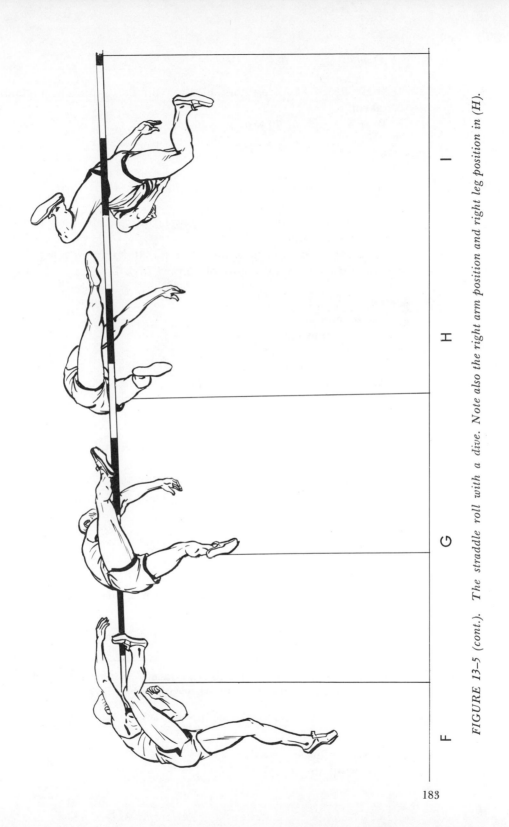

F   G   H   I

FIGURE 13–5 (cont.). The straddle roll with a dive. Note also the right arm position and right leg position in (H).

   4. Jump 15 to 25 times, concentrating on the approach run and takeoff.
   5. Run 5 flights of 70-yard low hurdles.

Tuesday
   1. Jog ¼ mile.
   2. Do stretching exercises for 15 minutes.
   3. Run wind sprints for ½ mile.
   4. Do "bounding exercises" by springing off on alternate feet on grass for 10 minutes.
   5. Do exercises on the horizontal bar for 10 minutes.
   6. Run through several flights of 70-yard high hurdles.

Wednesday
   1. Jog ¼ mile.
   2. Do stretching exercises.
   3. Run wind sprints for ¼ mile.
   4. Jump 15 to 25 times, working on the takeoff and bar clearance.
   5. Run 5 flights of 70-yard low hurdles.

Thursday
   1. Jog ¼ mile.
   2. Do stretching exercises.
   3. Run wind sprints for ½ mile.
   4. Run through 3 flights of 70-yard high hurdles.
   5. Exercise on the horizontal bar for 10 minutes.

Friday
   1. Jog ¼ mile.
   2. Do stretching exercises.
   3. Run wind sprints for ¼ mile.
   4. Jump 15 to 25 times, practicing on form at maximum heights.
   5. Run 3 flights of 70-yard low hurdles.

AFTER MEETS START

   This schedule is set up for Saturday meets. If meets are held on Friday the schedule should be altered accordingly.

Monday
   1. Jog ¼ mile.
   2. Do stretching exercises.
   3. Run wind sprints for ¼ mile.

4. Jump 10 to 15 times. Practice on the run and the jump. Concentrate especially on the last 3 steps and the takeoff.
5. Run 3 flights of 70-yard low hurdles.

Tuesday
1. Jog ¼ mile.
2. Do stretching exercises.
3. Run wind sprints for ½ mile.
4. Run 3 flights of 70-yard high hurdles.
5. Do exercises on the horizontal bar for 10 minutes.

Wednesday
1. Jog ¼ mile.
2. Do stretching exercises.
3. Run wind sprints for ¼ mile.
4. Jump 10 times at maximum height.

Thursday
1. Jog ¼ mile.
2. Do stretching exercises.
3. Run wind sprints for ½ mile.

Friday
Rest, study movies taken in meets and in practice.

WEIGHT-TRAINING SCHEDULE

1. Do 2-arm military press, one set of 10 repeats using 50 to 75 pounds.
2. Do deep knee bends (feet flat on the floor), barely jumping off the floor, 2 sets of 10 repeats using 75 to 100 pounds.
3. Do leg lunges with barbell on shoulders, 2 sets of 10 repeats using 75 to 100 pounds.
4. Do toe raises with toes on 2-inch blocks, barbell on shoulders, 3 sets of 10 repeats using 75 to 100 pounds.

helpful hints

1. Condition the entire body properly *before* starting to high jump. Some athletes go out the first day of practice and jump higher than they will again for several weeks! Stretching exercises to loosen

up hamstring muscles, the groin region, the calf muscles, ankles, and feet are necessary and help prevent injury to these areas. Running the high and low hurdles also helps to stretch the leg muscles.

2. Constant work on the proper foot plant is important. The heel should strike the ground first, and the foot is placed along the direct path line of the run.

3. Dropping the left shoulder and leaning in toward the bar at the takeoff should be avoided.

4. The jumper should work on *timing* the lead leg swing-up with the takeoff. The spring off the big toe should be made just as the lead leg reaches its highest point.

5. The jumper should be relaxed when he is on top of the bar; he should avoid thinking about picking up the trail leg.

6. Most practice jumping should be done before the regular meets begin. Many jumps should be taken to perfect form and timing before the important meets occur.

7. A rubber cup used in the heel of the takeoff shoe in practice will prevent stone bruises.

8. If the spikes of the lead leg drag the ground at the takeoff, the jumper should try jumping without a shoe on the lead foot.

9. Heights for practice jumping which are high enough to offer a challenge and call for almost top effort should be those that the jumper can make without losing proper form.

10. The jumper should be convinced that there is no "ultimate" height that he can jump.

11. The takeoff area should be very firm. Many schools are now using a type of rubberized macadam that has proved to be very satisfactory for takeoff purposes.

12. The coach may be able to get a good view of the jumper's bar clearance by watching from a position at the end of the crossbar. The jumper's maximum height should be attained as he is directly above the crossbar.

13. Since soft landing surfaces (inflated rubberized material) are now in use in most situations, a jumper has an environment that provides him with an opportunity to experiment with many types of jumping styles. Tumbling-like crossings of the bar will be more evident in the future because of the soft landing surfaces.

14. Some resistance, such as weights, should be used by the jumper in practice simulating the proper leg action he uses when jumping in meets.

POLE VAULT

14

yesterday's vaulters

By conjecture, the pole vault can be traced to the days of primitive man. He vaulted across streams and obstacles too board or high to jump when he sought food, or when he escaped from or attacked an enemy. Thus, at first, vaulting was done to gain distance rather than height.

Much later, the pole vault began to be used in athletic contests as a height event, and by 1877 it became a part of the track program. The original vaulting poles, made of ash and hickory wood, were long and heavy, and had a tripod of iron attached to the ground end, instead of using a box. The early competitor ran slowly to the takeoff spot (because of the great weight of the pole and the awkward carrying position that entailed) and planted the tripod in the ground about 3 feet from the bar. As the pole started up he would climb it hand over hand until it started to fall forward. Then he would pull his knees up first, followed by his body, and go over the bar in a sitting position.

However, in 1889, the rules were changed to prevent the performer from climbing the pole in this manner. Now the top hand cannot be moved toward the top end of the pole after the takeoff.

The early vaulters used the widespread hand position (hands about 3' apart) because of the weight of the poles. With this wide hand position, Hugh H. Baxter held the world record (11'5") from 1887 to 1898. However, in 1898, R. G. Clapp of Yale established a world record of 11'10½", using a lighter pole and the same type of hand position in use until recently. The hands of the metal vaulter were placed anywhere from 2" apart to a position almost touching one another.

The next distinctive change in vaulting came with the introduction of the bamboo pole. Its lightness made it possible for the vaulter to carry the pole with a closer hand grip, thus enabling him to run faster down the runway.

By 1912, most main elements of modern vaulting had been established. For example, the run, the hand shift (which we believe will be used by the vaulter more and more in the future, in connection with the fiber glass pole), the swing, the pull, and the jackknife over the bar were used by M. S. Wright of Dartmouth when he vaulted 13'2¼" in 1912. The modern history of the pole vault has been as dynamic as the event itself. The type of pole used has played an important part in the progress of pole vaulting. Poles progressed from the heavy wooden poles of ash and bamboo to the safer steel and metal poles, and finally to the fiber glass pole, which helped raise the world record by nearly 2 feet.

Such men as Charles Hoff, Lee Barnes, Sabin Carr, Bill Sefton, Earle Meadows, George Varoff, Don Laz, Bob Richards, and Cornelius Warmerdam have all contributed to the development of the method now considered the most efficient way to pole vault.

Warmerdam is thought of by many as *the* vaulter of premetal times. Perhaps his greatest contribution was in proving that most vaulters can vault with a much higher hand hold than was previously thought possible. His increase of length of run, strong pull-up, unusual action over the bar, as well as his higher hand grip, gave him superior form as a vaulter for more than 15 years. In 1942, he set a world's record of 15'7¾", and in 1943 an indoor record of 15'8½". For nearly 10 years he was in a class by himself, clearing 15' more than 50 times, using a bamboo pole. During the early 1950's, his records were challenged, but never surpassed, by Bob Richards, the 1952 and 1956 Olympic champion. Richards used a metal pole and became the world's most consistent vaulter, clearing 15' over 100 times in his career. Bob Richards' best vault (15'6½") was made in 1957, when he was well over 30 years old.

Bob Gutowski set a new world's record (15'8¼") using a metal pole in 1957. Don Bragg, the 1960 Olympic champion (15'5"), broke the world record during that same year with a vault of 15'9½", and set what will probably remain the best vault ever achieved with the use of the metal pole.

The fiber glass pole was introduced during the early 1950's, but was not fully developed, accepted, or even close to being mastered until George Davies used a fiber glass pole in 1961 to set a world's record of 15'10½". In 1962 the world's first 16' vault was made by John Uelses. The following year John Pennel became the first 17' vaulter, and once held the world record at 17'6¾". Other vaulters to clear 17' are: Fred Hansen, 1964 Olympic champion (16'8¾") and one-time world record of 17'4"; Paul Wilson, former world record holder (17'7¾"), and the first high school vaulter to clear 16'; Bob Seagren, 1968 Olympic champion and present world record holder (17'9"); and Casey Carrigan, 1968 Olympic vaulter and first 17' high school vaulter. Other 17' vaulters are Dennis Phillips, Dick Railsback, and Sam Kirk. The best pole vault heights in Olympic history were accomplished in the 1968 Olympics in Mexico, with 9 vaulters clearing over 17'. The results were as follows:

finals (Oct. 16)

1. Bob Seagren (United States)	17'8½"
2. Claus Schiprowski (West Germany)	17'8½"
3. Wolfgang Nordwig (East Germany)	17'8½"
4. Chris Papanicolaou (Greece)	17'6¾"
5. John Pennel (United States)	17'6¾"
6. Gennadiy Bliznyetsov (Soviet Union)	17'4¾"
7. Herve D'Encausse (France)	17'2¾"
8. Heinfried Engel (West Germany)	17'¾"
9. Ignacio Sola (Spain)	17'¾"

characteristics of pole vaulters

Generally speaking, vaulters should be rather tall (over 6'), with good speed, strength, coordination, and tremendous courage. However, there have been, and will continue to be, great vaulters who may seem too short, too slow, or have other shortcomings which they overcome by their exceptional desire, skill, and daring.

Young men who have enjoyed vaulting with poles across streams or in their own yard when boys may become vaulters in high school or college if given the opportunity. The mechanics of the pole vault are quite involved; they require concentrated study and understanding from the performer if he is to be successful. The vault is, in essence, a run, jump, rope climb, gymnastic stunt, fall, and tumble.

Boys who are weak in arm strength and afraid of heights should probably be discouraged from participation. Boys with good speed, average or better height, strong arms, light legs, handstanding ability, and keen analytical minds should become fine vaulters (*see* Chapter 1).

proper form

Fiber glass pole vaulting is one of the most complex and difficult of all track and field events. It takes an exceptional athlete to be a champion in pole vaulting. He must combine the speed of a sprinter with the courage, strength, and ability of a gymnast. (*See* Fig. 14-1.)

The vault must be thought of as a complete action from the beginning of the run until the landing in the pit. The action must be broken down into several important phases in order to explain it clearly. They are presented in the following pages (for the right-handed vaulter with a left foot takeoff).

THE POLE CARRY

The distance between the hands when carrying the pole in the approach varies from 24″ to 36″. The high grip used in fiber glass vaulting forces the vaulter to use a high pole carry (the tip of pole is held slightly above the head) at the start of the run. The pole may be placed slightly across the body at the beginning of the run. This helps the vaulter to gain speed more efficiently (the pole is actually lighter to the vaulter when carried in this position), but the pole must be carried horizontally and directed toward the vaulting box during the last third of the run. The left hand and thumb support much of the pole's weight, while the right hand and thumb apply pressure downward.

The pole carry should be as relaxed as possible (the fingers and hands should not grip the pole tightly), since tenseness generated from the hands and arms is quickly transferred to the rest of the body and causes a decrease in speed, relaxation, and coordination.

HEIGHT OF HAND GRIP

The height a vaulter can grip on a pole is relative to his experience, height, weight, speed, and the flexibility of the pole. Most fiber glass poles should be purchased with the age group, vaulter's weight, and height of grip on the pole kept in mind. Commercial sporting goods firms will supply the correct weight pole for a boy if given this information at the time of purchase. Normally, the vaulter must learn to grip the pole at a constant height and within a foot of his maximum jumping height.

THE RUN

The length of the run is usually determined by the speed and skill of the vaulter. Another factor to consider is how far he has to run to attain maximum speed. Most world class vaulters possess good running speed, but this is not an absolute prerequisite for the out-standing vaulter. The length of the run should be determined on the running track, and the measurements transferred to the runway. The vaulter should make several runthroughs at approximate distances of 110 to 140 feet. He should start at a specific point and have someone mark the place at which his takeoff foot hits the track surface near the finish of his run. Several trials should be made until the check marks become consistent at both the midway and the takeoff spots. The total distance of the run and the distance between check marks should be measured off on the track, and then transferred to the pole vault runway. In the transferral, the measurements must be taken from the takeoff spot, not from the back of the vaulting box. The 8 to 12 feet from the takeoff spot to the vaulting box may then be added to the total distance. The check marks will vary in accordance with the type of runway surface and the direction of the wind. Another factor that may affect the placement of the check marks is the length of time the vaulter has been in training during the season. As he becomes more efficient, the check marks may have to be changed.

THE POLE PLANT

The pole plant and takeoff are the 2 most important phases in the vaulting action. Nearly all problems encountered during the final phases of the vaulting movement can be traced to inefficient pole plant and takeoff mechanics. The pole plant should be started about 2 strides or less from the takeoff point. Before the left foot lands in preparation for the takeoff, the pole should be planted in the box and the hands placed directly above the head in good takeoff position. The action of the arms during the last 2 strides can best be described as a side arm circling-like movement. The right shoulder is rotated slightly to the rear as the right hand brings the pole upward in a

FIGURE 14-1. *Fiber glass pole vaulting form. (A) The pole is planted while on left foot (right-handed vaulter), 2 strides from the takeoff, with a side arm circling-like movement. (B) The pole is almost planted as it is moved forward and above the head while the vaulter is on right foot. It is planted for the takeoff as the left foot lands. (C) and (D) Excellent takeoff and hang techniques as the vaulter drives forward horizontally. (E) and (F) The swing-up begins just after the hang. The left leg remains straight and is swung upward toward the right leg, which is flexed and is leading the action.*

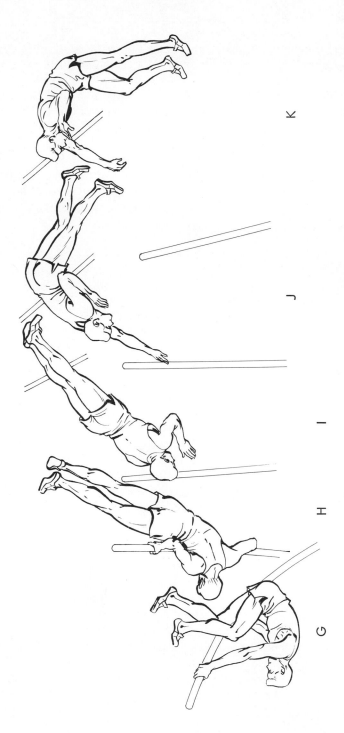

G   H   I   J   K

FIGURE 14–1 (cont.). Fiber glass pole vaulting form. (G) The roll back and vertical extension are the continuation of the swing. Both legs flex as they are driven back and toward the top of the pole at a 75-degree angle. The arms maintain their takeoff position, keeping the body behind the pole. The shoulders are the horizontal axis of rotation. Notice that the head is never thrown back in a hyperextended position. (H) The vaulter attempts to keep his back to the bar as long as possible during the vertical extension of the body in preparation for the clearance. This also delays the pull and turn actions until after the hips pass the head. The pull, turn, and push-up are continuous powerful moves made to maintain vertical lift. (I), (J), and (K) The push-up and arch-fly-away clearance. The arms are extended quickly down the pole, the left arm being released first, followed by the right arm. Notice that the head and eyes remain down as the body drapes around the bar in an arch-fly-away clearance.

circling-like movement to the side and above the head. The left hand directs and supports the pole while it is being planted firmly in the box.

The left hand is shifted upward on the pole just before the pole makes contact with the box. Some vaulters do not shift their hands, keeping the same takeoff hand spread used during the pole carry. The hand spread used by present-day vaulters during the takeoff varies a great deal, ranging from about 8 to 30 inches. However, the hand distance used by most outstanding vaulters varies from 12 to 24 inches. Generally, the last stride just prior to takeoff is 6 to 10 inches shorter than the normal strides. This allows the vaulter more control over his actions in order to gather for the takeoff.

THE TAKEOFF AND HANG

The takeoff should resemble that used in the long jump. However, the vaulter must drive off the ground in more of a horizontal than a vertical direction. The lead leg is driven forward and up at a 20 degree angle. The left foot pushes off and remains in a nearly straight extended position. The vaulter appears to be hanging momentarily in the takeoff position, with the right knee and foot leading and the left leg extending backward. The right arm is extended to nearly a straight position, and is above and in back of the vaulter's head at takeoff. The left arm is flexed at nearly a 90 degree angle and remains fixed throughout the vault until the turn is begun.

The position of the takeoff foot relative to the top hand varies from a foot back to a foot in front of a plane parallel to it. Ideally, the takeoff foot should be placed directly below the top hand, or 6 to 12 inches ahead at a point just below the midpoint of the hand spread.

THE SWING-UP

The body is in an extended position during the swing-up, with the straight left leg being swung upward in an attempt to catch up with the right leg, which remains in the flexed takeoff position (90° to 120°). As the vaulter's back reaches the horizontal, the left leg is flexed, with both knees being brought back toward the shouders. This action, when properly executed in a fast, powerful manner, aids in bending the pole and keeps the hips square (not tilted right or left) during the roll back.

The Roll Back and Vertical Extension

The roll back is a continuation of the swing-up. The shoulders are the horizontal axis of rotation as the legs are flexed and driven back and up toward the hands. Combined with this flexing and upward thrust of the hips and legs is the roll back of the head and shoulders. The head and shoulders act as a unit at this stage; the head is not thrown back excessively or separately during the swing, roll back, and vertical extension of the body. During the roll back, the legs are not just brought up vertically, but backward at a 75 to 80 degree angle to the runway. The right arm remains relatively straight, while the left arm is flexed, but fixed, keeping the vaulter behind the pole.

The vertical extension of the vaulter's body takes place as the hips rotate up and past the shouders. The vaulter should attempt to keep close to the pole by bringing the hips in toward the pole and extending the legs vertically.

The Pull and Turn

The pull and turn should be delayed as long as possible to insure that maximum vertical lift takes place. During this phase, the vaulter is being raised quickly by the pole, and the pull and turn should therefore be a very quick, catlike movement as he positions himself for the push-up and clearance of the bar.

Push-up, Clearance, and Landing

The push-up and clearance is a continuation of the pull and turn. A push downward is made by the arms, with the elbows held outward. The left arm is released first, and flexed and kept away from the cross bar. The right arm then completes its extension as a push backward is made with an outward flick of the thumb. After the release of the pole, the thumbs of both hands are rotated inward, causing the elbow to rotate out and away from the cross bar.

The head remains down during the clearance, with the eyes focused on the box or landing area. The head should not be thrown back too soon, even during a poor clearance; this forces the chest down and into the bar. During mechanically sound vaults, the head is never thrown backward; this aids the vaulter in obtaining a good arch-fly-away clearance of the bar.

The position of the standards is very important to the success of the vault. The best mechanical clearance is obtained with the standards set back 8 to 24 inches from the front of the pit. During practice, it is recommended that the standards be placed 8 to 24 inches toward the rear of the pit. This will help cause the vaulter to drive horizontally during the takeoff and hang, thus preventing a premature roll back, pull, and turn.

The landing should be made on the back when conditions permit. The vaulter should attempt to distribute the impact of landing over the area of the hips, back, and shoulders. When poor facilities prohibit this type of landing, the athlete should land on his feet with the legs flexed, and then roll backward, shifting the weight in a rolling action to the hips, back, and shoulders. Proper landing techniques are a necessity to conserve the athlete's strength and energy during the long demanding periods of competition.

Note: Effective May 1, 1969, it is no longer a miss when the vaulter's pole passes under the bar as he crosses over it. Bob Seagren of the U.S. lost 2 world records because of the rule declaring it a miss, and Casey Carrigan failed to qualify for the U.S. Olympic finals due to the enforcement of this rule. John Pennel cleared 17'8½" only to have it declared a miss because his pole passed under the cross bar.

training program

This first workout schedule assumes that at least 60 days have previously been spent in a regular program of weight-training and general body-building exercises. The training program followed by the vaulter is strenuous, and tumbling and rope climbing should be participated in during the fall. The following sample schedules are presented with the idea that the coach will modify them to fit each individual athlete.

WORKOUT SCHEDULES

Four Weeks Prior to the First Competition

Monday
1. Jog ¼ mile.
2. Do stretching exercises that include:
   a. Push-ups.
   b. Walking on hands.
   c. High kicking.

    d. Hurdle exercises from sitting position.

    e. Touching toes to loosen hamstring muscles.

    f. Situps raising feet and touching toes in a jackknife position.

3. Run ½ mile of wind sprints.

4. Work for 15 minutes on the run-up. Check the takeoff point accurately.

5. Take 6 vaults, using a run of 40 to 50 feet, with a "soft pole" (10 to 20 pounds under weight of vaulter).

6. Take 10 to 14 vaults using a full run (pole equal to or above vaulter's weight).

7. Work for 10 minutes on the horizontal bar. Do pull-ups and kick-ups.

Tuesday

1. Jog ¼ mile.

2. Do stretching exercises.

3. Run ½ mile of wind sprints.

4. Run 5 flights of 70-yard low hurdles.

5. Work for 15 minutes on parallel bars and rope.

Wednesday

1. Jog ¼ mile.

2. Do stretching exercises.

3. Run ½ mile of wind sprints.

4. Work for 15 minutes on the hand shift and pole plant, doing the last 4 strides of the run only.

5. Take 6 vaults, using a short run and "soft pole."

6. Take 10 to 15 vaults, doing full runs with regular pole.

7. Take 6 starts, running 25 yards each time.

Thursday

1. Jog ¼ mile.

2. Do stretching exercises.

3. Run ½ mile of wind sprints.

4. Run 5 flights of 70-yard low hurdles.

5. Lift weights.

Friday

1. Jog ¼ mile.

2. Do stretching exercises.

3. Run ½ mile of wind sprints.

4. Work for 10 minutes on the run-up.

5. Take 5 vaults, using a short run and "soft pole."

6. Take 10 to 15 vaults, doing a full run. Place the bar high enough to require work to get proper clearance.

After Meets Start

This schedule is set up for Saturday meets. If meets are held on Friday, alter the schedule accordingly.

Monday
1. Jog ¼ mile.
2. Do stretching exercises.
3. Run ½ mile of wind sprints.
4. Take 5 vaults, using a short run and "soft pole."
5. Take 10 to 15 vaults, using a full run and regular pole.
6. Run 5 flights of 70-yard low hurdles.

Tuesday
1. Jog ¼ mile.
2. Do stretching exercises.
3. Run ½ mile of wind sprints.
4. Take 6 starts, running out of the blocks for 25 yards each time.
5. Lift weights.

Wednesday
1. Jog ¼ mile.
2. Do stretching exercises.
3. Run ½ mile of wind sprints.
4. Work for 10 minutes on the hand shift and pole plant, using just the last 4 strides of the run.
5. Do 10 to 15 vaults (regular pole). The last 6 are to be done at maximum height.
6. Run 3 flights of 70-yard low hurdles.

Thursday
1. Jog ¼ mile.
2. Do stretching exercises.
3. Run ½ mile of wind sprints.
4. Take 6 starts, running out of the blocks for 25 yards each time.
5. Work for 15 minutes on the bars and rope.

Friday
Rest, or study movies of practice jumps and jumps taken in meets.

Saturday

Day of the meet. Arrive at the stadium early enough to dress slowly. Be on the track early enough to check the run distance *accurately*. Check the run at least 4 or 5 times. Vault at medium height 4 or 5 times before competition begins. Be confident and relaxed.

WEIGHT-TRAINING PROGRAM

Use 1 to 4 sets of 1 to 10 repetitions with a weight that can be lifted only 10 times. Increase weight used as strength is gained.

1. Do 2-arm military press.
2. Do curls.
3. Do partial squats and heel raises.
4. Do bent arm pull overs.
5. Do incline bench presses.
6. Do 1-hand dead lifts with dumbbell.
7. Do situps with weight behind neck and legs flexed.
8. Run and hop stairs with weighted vest.

helpful hints

1. Train and condition properly before beginning to vault. Weight-training and body-building exercises on the bars and rope for at least 3 months before the competitive season begins are necessary if the vaulter wants to develop into a top performer.

2. Do constant work on the run-up and pole plant phases. Proper accomplishment of these parts of the vaulting procedure is necessary to insure that the takeoff foot is placed properly.

3. Relax on the run-up. Do not punch the pole forward and backward during the run.

4. Be sure the last 2 steps prior to the takeoff are somewhat shortened.

5. Check each vault for actual foot placement.

6. Delay pull and turn as long as possible.

7. Emphasize driving forward horizontally with the lead leg (right leg if right-handed vaulter).

8. Pull the knees in toward the chest as the hips swing up.

9. Keep the center of gravity behind and below the hands during the swing-up.

10. Delay the pull, turn, and push-up as long as possible to gain maximum vertical lift.

11. Do not stay on the pole too long. The push-off should be completed before the hips start to drop down.

12. Use type of tape and hand-grip substance that will keep the top hand from slipping down on the pole during the takeoff.

13. Participate in the following preseason activities:

    a. Use the rope vault to develop good roll back and vertical extension.

    b. Use the rope climb to develop arm strength for the pull-up.

    c. Do dips on the parallel bars from the headstand position.

    d. Use fiber glass pole vault trainer to simulate desired technique.

FIVE

WEIGHTS

SHOT PUT

The history of shot putting involves a steady course of achievement from a period beginning in 1887, when the world record was 43'11", to the present record of 70'7", made in 1967.

During this nearly 80-year period there have been many changes in shot putting form. Ralph Rose's 1909 record of 51' stood for 19 years, and many thought it would stand for all time. However, men such as Bud Houser, John Kuck, John Lyman, Jack Torrance, Wilbur Thompson, and Charles Fonville produced better results and contributed to improvements in techniques as they arrived on the scene.

In recent times, Jim Fuchs of Yale started a new trend in shot putting form that produced outstanding results. In 1950 he established a new world record of 58'10¾". Fuchs was not a big man, but he had great speed; he was timed at 9.8 seconds for 100 yards.

The main change introduced by Fuchs was the backward pointing of the right foot at the starting position, which kept his hips from rotating or "opening up" too soon and allowed him to get his body much lower over his right leg. This latter action permitted his hand to be in contact with the shot for a longer time before the release. It also added to the upward and outward action of his arm, enabling him to release the shot at a higher angle (nearer 45°, which is *mathematically* the optimum angle).

Parry O'Brien of the University of Southern California, who came after Fuchs, used the same type of starting position, with a few exceptions. The main differences in the O'Brien style, in comparison with Fuchs' style, are in the position of the eyes, head, and shoulders throughout the put, and the starting position of the right foot. Basically, what O'Brien tries to achieve is application of the force of the hand to the shot over a longer distance (his arm moves through a larger arc) and a quicker explosion as the release is made. O'Brien recently reached his peak at the age of 35 by throwing the shot nearly 65 feet.

Since its introduction, several men have imitated the O'Brien style and surpassed his all-time mark. Leading the list is Randy Matson, 1968 Olympic champion, with the world record of 70'7" (May 8, 1965); George Woods, 66'1/4"; Dallas Long, 1964 Olympic champion with the top mark of 67'10" (July 25, 1964); Dave Maggard, who threw 67'4 1/4" in the Olympic trials and fifth in the 1968 Olympics (63'9"); and Neal Steinhauer, 67'3/4", thrown on June 2, 1965. All these men use the O'Brien style with a few variations. The 1968 Olympic results are as fellows:

1.	RANDY MATSON (United States)	67'4 3/4"
2.	GEORGE WOODS (United States)	66'1/4"
3.	EDUARD GUSHCHIN (Soviet Union)	65'11"
4.	DIETER HOFFMAN (East Germany)	65'7 1/2"
5.	DAVE MAGGARD (United States)	63'9"

proper form

Position at the back of the circle. The form discussed in the subsequent pages is that used by ex-Olympic and world champion Parry O'Brien as slightly modified by Randy Matson and others. A stance is assumed in which the putter faces toward the back of the circle. The shot is held in the hand well to the rear of the jaw line, resting on the neck just back of the ear. The shot is held in the hand well up toward the tips of the 3 middle fingers, which are slightly spread, with the thumb and little finger helping to hold the shot in the hand.

The shot putter stands erect, with his chest well out and up. His right foot is pointed toward the rear of the ring, 90 degrees from the direction of the proposed flight of the shot. His back is toward the center of the toe board, and his eyes are fixed on a point about 10 feet to the rear of the ring. Keeping his eyes on this spot back of the ring helps keep his shoulders and hips in a position enabling him to start the put in almost exactly the same position each time (*see* Fig. 15-1).

The glide across the circle. The shot putter then does a deep body bend over his bent right leg, with his back kept in a plane almost parallel to the ground. This deep bend will give him a very low starting position.

As he begins his move across the ring close to the ground, the left foot kicks up and out across the ring, with the left knee pointing toward the ground. This high kick helps the putter accumulate speed across the ring, and helps keep his upper torso directly over his right leg. (However, in the glide the lead foot is close to the ground.)

The putting position at the end of the circle. The shot putter is still facing the back of the circle. His right foot is planted in the center of the ring, but now has come around from an angle of 90 degrees to one of about 35 degrees. The left foot forms an angle of approximately 30 degrees with the board, and the toes are jammed against the toe board on a line through the center of the ring and along the line of the flight of the shot.

The putter, still maintaining the back facing position (even though his right foot has moved around to the 35 degree angle posi-

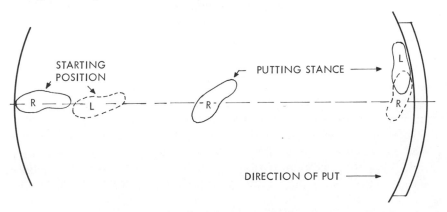

FIGURE 15–1. *Placement of feet in the O'Brien shot putting style.*

tion), explodes in a combination of power and timing, swinging his shoulders and finally his hips to the so-called "orthodox" front position. There is a right-to-left rotation of the hips and shoulders, plus an upward thrust off the right foot, in this final movement. At the same time, the back muscles are utilized (since the largest one is attached to the arm) as the right arm and finally the hand turn inward in releasing the shot. It is important not to let the elbow of the throwing arm get too high or too low. It should be in a direct line with the shoulder and hand at the time of release.

Maintaining the hips and shoulders in their own separate but parallel planes is very important. Speed across the ring is equally important. A fast arm thrust using strong wrist and finger snap, followed by a good follow-through of the body over the left leg, completes the put. In this form more hip "drive" and more "lift" from the large muscles of the back can be utilized. The longer pushing radius achieved (range of motion), the longer time the shot is pushed by the body. The longer time the shot is pushed, the greater momentum the moving object gains and, consequently, the longer the throw will be. Actual measurements show that putters using the O'Brien style get a pushing range 12 inches longer than that attained by the old upright style (*see* Fig. 15-2). Randy Matson may have a pushing range of as much as 18″ because of his greater height and longer arm.

The sequence of movements involved in putting the shot are: rear leg push, hips forward, shoulder push, forearm push, arm pronation, hand supination (so palm is almost facing upward), and, finally, the fingers push. The momentum should be so great that as the shot leaves the hand it feels "as light as a feather." Many shot putters think they must stop and feel the fingers pushing against the shot. They do not realize that this will lose them much of the momentum they have gained.

The follow-through and reverse. A proper long follow-through shows that a long time was taken in giving momentum to the shot. After the shot has left the hand, no more momentum can be accumulated. However, if the right side of the body does not follow up and into the put, it will fall many inches short of the possible distance. A good follow-through means that the putter rises high on the toes of his left foot and continues the "drive" of the right arm and fingers as far as possible, without fouling, in the direction of the put. The reverse, also an important part of the follow-through, is done so that balance in the ring may be maintained. Exchange of the feet in the reverse hop as the body weight is moved well over the leading foot is shown in Figure 15-2. It is impossible to achieve a complete follow-through without using the reverse. If special care is not taken to avoid reversing too early, some distance in the put will be lost.

Movement of the shot during the body action across the ring. A 12- or 16-pound ball is heavy enough to make it important that the shot putter keep his body weight moving from the time he takes his body dip over his right leg until his fingertips apply the last force against the shot. This simply means that he must not stop his action in the ring to get the feeling of balance and power that many beginners think is necessary before they continue the put. Many top shot putters have felt that they have not gotten all of their strength behind the shot in their better puts because the shot developed so much momentum from leg force and back lift. The shot seems to move of its own accord when the shot putter moves across the ring with no stop or hesitant movement.

Some suggestions on how to avoid fouling. Fouling is caused by 2 or 3 minor mistakes that can be avoided with proper practice. Some suggestions are mentioned below.

1. Form proper habits by practice putting out of a regulation ring. Carelessness in practice is one of the major reasons for fouling in competition.

2. Maintain proper balance during the move across the ring so that recovery can be accomplished when the reverse is finished.

3. Do not follow-through too far. This fault is often caused by starting the "explosion" too late.

4. Be sure the trajectory of the shot' is such that the arms are reaching up, not out, as the shot is released. The angle of flight should be between 40 and 45 degrees.

5. Do not watch the shot in flight. Keep original spot of focus; failure to do so may cause fouling.

training program

Remember that in any event, including the shot, it is impossible to judge whether each individual should follow any training plan to the letter. Allowances must be made for those who may have a very heavy work and study program in school; the age and maturity of each athlete should also be considered. Some of the older, stronger men may need more work than is contained in most schedules. The coach and athlete should determine the exact workout program that is needed. The schedule presented below is suggested for the 4-week period prior to participation in the first meet.

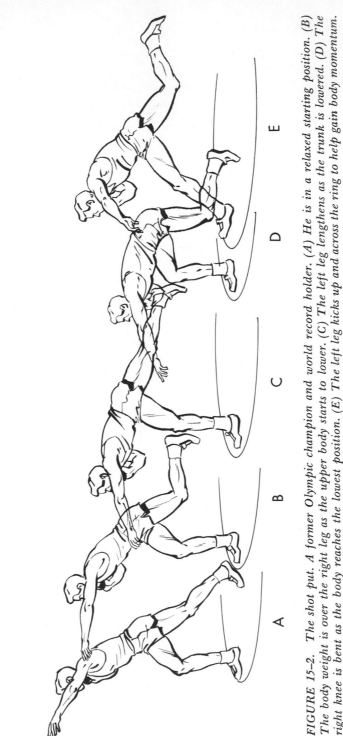

A B C D E

FIGURE 15–2. The shot put. A former Olympic champion and world record holder. (A) He is in a relaxed starting position. (B) The body weight is over the right leg as the upper body starts to lower. (C) The left leg lengthens as the trunk is lowered. (D) The right knee is bent as the body reaches the lowest position. (E) The left leg kicks up and across the ring to help gain body momentum.

F G H I J K

FIGURE 15-2 (cont.). The shot put. (F) He has landed with his weight over the bent right leg. (G) The right leg has extended and the hips and shoulders have started to turn. (H) The chest lifts as the hand leaves the shoulder. (I) Note the push-off by the right foot and position of the right elbow and hand. (J) The full extension of the right arm (forearm and hand inwardly rotated) is seen. The final push-off by the left foot is made. (K) The completion of the reverse is accomplished.

WORKOUT SCHEDULES

Monday
1. Jog ¼ mile.
2. Run wind sprints for ½ mile, sprinting 50 yards and walking 50 yards.
3. Do stretching exercises involving the large muscles of the back and shoulders.
4. Do 10 push-ups (repeated 3 times) executed from the fingertip position.
5. Do 20 puts from a standing position, concentrating on leg lift and proper delivery.
6. Do 20 to 30 puts by gliding across the ring and concentrating on form. Remember, the shot should be carried low in the hand for the first 4 weeks.
7. Take 6 to 10 starts from the blocks, running 25 yards each time.

Tuesday
1. Jog ¼ mile.
2. Run wind sprints for ½ mile.
3. Do stretching exercises.
4. Do 10 push-ups (repeated 3 times) from the fingertip position.
5. Put the shot 10 times from a standing position.
6. Do 10 to 20 puts, using the whole circle. Work on proper form.
7. Take 5 starts from the blocks.
8. Lift weights (*see* weight-training program).

Wednesday
1. Jog ¼ mile.
2. Run wind sprints for ½ mile.
3. Do stretching exercises.
4. Do 10 push-ups (repeated 3 times) from fingertip position.
5. Put 10 times from a standing position.
6. Take 20 puts, using the whole circle. Put hard enough to get proper timing, but not at an all-out effort for the first 4 weeks.
7. Execute a high jump at reasonable height, or a standing long jump.

Thursday
1. Jog ¼ mile.
2. Run wind sprints for ½ mile.

3. Do stretching exercises.
4. Take 10 puts from a standing position.
5. Do 10 to 20 puts across the circle.
6. Lift weights (*see* weight-training program).

Friday

1. Jog ¼ mile.
2. Run wind sprints for ½ mile.
3. Do stretching exercises.
4. Do 10 push-ups (repeated 3 times) from the fingertip position.
5. Take 10 to 20 puts from a standing position.
6. Take 20 to 30 puts, using the circle. Retrieve your own shot after each put; this gives you time to think about your faults and prepare for the next put.

Saturday

Lift weights if time and facilities are available (*see* weight-training program).

AFTER MEETS START

This schedule is set up in preparation for Saturday meets. When meets are held on Friday the schedule should be altered accordingly.

Monday

1. Jog ¼ mile.
2. Run wind sprints for ½ mile.
3. Do stretching exercises.
4. Do 10 push-ups (repeated 3 times) from the fingertip position.
5. Take 10 puts from a standing position.
6. Take 15 to 25 puts, using the whole circle.
7. Take 6 to 10 starts from the blocks, running 25 to 50 yards each time.
8. Check action pictures of your competition taken the previous Saturday.

Tuesday

1. Jog ¼ mile.
2. Do stretching exercises.
3. Do 5 push-ups (repeated 3 times) from the fingertip position.
4. Take 10 puts from a standing position.
5. Take 10 puts at all-out effort in competition with teammates.
6. Take 6 starts from the blocks, running 25 to 50 yards each time.

Wednesday
1. Jog ¼ mile.
2. Run wind sprints for ½ mile.
3. Do stretching exercises.
4. Do 5 push-ups (repeated 3 times) from fingertip position.
5. Take 10 to 15 puts from a standing position.
6. Do 15 to 25 puts, using the whole circle.
7. Lift weights (*see* weight-training program).

Thursday
1. Jog ¼ mile.
2. Run wind sprints for ½ mile.
3. Do stretching exercises.
4. Do 5 push-ups (repeated 3 times) from fingertip position.
5. Take 10 puts from a standing position.
6. Take 7 puts under meet conditions.
7. Take 6 starts from the blocks, running 25 to 50 yards each time.

Friday
Study motion pictures of yourself and others in action. Get plenty of sleep and rest. Prepare yourself mentally for a great performance on Saturday. Be confident!

Saturday
The day of the track meet. Be prepared to compete at your best.
1. Arrive at the stadium in plenty of time to dress slowly and get properly warmed-up for competition.
2. Jog 1 lap.
3. Do stretching exercises.
4. Take 3 starts, and run 25 yards each time.
5. Take 10 puts from a standing position.
6. Take 5 puts, using the whole circle. Do not put with all-out effort. Try to time your action so that you are effective.
7. Do your best on each throw after competition begins. It is unwise to save up for any one all-out effort.

WEIGHT-TRAINING PROGRAM

The concept of using weights to improve performance in various track and field events is a well-accepted principle. For many years track coaches believed that lifting weights would make the athlete slow and "musclebound." However, most outstanding athletes in the past 10 to 15 years have taken part in weight-training, especially those in throwing and field events. All of the athletes referred to in this chapter are dedicated weight-trainers. All world caliber shot putters train regularly with weights, some as much as 4 out of each 5 days of practice. However, it is believed that at least 2 out of each 5 days should be devoted to the skill of putting the shot. Although the results from studies are somewhat controversial, it may be stated that weight-lifting has increased coordination, speed, or timing of some performers, and in most instances will increase strength.

The weight-training program presented here is not considered a magic formula, but it may be used as one way to help develop strength and coordination. Furthermore, tangible results cannot be obtained overnight; time and consistent work under proper super-vision are required to obtain the best results. The athlete preparing for a given track season should begin weight-lifting 3 times a week at least 8 months before the season begins. During the competitive season the lifting should be on a somewhat limited basis (only twice a week), depending on the strength and maturity of the performer. The weight-training program should involve exercises that simulate the arm and leg action used in shot putting.

How far the athlete should increase the weight pounds as he progresses in his training depends upon many factors, the foremost being his strength and experience in weight-lifting. Other factors include his need for increased strength, the progress he has made, and the amount of time he devotes to this phase.

TWO-ARM EXERCISES

A. Standing position
   1. *Two-arm barbell military press (simulating the shot putting arm action):*
      Do 5 sets of 3 to 5 repeats. The starting weight should be 70 to 100 pounds. The lifting action should be done rapidly to help develop explosive power.
   2. *Two-arm barbell snatch:*
      Do 3 sets of 5 repeats, starting with weight from 70 to 100 pounds. Make very quick lifts.
   3. *Curls:*
      Do 3 sets of 5 repeats.
   4. *Deep knee bends (not more than 90° bend):*
      Do 3 sets of 5 repeats, starting weight 70 to 150 pounds.
      Do 1 set of 5 repeats, jumping off the floor with the weights.

Be careful to bend the knees only to the position where the thighs are parallel to the floor.

5. *Dumbbell military press (one arm):*
    a. Do 3 sets of 8 repeats, starting weight 20 to 40 pounds.
    b. Start the action in a shot-putting stance, using the legs, back, and arm in same manner as when putting the shot from a standing position.
6. *Wrist and finger curls:*
    Do 3 sets of 5 repeats, starting weight 50 to 100 pounds.

B. Prone position
   Two-arm barbell prone press on a bench:
   Do 3 sets of 10 repeats, starting weight 70 to 100 pounds.

It is interesting to note that many mature men progressed to the point of using 300-pound weights in many of these exercises. They always emphasize speed with this amount of weight. In early season, some of the top shot putters lift up to 350 pounds or more to gain strength.

helpful hints

1. Keep the shot down in the palm of the hand to avoid injury to fingers early in the season. The injury most common to shot putters is strain of the fingers and the tendons in the hand and wrist.

2. Be sure to dip the body low at the back of the circle and keep the same position during the glide. Many beginning shot putters straighten up in the center of the circle and get little or no "lift" from the right leg and back muscles.

3. Keep the eyes, shoulders, and hips in the same parallel plane during the glide. This will give the shot putter the "around-up-and over" movement that he should be trying to accomplish in the put.

4. Be sure the left foot is not placed in the "bucket" at the end of the glide. The left foot must be placed near the center line. Many of the best putters' puts are made with their left feet placed just 4 inches to the left of the center line. This prevents their hips from "locking."

5. Keep the elbow directly behind the putting hand. Do not try to get the correct altitude by dropping the elbow down. The entire lifting action must be in a straight-line direction. Conversely, if the elbow is raised too high, the shot will probably land to the right of

the line of proposed flight and a loss of force (and, consequently, distance) may occur.

6. Do not stop and gather in the center of the circle. A "rock back" of the body will occur as an opposite reaction if the shot putter stops. The stopping and gathering action is called "cocking," one of the most common faults among shot putters. This can be eliminated by making sure that the shoulders are kept low in the glide across the ring so that the putter is in a position to "lift" or "thrust" when his right foot lands in the center of the ring.

7. Remember that the "lift" begins with the right leg and hips. Do not start the arm explosion too soon. The arm, then the hand, and finally the finger movements are involved in the last part of the put.

8. The left arm is held about eye level and is in a relaxed position, reaching toward the rear in a slightly flexed position. Keep it there until the last instant to make sure that the shouders do not rotate too soon. However, it should be thrust toward the rear as the shot is being released.

9. Spend many practice hours on "form putting." It is necessary to work at full effort occasionally, but many athletes erroneously feel that they must break their all-time best effort in practice or they are not progressing fast enough. It is usually normal in practice for the athlete to put 2 or 3 feet shorter than his best effort. Do not get discouraged. It takes great determination and long hours of concentration to become a champion.

DISCUS THROW

discus throws of the past

The Greeks are known to have thrown the discus. Aristotle discussed the form used by the heroes of his day, and it appears that they threw from a stationary (nonspinning) position. Many changes in form have occurred in America, where discus throwing began with the Greek "standing position." This form produced the first accepted world record of 118'9". Gradually, the spin was added. Martin J. Sheridan, a New York policeman, was one of the first real stars in the period from 1901 to 1911. Throwing from a 7' circle, his best distance of 141'4⅜" was made in his last year of competition.

In 1912, because of the frequency of fouling while throwing that resulted from using a 7' circle, the size of the circle was changed to 8'2½". From 1912 until 1939, most performers used the orthodox pivot method of spinning around the ring, using only 1½ turns. Such great American discus throwers as Hartanft and Krenz of Stanford and Carpenter and Houser of the University of Southern California undoubtedly would have far exceeded their best performances if they had used the newer method of executing 1¾ hop turns around the circle (*see* Fig. 16-1).

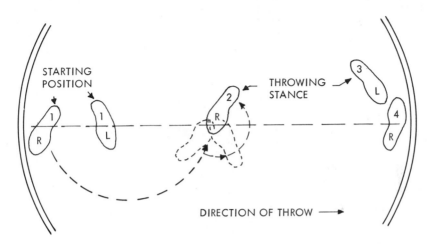

FIGURE 16–1. Old style discus footwork. The 1½ turns shown were used in discus throwing in the past.

Two and even three turns have been tried in the past, and probably will be experimented with and perfected in the future. In fact, several men are now trying to use 2 full turns, and a few are finding that this additional quarter turn increases body and arm momentum sufficiently to add several more feet to their throws (*see* Fig. 16-2).

Probably the most important change in style in recent years has been the introduction of the 1¾ hop turn (hop, not pivot) as a means of adding momentum to the throw. This new style was made popular by several national champions who had the adventurous spirit to change successfully from their old 1½ turns to 1¾ turns.

The 1¾ turn throw is executed with the performer starting with his back to the direction of the throw. His right toe (right-handed performer) is placed at the back of the circle, the left foot is placed about 8 inches laterally from the rear of the right foot, and, as the right arm and shoulder are swung back in a throwing position, the left foot is moved to the back of the circle, about 18 inches from the right foot. The performer then pivots or hops around the left leg so that his right foot lands in the center of the ring on a straight line drawn through the middle of the circle that bisects the toe board. His left foot then comes around and is placed about 6 inches to the left of this center line. (The correct placement of the left foot will

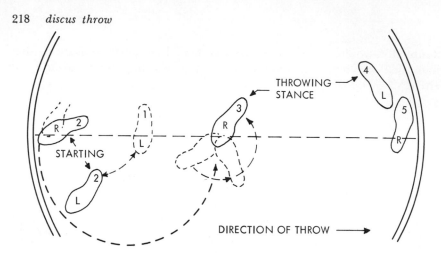

FIGURE 16–2. *Modern discus footwork. This style of footwork is used by most discus throwers.*

help keep the hips from "locking," and allow them to lead the body when the throw is made.) The discus is then thrown from this wide stance position.

A reverse at the end of the throw has become the recognized method of maintaining balance after releasing the discus. Most discus throwers spin several times about on the right foot (right-handed throwers) after releasing the discus.

There are now several athletes throwing over 200 feet in the discus. The present world record holder is Jay Silvester, U.S., with a mark of 218′3½″. Ludvik Danek of Czechoslovakia was the former record holder, with a throw of 213′11½″. Al Oerter, U.S., became the first Olympic athlete to win 4 consecutive gold medals, with his best throw a new Olympic record of 212′6½″. Other standouts are Randy Matson (210′), Rink Babka (209′5″), Gary Carlsen (205′2″), and Dave Weill (200′3″).

The 1968 Mexico Olympics had 5 athletes with throws over 200 feet. The discus results were:

1. AL OERTER (United States)	212′6½″
2. LOTHAR MILDE (East Germany)	206′11½″
3. LUDVIK DANEK (Czechoslovakia)	206′5″
4. HARTMUT LOSCH (East Germany)	203′9½″
5. JAY SILVESTER (United States)	202′8″

characteristics of the discus thrower

Discus throwers are usually tall, heavy men with long arms and large hands. Smaller men with good speed may become good performers, but most of the top competitors are reasonably tall and heavy. Rangy football tackles have the physical requirements to become good discus throwers. The high school or college coach should have several informal early competitive situations so that potential performers can compete. As many men as possible should try to throw in the first weeks in order to give the coach an idea as to the best candidates. Of course, the coach at a large university knows most of his potential candidates, but even he may discover a "find." An off-season informal meet may aid in the discovery of other candidates.

Discus throwing requires years to master. Boys who are not able to make the track team in any other event because of slowness, great weight, or lack of strength may have the necessary qualifications to become successful as discus throwers. (*See* Chapter 1 for further infomation on this topic.)

proper form

The grip. The hand should be placed on the discus so that the first joints of each of the first 3 fingers are hooked over the edge of the discus. The fingers are spread so that as much of the discus as possible is covered by the hand. The thumb and small finger are kept in a relaxed position. The discus is gripped with the fingers toward its rear half, and the wrist is cocked toward the rear in order to get a good wrist whip when throwing. The discus must be released so that it leaves the index finger last, thereby making it rotate clockwise (*see* Fig. 16-3).

Learning to throw from the standing position. Throwing from the standing position is a good way for the performer to warm up. It

FIGURE 16–3. Discus handhold.

gives him the feeling for the proper position needed later when he uses the turn with the throw.

In the standing position, the feet are placed apart about shoulder width, with the left side of the body toward the direction of throw. The left foot is placed 6 inches to the left of the center of the ring. The weight is evenly distributed over both feet. As the performer turns his body toward the right and to the rear, the weight transfers to the right foot, with the right knee kept slightly bent. The left arm is bent and placed across the chest, and remains there until the shoulders begin their turn. The right arm is forced back and around in a clockwise movement, and remains extended at all times during the turn. From the standing position, the "lift" is started from the right foot, leg, and hip. The body weight moves up on the toes of the right foot and then over the left leg as the shoulders and arm are pulling the discus around and up. This is a steady pull, with a final whip being made across and in front of the face. This action is like the uncoiling of a spring, starting with the right foot and finishing with the right hand.

A reverse is not necessary in throwing from the standing position, because the momentum created is not great enough to demand its use in order to stay in the ring. Moreover, it may cause the performer to form the bad habit of leaving the ground before the throw is completed, which would result in less momentum being imparted to the discus.

Learning to release the discus. The discus in flight develops aerodynamic qualities and tends to rise. (A low throw into the wind will go farther than a throw with the wind because of aerodynamics.) Much time and practice will be needed to learn how to release the discus so that it will sail at the proper angle without a wobble. Because of the centrifugal force, the discus will stay in the performer's hand during the motions he makes while he spins.

Many practice throws should be made from the standing position to learn the proper release. The angle of the discus as it is released should be from 30 to 45 degrees to the ground. Experimental evidence and observation of actual competitive throws seem to bear out the conclusion that, in normal throwing situations, a 40 degree angle of release gets the best results. The angle of release with the wind should be somewhat higher than 40 degrees. The throw is accomplished by adding to the arm momentum that of the legs, hips, and back. So that the proper altitude can be secured, the discus hand should never be dropped below the level of the hips. If this occurs, the discus goes up in the air too high and the performer has a "scooped" motion. If the discus is turning up on its right side when released, the performer has pressed down too hard with his thumb, or he has dropped his left shoulder too low and the right arm and hand have come up above the right shoulder. Frequently, a beginner will not keep the wrist of his throwing hand in line with the anticipated flight of the discus, and it wobbles in flight. The release must be made so that the right hand goes across the body at eye level during the follow-through, thus assuring that a good spin has been given to the discus and that good forearm, wrist, and finger snap have been used.

Learning to turn in the circle. This is the most difficult of the movements involved in throwing the discus. The problem is to attain as much speed as possible and still maintain balance and proper form. This will take many hours of practice. It is of *little or no value to walk through the turn,* because an entirely different set of moves must be made in order to execute the throw when using a faster turn. Many practice turns can be made without the discus, with a performer making his turns at competitive speed and simulating release of a discus. Another satisfactory practice method is to hold the discus farther up in the hand than usual, or tie it to the hand so that it cannot be released after the turn is completed.

The turn in the circle is started with the performer's back to the front of the circle and right toe against the back of the circle. As his right arm is forced back to a throwing position, the left foot is moved to the back of the circle about 18 inches from the right foot. As his right arm is being forced back in a clockwise direction, most of the body weight is shifted to the right foot. His knees are bent so that the performer can get his body low enough to get a good lift. When he starts to pivot on his left foot, his weight begins to shift to the left foot. Then, as the right leg is thrown around the left leg, he pushes off with the left foot to help gain speed and momentum. At this point both feet will be off the ground momentarily, as in a run. During this part of the turn the right arm is still kept back to the rear and the left arm is kept folded across the chest. The turn should not be started by diving forward with the left shoulder. Instead, the turn is made with the legs and by a forward shifting of the body weight. The head and shoulders must stay in the same vertical parallel plane throughout the turn. The right foot lands in the center of the circle, with the knee still bent, as the left foot comes down about 6 inches to the left of the center line. As the left foot hits the ground, the left arm starts a pulling motion and the hips turn in advance of the right arm. The weight is now over the bent right leg, and the left leg is almost extended. The actual throw is made from this position, with motion continuous as the last turn is made. The right leg begins to extend, and the hips are "opened" and lead the rest of the body in the turn. The chest is also thrust out in advance of the trailing right arm. As the arm comes around, the weight is shifted to the left leg, and the tremendous whip of the arm as the discus is released will necessitate execution of a follow-through and reverse (*see* Fig. 16-4).

training program

The discus throwing movement is not strenuous, but the performer should be in top physical condition in order to perform at his best. The workout schedule should include running and arm strengthening exercises. A definite program of weight-training should be participated in during the entire season.

WORKOUT SCHEDULES

FOUR WEEKS PRIOR TO MEETS

Monday
1. Jog ¼ mile.
2. Run wind sprints for ½ mile, sprinting 50 yards and walking 50 yards.
3. Do stretching exercises that involve the large muscles of the back and shoulders.
4. Throw 15 or 20 times from the standing position.
5. Practice the turn 10 minutes without throwing.
6. Make 15 or 20 throws with the turn, concentrating on form rather than speed.
7. Do pull-ups on the horizontal bar for 15 minutes.

Tuesday
1. Jog ¼ mile.
2. Run wind sprints for ½ mile.
3. Do stretching exercises, same as on Monday.
4. Throw 15 times from the standing position.
5. Practice the turn for 10 minutes without throwing.
6. Practice 15 to 20 throws with the turn; always throw from a circle. Work on form—no all-out throws should be taken for the first 4 weeks.
7. Lift weights (*see* weight-training program).

Wednesday

1. Jog ¼ mile.
2. Run wind sprints for ½ mile.
3. Do stretching exercises, same as on Monday.
4. Take 15 or 20 throws from the standing position.
5. Work for 10 minutes on the turn without throwing.
6. Throw 15 or 20 times out of the circle with the turn.
7. Do 6 starts out of the blocks, running 25 yards each time.

Thursday

1. Jog ¼ mile.
2. Run wind sprints for ½ mile.
3. Do stretching exercises.
4. Make 10 throws from the standing position.
5. Practice the turn for 10 minutes without throwing.
6. Do several throws (15 or 20) out of the circle with turn. Work on form for timing and follow-through.
7. Lift weights.

Friday

1. Jog ¼ mile.
2. Run wind sprints for ½ mile.
3. Do stretching exercises.
4. Make 15 throws from the standing position.
5. Practice 10 minutes on the turn.
6. Throw 15 to 20 times out of the circle with turn. Work on timing and speed.
7. Take 6 starts from out of the blocks, running 25 yards each time.

Saturday

Lift weights if time and facilities are available.

AFTER MEETS START

This schedule is set up for a program which climaxes each week with a Saturday meet. When meets are held on Friday, the schedule should be altered accordingly.

Monday

1. Jog ¼ mile.
2. Run wind sprints for ½ mile.

FIGURE 16–4. The discus throw. A former NCAA co-champion and National AAU champion. (A) He is assuming a relaxed position preparatory to making the turn. (B) Both feet are placed at the back of the circle. The right shoulder and arm are swung to the rear. (C) The weight has shifted forward to the bent left leg. (D) He is pivoting on the ball of the left foot as the right leg starts moving around the left leg. (E) Note the sprintlike action of the right leg, and that the right arm is still extended to the rear as he moves. (F) He appears to be landing off balance because of the angle from which the drawing is made. He is in a running position.

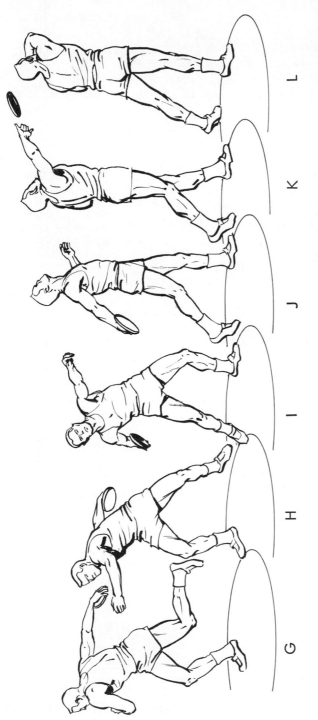

FIGURE 16-4 (cont.). The discus throw. (G) The weight is over the bent right leg. The right arm is still extended to the rear. (H) He demonstrates an almost perfect position for the beginning of the leg lift. (I) The hips start to rotate forward as the left arm pulls around. (J) The chest is pulled up and expanded, following in order the action of the hips. The placement of the feet here is good. (K) The hand has released the discus at about the correct angle. (L) He has completed the follow-through is over the left leg. (L) Note that the reverse, and will spin about on his right foot several times.

3. Do stretching exercises.
4. Take throws from the standing position.
5. Practice the turn in the circle without throwing for 10 minutes.
6. Throw 15 to 20 times out of the circle with turn. Work on timing and speed.
7. Do pull-ups on the horizontal bar for 10 minutes.

Tuesday
1. Jog ¼ mile.
2. Run wind sprints for ½ mile.
3. Do stretching exercises.
4. Take 10 throws from the standing position.
5. Throw 10 times with turn with all-out effort, competing against teammates.
6. Take 6 starts out of the blocks, running 25 yards each time.

Wednesday
1. Jog ¼ mile.
2. Run wind sprints for ½ mile.
3. Do stretching exercises.
4. Take 10 throws from the standing position.
5. Practice the turn in the circle for 10 minutes, working on speed and timing.
6. Throw 10 to 15 times out of the circle with turn, working on speed and timing.
7. Lift weights.

Thursday
1. Jog ¼ mile.
2. Run wind sprints for ½ mile.
3. Do stretching exercises.
4. Take 10 throws from the standing position.
5. Throw 7 times with turn from the circle under meet conditions.
6. Take 6 starts out of the blocks, running 25 yards each time.

Friday
Study motion pictures of yourself and others in action. Get plenty of sleep and rest. Prepare yourself mentally for a great performance on Saturday. Be confident. Be prepared.

Saturday
1. Arrive at the stadium in plenty of time to dress slowly and get properly warmed up for the competition.

2. Jog 1 lap.
3. Do stretching exercises.
4. Take 3 starts and run 25 yards each time.
5. Take 5 throws from the standing position.
6. Throw 5 times with turn from the circle; do not throw with all-out effort.
7. Do your best on each throw after competition begins. It is unwise to save up for one all-out effort.

WEIGHT-TRAINING PROGRAM

The same program as suggested for the shot put should be followed, with the following additions:

1. Execute bent arm pull-overs lying on bench. Do 2 sets of 10 repeats, beginning with 50 pounds.
2. Do lateral raises with dumbbells lying on bench. Do 2 sets of 10 repeats, beginning with 20 pounds.
3. Do arm swing with wall pulleys. Do 3 sets of 15 repeats, beginning with 25 pounds. The arm must be kept extended from the side as in throwing the shot. (*See* Chapter 15.)

helpful hints

1. Relaxation throughout the turn is imperative. The discus cannot be "muscled." The momentum gained in the turn ($1\frac{3}{4}$) will accomplish the task.

2. The right arm must be forced back during the turn so that it trails the rest of the body.

3. The performer spins on the ball of the left foot.

4. The turn must not be made by "diving" forward with the left shoulder, but by the legs and by shifting the hips forward. At the beginning of the last turn, the hips lead the rest of the body.

5. The shoulders, head, and eyes are kept on the same vertical parallel plane during the action.

6. The discus should never drop below the level of the hips during the turn. If it does, the performer will lose most of the power from his shoulders and back.

7. The performer must not hop too high as he turns. He should hop across the ring, not up and down.

8. He should not hesitate or stop at the end of the last turn, but should continue his action on into the follow-through.

9. The discus should be kept low if thrown into the wind. If possible, the throw should be executed so that the wind comes in slightly to the right of the direction of the throw in order to utilize its force.

10. The performer should keep his chest out and his left shoulder in a normal position during the final pull on the discus. If the left shoulder drops at this time, the right arm has a tendency to come above the shoulder and the head to pull away from the line of throw, thus interfering with the final momentum given to the discus.

11. The finish of the action should find the thrower well up on his toes to insure having accomplished a good "lift."

12. A hand gripper may be used to help strengthen the fingers.

JAVELIN THROW

historical background

The history of javelin throwing can be traced to primitive man's use of a spear for hunting and fighting. Later, men used the spear in athletic competition. The Greeks had a spear throwing event in the Olympic Games. A leather strap or thong was bound around the shaft near the center of the javelin (spear), which was about a man's height. The javelin was carried between the thumb and first finger in an over-the-shoulder position. It was thrown by imparting momentum to it with a terrific whip of the right arm and hand. The unwinding of the strap as it was thrown gave the javelin a bullet-like spinning motion.

Sweden and Finland have been the greatest contributors to the modern era of javelin throwing. It was Sweden that requested its inclusion in the Olympics in 1906. However, the Finns have made most of the records in the event since that date. Their greatest star was Matti Jarvinen, who set a world record of 253′4½″. Robert Peoples of Southern California threw the javelin 234′1⅞″ in 1939 after changing to the

Finnish form. The Americans seemed to have mastered the event in the 1952 Olympic Games at Helsinki; two United States performers, Cy Young and Bill Miller, finished first and second, to the surprise of everyone. But in the 1956 Olympic Games a Norwegian, Egil Danielsen, set a new world record of 281'2", and the American representatives did not place. The 1968 Olympic results are as follows:

1.	JANIS LUSIS (Soviet Union)	295'7"
2.	JORMA KINNUNEN (Finland)	290'6"
3.	GERGELY KULCSAR (Hungary)	285'7½"
4.	WLADYSLAW NIKICIUK (Poland)	281'2"
5.	MANFRED STOLLE (East Germany)	276'11½"
6.	AKE NILSSON (Sweden)	273'10½"
7.	JANUSZ SIDLO (Poland)	264'4½"
8.	URS VON WARTBURG (Switzerland)	264'3½"
9.	MARK MURRO (United States)	262'8½"
10.	WALTER PEKTOR (Austria)	253'11"

Janis Lusis of the Soviet Union is the present world record holder and 1968 Olympic champion, with 301'9". Terje Pedersen, Norway, held the record at 300'10" in 1964. The American Collegiate record is held by John Tushaus, Arizona, with a throw of 284'0".

Until the Americans changed their style of throwing from one similar to baseball pitching to an over-the-head pull throw and a Finnish front cross-over step, they were notably unsuccessful. At times in the recent past, however, Americans have achieved world recognition in this event. Two were especially noteworthy in their accomplishments—Franklin W. Held and Stephen A. Seymour. Seymour was the first American to throw the javelin beyond 240 feet, winning the 1947 National AAU title with a throw of 248'10". Held threw the javelin 270 feet. He has constructed a special javelin that can be thrown with greater ease than the regular types, but it was outlawed by the international body.

At the present time, the United States performers are not among the world's best. Techniques and length of training are part of the explanation. Many high schools and some colleges have discontinued the javelin as an event in their track programs, although a few have added it in the last 2 years. The reasons most often given for excluding the javelin are lack of space and potential danger to spectators in the stand and on the field. This has affected the number of potential performers available for track teams representing the United States. However, companies now have rubber tipped javelins for high schools and colleges that are balanced and have proven safe. This should in time improve the quality and quantity of American javelin throwers.

Most coaches believe that it takes at least 8 years for a performer to master the finer techniques of the Finnish style of throwing. Nevertheless, a few dedicated throwers who started as rank beginners have been known to throw exceedingly well at the end of a 4-year period.

characteristics of the javelin thrower

Javelin throwers have various body builds. Some are tall and thin, others are short and heavy. However, they generally tend to be average and above in height, with long arms and good body proportions. Probably the most important physical characteristic is a good throwing arm. The whip-like arm action used in football passing and outfield throwing is similar to javelin throwing.

A desire to excel and a temperament that will stick to constant practice is considered necessary for success. Ability to be analytical and to accept criticism are other good assets (*see* Chapter 1).

analysis of the Finnish form

The handhold. The javelin is placed in the palm of the hand and alongside the inner portion of the forearm. The fingers and thumb are curled around the "grip" in a relaxed manner, with the second finger hooked slightly over the back of the grip and around the javelin to help maintain proper balance and to enable the fingers to release the javelin at approximately a 45 degree angle (*see* Fig. 17-1).

The full run and carry of the javelin. The generally accepted method of carrying the javelin during the run is to hold it in the palm of the hand, with the second finger curled behind. The elbow is bent above the shoulder at eye level. The front point of the javelin is held slightly higher than the rear. The arm must be relaxed at all times during the run.

The length of the run varies with individuals. It should be a sufficient distance to allow the performer to gain enough speed and to allow him time to get properly prepared for the final action. Twelve steps, or about 70 feet from the starting point to the final check mark, is usually a sufficient distance for a proper run. The distance from the final check mark to the foul line will vary, depending on the performer's speed and length of stride. Normally, a distance of 30 to 35 feet is allowed for the last 5 steps.

Speed of the run. The speed of the run is determined by the ability of the thrower to transfer his speed (momentum) to his throw.

FIGURE 17–1. Finnish javelin handhold.

Each individual has a so-called "critical" momentum. Any faster or slower speed will result in a needlessly poor performance. The run should be started slowly and gradually accelerated until the final action. Many aspirants start out incorrectly at full speed and slow down to an almost complete stop on the last 3 steps. The last 5 steps must be taken so that the competitor is *gaining* speed. A special effort must be made to get the left foot down on the ground as the javelin is released. The increased speed enables the thrower to get both feet on the ground before throwing, and the momentum from the legs can be transferred to the arm, and thence to the javelin (*see* Fig. 17-2).

The throwing action. As the final check mark is reached, the javelin is moved back and the arm straightens out to the rear. The body then begins to assume a slightly backward lean. Attaining the backward lean can be aided by using high knee action during the run. As the right foot hits the final check mark, it is pointed straight ahead, and the left foot follows suit. Then, in the next step, the right foot lands at a 45 degree angle to the direction of movement; the left foot again follows suit. The final cross-over step is made with the right foot landing at a 90 degree angle to the direction of the run, with the left foot landing at an angle of 25 degrees. The right knee is then bent and the left leg kept straight to assure a good backward lean and sufficient "breaking" action of forward momentum which can be transferred from the body to the javelin. The upward lift of the body is started from this last position with a thrust forward of the right hip, followed by holding the chest high and by the elbow leading the rest of the arm. The pull is started from a position of an almost straight (elongated) arm. The elbow should move straight over the shoulder from a "high" position. The javelin's path of flight should be in the direction of the run and the throwing action. The angle of release is between 45 and 50 degrees, depending somewhat on wind conditions. If the wind is blowing against the performer's direction of throw, he will throw at a lower angle than if the wind is blowing in the direction of the throw (*see* Fig. 17-3).

Steps in learning proper release of the javelin. In practicing the release of the javelin: (1) Hold it with a relaxed grip and bring it back over the shoulder until the arm is almost straight. (2) Throw at an object about 30 or 40 feet away, bringing the javelin directly over the shoulder during the pull-through. The point or front of the javelin must be slightly lower than the rear in order for it to stick in the ground when it lands. (3) After several days' practice on these techniques, start throwing at an object at a distance of about 60 to 80 feet. This will necessitate taking a throwing stance much like that used in shot putting, the right leg being bent and the left leg kept straight. The angle of the release of the javelin will be a little higher when using a standing throwing position than if it is thrown from a run. (4) Next, take a few short steps, using the Finnish cross-over step, and then release the javelin (*see* Fig. 17-4). Reach back to the rear with the javelin arm when throwing. This will help to keep the arm straight and will also move the weight of the body back further over the right leg and foot. Get the left foot on the ground as quickly as possible before throwing to prevent rocking forward too soon and interfering with the momentum transferred to the javelin from the hand.

training program

The training program followed by javelin throwers is not strenuous. However, the javelin thrower must be in good physical condition and not be carrying excess weight. He should participate in a weight-training program in the early season.

WORKOUT SCHEDULES

Four Weeks Prior to Meets

Monday
1. Jog ¼ mile.
2. Run ½ mile of wind sprints.

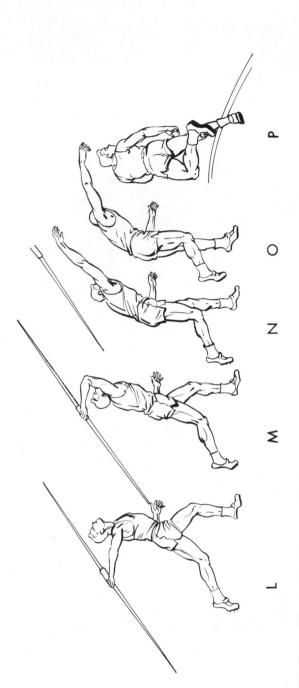

L   M   N   O   P

FIGURE 17–2. The javelin throw. A former top performer is seen in action here. (A) and (B) He is using a rather unusually high carry of the javelin. (C) and (D) Proper high knee lift is used in the run. (E) and (F) The arm starts to drop back preparatory to the execution of the last cross-over step. (G) He is finishing the preparation for the last cross-over step. (H) The body starts to assume a backward lean. (I) Note the straight-ahead position of the right foot. (J) The right arm is extended. The placement of the feet at this stage is considered good. (K) Note the arched back and the angle at which the javelin will be released. (L) He has pushed off with the right leg. (M) Note how the right elbow leads the hand in the throw. (N) A good shoulder lift is shown. (O) He has finished the throw. Note the good lift that has occurred from the left leg. (P) The finish of the reverse with the proper landing at the scratch line is seen.

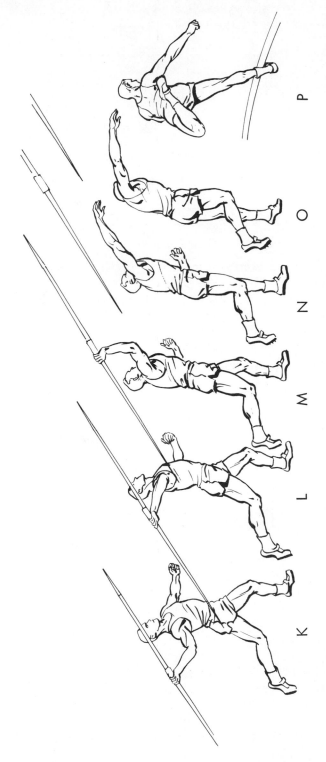

K L M N O P

FIGURE 17-3. The javelin throw. A former National AAU champion is shown here. (A) He is using a rather low javelin carry. (B) and (C) He has started to drop the javelin back in preparation for the throw. (D) Note the high knee lift used at the start of the first cross-over step. (E) The shoulders and hips have started to turn back toward the rear. (F) and (G) The beginning of the last front cross-over step is seen. (H) Note how the right leg crosses in front of the left leg. (I) The body is leaning backward at this stage. (J) Note the position of the right and left foot, and the nearly extended rear arm position. (K) His right arm is just moving from the rear position extended as the pull is underway. (L) The chest is expanded and the right elbow is leading the hand. (M) The javelin is pulled through and almost over the right shoulder. (N) Note the shoulder lift and the angle of release of the javelin, along with the head inclination to the left. (O) and (P) The proper follow-through is shown.

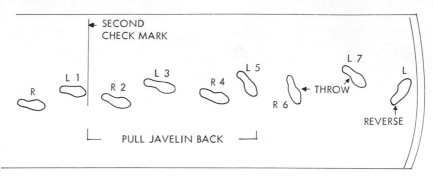

FIGURE 17–4. *The javelin front cross-over step.*

3. Do stretching exercises to loosen up back, side, and groin muscles.
4. Throw the javelin for 15 minutes at a target 30 feet away to loosen up elbow and arm.
5. Run through the steps to the foul line for 15 minutes.
6. Take 15 to 20 throws, working on timing. Start with a slow run and gradually increase speed. Do not throw hard; let the momentum of the run take care of the distance attained.
7. Take 10 puts with 16-pound shot.
8. Work for 15 minutes on parallel-bar exercises and the rope climb.

Tuesday
1. Jog ¼ mile.
2. Run ½ mile of wind sprints.
3. Do stretching exercises.
4. Throw the javelin for 15 minutes at a target at a distance of 50 feet.
5. Run through the steps to the foul line for 15 minutes.
6. Take 15 to 20 throws, working on form. Always work from behind the foul line.
7. Lift weights.

Wednesday
1. Jog ¼ mile.
2. Run ½ mile of wind sprints.
3. Do stretching exercises.
4. Throw for 15 minutes at a target at a distance of 50 feet.
5. Run through the steps to the foul line for 15 minutes.
6. Take 15 to 20 throws, working on release and angle of flight.

7. Take 10 puts with 16-pound shot.
8. Take 6 starts out of the blocks, running 25 yards each time.

Thursday

1. Jog ¼ mile.
2. Run ½ mile of wind sprints.
3. Do stretching exercises.
4. Do short throws for 10 minutes to loosen up the elbow.
5. Run for 15 minutes up and down the field, carrying the javelin as if in a regular competitive run. Stay relaxed. Practice the front cross-over step during the run.
6. Take 10 to 15 throws, using a regular run; throw with ¾ effort.
7. Lift weights.

Friday

1. Jog ¼ mile.
2. Run ½ mile of wind sprints.
3. Do stretching exercises.
4. Do short throws for 10 minutes to loosen up elbow and arm.
5. Run through the steps to the foul line for 15 minutes.
6. Take 15 to 20 throws, working on form.
7. Check form as seen in movies of yourself and others throwing the javelin.

AFTER MEETS START

This schedule is set up for Saturday meets. When meets are held on Friday, alter the schedule accordingly.

Monday

1. Jog ¼ mile.
2. Run ½ mile of wind sprints.
3. Do stretching exercises.
4. Take short throws for 10 minutes to loosen up the elbow and arm.
5. Run through the proper steps to the foul line for 10 minutes.
6. Take 15 throws—10 throwing for form and 5 throwing for distance.
7. Work for 15 minutes on parallel bars, exercises, and the rope climb.

Tuesday

1. Jog ¼ mile.

2. Run ½ mile of wind sprints.
3. Do stretching exercises.
4. Take short throws for 10 minutes to loosen up the elbow and arm.
5. Run through the steps to the foul line for 15 minutes.
6. Take 10 throws, working on both speed of run and form in throwing.
7. Do high jump and standing long jump a few times.

Wednesday
1. Jog ¼ mile.
2. Run ½ mile of wind sprints.
3. Do stretching exercises.
4. Take short throws for 10 minutes to loosen up the elbow and arm.
5. Run through the steps to the foul line for 10 minutes.
6. Take 7 throws for distance, competing against teammates.
7. Take 6 starts out of blocks, running 25 yards each time.

Thursday
1. Jog ¼ mile.
2. Run ½ mile of wind sprints.
3. Do stretching exercises.
4. Take short throws for 10 minutes.
5. Run through steps to the foul line for 10 minutes.
6. Throw easy 10 times, working on form. During the last part of the season it is possible that no throwing will be done on Thursday.

Friday
Rest. Check the form exhibited in meets as shown in the movies.

WEIGHT-TRAINING PROGRAM

1. Do deep knee bends—2 sets of 10 repeats using a 100-pound weight.
2. Do curls—2 sets of 5 repeats using 50 pounds.
3. Do pull-overs—2 sets of 10 repeats, 1 set with arm straight, 1 set with the arm bent.
4. Do toe raises—3 sets of 10 repeats using 100 pounds.
5. Do arm pulls with wall pulley—5 sets of 10 repeats using 25 pounds.

6. Do situps and leg raises many times, according to a graduated progressive schedule.

7. Practice on a simulated device to perfect the throwing action.

helpful hints

1. Take plenty of time in warming up before throwing vigorously. Elbow injuries occur among javelin throwers quite frequently, and it often takes many weeks to make a recovery. Prepare weeks in advance by training properly with weights and doing exercises to avoid elbow and back injuries. Try to simulate javelin throwing arm action when doing weight-training.

2. Stay relaxed throughout the run and actual throw. All arm and back muscles must be relaxed so that the arm is kept "loose." The arm and hand must react like a whip to get the proper snap as the javelin is released.

3. Be sure to have an exaggerated backward lean as the throwing action takes place. This can best be accomplished by keeping the right knee bent and the left leg straight at the moment of release.

4. Get the left foot down on the ground as fast as possible as the final throwing position is assumed. If the left foot moves down too slowly, there will be a tendency for the body to move forward, and the "lift" in the throwing motion will be lost.

5. Do not step in the "bucket" with the left foot. The left foot must be placed near the line and not out to the side. This proper movement of the left foot should keep the hips from "opening up" too soon, and will help to get the proper pull from the left side so that the finish position is over the left leg.

6. Lead with the elbow, and keep the javelin up over the shoulder. This will help prevent making the throw with the side arm motion, and will also aid in preventing injury to the elbow and the arm.

7. Start the "pull" with the arm almost straight, and pull along the line of flight of the javelin.

8. Do not pull down on the javelin. This downward pull is often caused by starting the pull too late.

9. Do not try to get height simply by raising the tip of the javelin. A correct angle of release can be accomplished by proper leg and shoulder lift.

10. Use field shoes with long spikes when throwing from dirt runways.

11. Use baseball shoes when throwing from grass runways.

12. When throwing into and against the wind, keep the javelin a

little lower than normal and try to keep it level during flight. If the tip points too high upward during flight, distance will be lost.

13. Practice the run and steps many times. This can be done without throwing for distance.

14. Study and try to emulate the world's best throwers.

HAMMER
THROW

history of hammer throw

The hammer throw has been traced back in history as far as 2000 B.C., when competition was held during the Tailteann Games at Tara, Ireland. This event is related to the log and stone throws used by other nations earlier than 2000 B.C. The hammer throw was introduced into the United States by Irish immigrants during the late 1800's. These Irish-Americans dominated the hammer event in the United States from about 1890 to the 1920's.

The 7' diameter circle was standardized in 1907. The hammer weighs 16 pounds and is attached to a 48-inch wire chain. Most throwers in the early 1900's were using 1 or 2 turns while spinning on the toes and heels, and even becoming airborne during the turns. Now the throwers turn 3 times while spinning from the heel to outer edge of foot, keeping the pivoting foot in contact with the ground throughout the turns.

Irish-Americans John J. Flanagan, Matt McGrath, and Pat Ryan held either the world's record in the hammer throw and/or were world champions from 1900 to 1920. For example, Flanagan was Olympic hammer champion 3 times, in 1900, 1904, and 1908. His all-time best was 172'11", which was a world's record. McGrath bettered this record twice and won this event in the 1912 Olympics. However, his world record of 187'4" was set during 1911.

For about 8 years after this, Pat Ryan dominated the hammer throw, setting a world record in 1913 of 189'6½" and winning the 1920 Olympics with a toss of 173'5¼". Ryan held the world record for 25 years. Then European throwers dominated the event from 1924 to 1956.

During 1956, Cliff Blair of Boston University set a new world record of 216'4½". The former record was held by Russia's Mikhail Krivonosov, who later that year reclaimed the world record with a mark of 217'9½". That same year, Harold Connolly of the United States set a new world's record of 220'8" and also won the 1956 Olympics. Connolly fought off challenges by the Soviet throwers during the next 10 years. In September, 1965, Connolly bettered his own 1962 world record of 231'10" with a mark of 233'9½". Connolly generally dominated the hammer record for about 10 years, but he was defeated in the 1960 Olympics by Vasiliy Rudenkov of the Soviet Union and in 1964 by Romuald Klim, also of Russia, with an Olympic record of 228'9½".

During September, 1965, Gyula Zsivotsky of Hungary bettered Connolly's world record with a throw of 241'11", and again set a new record of 242' just a few weeks prior to the 1968 Olympics.

Zsivotsky (Hungary) won at the Mexico Olympics with a throw of 240'8", defeating Romuald Klim (U.S.S.R.) by only 3 inches. The following are the first 5 winners at the 1968 Olympics in the hammer throw:

1. Gyula Zsivotsky (Hungary)   240'8"
2. Romuald Klim (Soviet Union)   240'5"
3. Lazar Lovasz (Hungary)   228'11"
4. Takeo Sugawara (Japan)   228'11"
5. Sandor Eckschmidt (Hungary)   227'10½"

Interest in and popularity of the hammer throw in the United States has increased greatly in recent years because of the efforts of Hal Connolly, Sam Felton, Jr., Fred Wilt, and other concerned Americans. Manufacturers are also producing "training hammers" with shorter wires, and underweight hammers which allow the beginner to progress gradually to the official 16-pound hammer.

fundamentals of the hammer throw

Starting position.   (*See* Fig. 18-1.) The thrower starts with his back to the direction of throw. The feet are placed shoulder width apart, with the legs flexed and the body in a sitting position. The back is straight, head upright, and eyes focused horizontally. The hammer rests on the ground directly in front of the thrower. The handle is held loosely in the right hand (right-handed thrower). When the throw is started, the hammerhead is swung to the rear of the right leg, while the head and shoulder simultaneously rotate about 90 degrees to the right. The gloved left hand is then slipped under the right hand, gripping the handle with the middle pads of the fingers. The left arm should remain straight as the hammer is pulled into orbit in a series of over-the-head swings.

Preliminary windups.   Generally 2 preliminary windups are used to build up the hammer head velocity. However, beginners often need 3 windups to build momentum. The windups are the foundation of the throw and must build up hammer head speed gradually in a controlled manner. The body (hips, back, and legs) are the main source of power countering and accelerating the hammer during the windups. The arms must be kept straight and the shoulders relaxed, allowing the hammer to sweep through the widest possible orbit that can be controlled.

The turns.   The purpose of the turns is to build up maximum peripheral velocity in the hammer head by increasing turning speed and the length of the radius through which the hammer head is swept. If maximum speed is to be reached at the time of release, it must be a gradual, controlled acceleration. This requires excellent technique, rhythm, balance, strength, and quick reflexes. The following are techniques which should be practiced and observed:

1. Work for a gradual increase of speed by sweeping the hammer smoothly and controlling it in the widest possible arc while keeping the arms extended and shoulders relaxed.

2. While turning, keep the left foot in contact with the ground. The left foot moves down the middle of the circle in a straight line, keeping contact with the ground from the start of the turn until the release. Rotate around the heel of the left foot to the outside of the foot toward the ball and toes, continue on to the heel of the other foot, and repeat in a series of continuous movements. The right foot remains grounded until the hammer is moved well to the left and is at shoulder height. The feet set the tempo of the throw and should work and drive hard to the left and ahead of the hammer.

FIGURE 18–1. Hammer throwing form. (A) and (B) The thrower is assuming a shoulder width stance, with the toes pointed slightly out. The hammer is held to the rear of the right foot and pulled upward by swaying the body to the left. (C) The hammer is held at head level during the first windup, as the upper body leans toward the hammer while the hips sway to the right. (D) The high point of the second windup is reached, with the upper body leaning left as the hips counter by moving to the right. (E) During the first turn the thrower's legs are flexed, while the head and hips lead the hammer. The turn starts on the heel of the left foot and the ball or toe of the right foot, with the arms and hammer kept low.

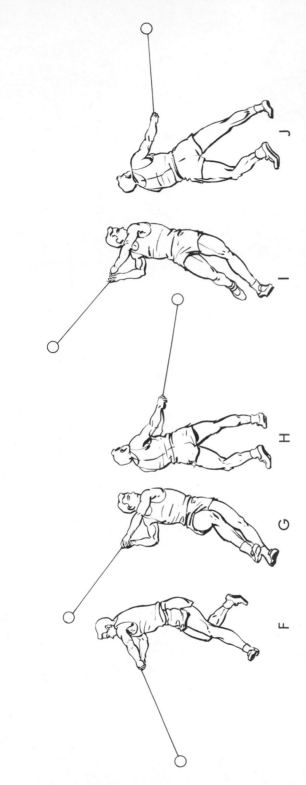

F   G   H   I   J

FIGURE 18–1 (cont.).   *Hammer throwing form. (F) Thrower continues to roll from heel around and on to the outside of the left foot. The right toe is kept in contact with ground during the first half of the first turn. (G) This second half of the initial turn shows the thrower continuing to roll on the outside of the left leg, as it is planted softly and with a slightly smaller leg spread than used initially. (H) At the finish of the first turn the body counters by moving to the left. The left shoulder dips to help keep the body weight on the left foot. (I) The second half of the second turn illustrates that a dynamic countermovement is made downward and opposite to the hammer's pull. The head and hips are leading the action, while the arms remain extended and semipassive. The right leg is brought around the left leg quickly and low, the feet being placed a few inches closer together during this turn. (J) Completion of the second turn, with the weight remaining on the left foot as left shoulder is lowered. The thrower counters by moving his body down and to the left.*

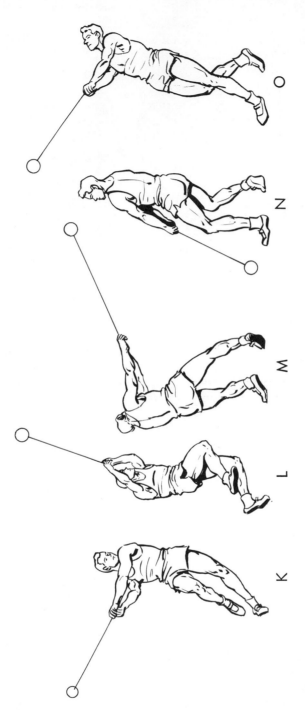

K   L   M   N   O

FIGURE 18–1 (cont.). Hammer throwing form. (K) The second half of third and final turn. The thrower again counters by force-fully leading with head, left shoulder, and hips. Arms remain as extended and relaxed as possible to increase the effective radius of movement. (L) Second half of final turn finds the thrower's weight placed over a well-flexed left leg as the thrower pulls down while leading with his head, shoulders, and hips. (M) The final turn is completed as the thrower quickly places his right foot down and into a more narrow stance than used in the earlier turn, with the legs noticeably flexed and the weight kept over his bent left leg. The upper body is countering by moving down and to the left. (N) The final movement shows the explosive burst of power as the legs extend, while the arms remain low and extended as the hammer sweeps through its low point. (O) The release is near with the complete extension of the legs and body. The release should be made at an angle of 42° to 45°.

3. To control the turns the right foot and leg must be shifted quickly, keeping the right foot low and close to the left leg. A loss of control and balance will occur if the shift of the right leg is too high or wide. The ball of the right foot should complete each turn well ahead of the hammer. Upon landing quietly, the right foot quickly but firmly presses on into the next turn. During the final sweep, the heel of the right foot should not touch the ground. During the turns, both legs must be well flexed until the ball of the right foot is in place, starting a strong lifting and pressing effort to the left.

4. The hammer's high point should not be forced. The hands should rise naturally to about eye level as the hammer reaches its high point. The hammer's low point should be kept well to the right because of the tendency of the low point to creep left during each turn. The correct low point can be achieved by making quick, tight turns while increasing torque from turn to turn.

5. The role of the arms and shoulders in the buildup is to increase the effective radius through which the hammer is swept. Since, in essence, the straight arms are an extension of the wire, the arms and shoulders must be relaxed and as passive as possible during the turns. The hammer head hangs directly in front of the chest during the turns.

6. The head plays an important role during the turns. The head and eyes should be kept up, particularly as the turns are completed. The head and hips lead the action to the left, but the head should not get ahead of the hips. A proper lead with the head makes it easier to hang from the hammer and leave the arms and shoulders behind. Beginners should not emphasize the head lead until they have mastered the fundamentals.

7. The throwing action begins after the completion of the last turn and just before the hammer reaches its low point. The thrower should be in a strong finish position, with the left shoulder down and legs flexed in a powerful lifting position. The thrower's arms remain extended as the legs straighten and the body extends upward and backward. The release takes place at shoulder level at an angle of 42 to 45 degrees. After release, recovery is made by completing another turn while staying in the ring.

training program

It must be remembered that it is impossible to judge whether each individual should follow any training plan to the letter. Allowances must be made for those who may have a very heavy work and study program in school. The age and maturity of each athlete should also

be considered. Some of the older, stronger men may need more work
than is contained in most schedules. The coach and the athlete should
determine the exact workout program needed. The schedule presented
below is suggested for the 4-week period prior to participation in the
first meet.

WORKOUT SCHEDULES

Four Weeks Prior to the First Meet

Monday
1. Jog ¼ mile.
2. Run wind sprints for ½ mile, sprinting 50 yards and walking
   50 yards.
3. Do stretching exercises involving the large muscles of the back,
   shoulders, and arms, always including 10 or more hip twists while
   hanging from chinning bar.
4. Do 10 push-ups (repeated 3 times) executed from the fingertip
   position.
5. Do 10 throws, concentrating on gradual build-up of hammer
   head speed.
6. Do 20 throws, working on form.
7. Take 6 to 10 starts from the blocks, running 25 yards each time.

Tuesday
1. Jog ¼ mile.
2. Run wind sprints for ½ mile.
3. Do stretching exercises.
4. Do 10 push-ups (repeated 3 times) from the fingertip position.
5. Do 10 throws, working on keeping arms extended and shoulders relaxed.
6. Do 10 to 20 throws. Work on proper form and getting into
   effective throwing position.
7. Take 5 starts from the blocks.
8. Train with weights (*see* weight-training program).

Wednesday
1. Jog ¼ mile.
2. Run wind sprints for ½ mile.
3. Do stretching exercises.
4. Do 10 push-ups (repeated 3 times) from fingertip position.
5. Throw 10 times, working on gradual acceleration and **relaxa-**

tion of arms and shoulders while sweeping hammer through widest possible radius.

6. Take 20 throws for form at near maximum, but not all-out, effort for the first 4 weeks.
7. Execute a high jump at reasonable height, or a standing long jump and vertical jump attempting to touch basketball rim or football goal cross support with one hand.

Thursday
1. Jog ¼ mile.
2. Run wind sprints for ½ mile.
3. Do stretching exercises.
4. Take 10 throws for form and position.
5. Do 10 to 20 throws at near maximum, working on gradual acceleration of hammer head speed.
6. Train with weights (*see* weight-training program).

Friday
1. Jog ¼ mile.
2. Run wind sprints for ½ mile.
3. Do stretching exercises.
4. Do 10 push-ups (repeated 3 times) from the fingertip position.
5. Take 10 throws, working on proper form and position.
6. Take 20 throws at near maximum effort, working on acceleration and getting good lifting action from legs.

Saturday
Train with weights if time and facilities are available (*see* weight-training program).

AFTER MEETS START

This schedule is set up in preparation for Saturday meets. When meets are held on Friday, the schedule should be altered accordingly.

Monday
1. Jog ¼ mile.
2. Run wind sprints for ½ mile.
3. Do stretching exercises.
4. Do 10 push-ups (repeated 3 times) from the fingertip position.
5. Take 10 throws for form and position.
6. Take 15 to 20 throws, working on weak points in your form.

    7. Take 6 to 10 starts from the blocks, running 25 to 50 yards each time.
    8. Check action pictures taken of your performance the previous Saturday.

Tuesday

1. Jog ¼ mile.
2. Do stretching exercise.
3. Do 5 push-ups (repeated 3 times) from the fingertip position.
4. Take 10 throws for form and position.
5. Take 10 throws at all-out effort, in competition with teammates.
6. Take 6 starts from the blocks, running 25 to 50 yards each time.

Wednesday

1. Jog ¼ mile.
2. Run wind sprints for ½ mile.
3. Do stretching exercises.
4. Do 5 push-ups (repeated 3 times) from the fingertip position.
5. Take 10 throws, working on weak points in your form.
6. Do 20 throws at maximum effort.
7. Train with weights (*see* weight-training program).

Thursday

1. Jog ¼ mile.
2. Run wind sprints for ½ mile.
3. Do stretching exercises.
4. Do 5 push-ups (repeated 3 times) from fingertip position.
5. Take 5 throws for form and position.
6. Take 7 throws under meet conditions.
7. Take 6 starts from the blocks, running 25 to 50 yards each time.

Friday

Study motion pictures of yourself and others in action. Get plenty of sleep and rest. Prepare yourself mentally for a great performance on Saturday. Be confident!

Saturday

The day of the track meet. Be prepared to comptete at your best.
1. Arrive at the stadium in plenty of time to dress slowly and get properly warmed up for competition.
2. Jog 1 lap.
3. Do stretching exercises.
4. Take 3 starts and run 25 yards each time.

5. Take 10 throws, working on form and position. Throw with near maximum effort, working on form and attaining best possible throwing position.
6. Do your best on each throw after competition begins. It is unwise to save up for any one all-out effort.

WEIGHT-TRAINING PROGRAM

The hammer thrower, like the shot putter and discus thrower, must make use of weight-training in order to develop into a top performer. Such performers often train as much as 4 out of every 5 days with weights. Perhaps this is too much effort expended in weight-training. A more reasonable approach might be to participate in weight-training 2 out of every 5 days.

Coordination in throwing the hammer should have top priority in the schedule in the other 3 days of training. It is recommended that the hammer thrower do 1 to 5 sets, repeating each set 1 to 8 times. The starting weight should probably be around 75 pounds. This may be gradually increased to the maximum that can be handled 2 to 4 times.

STANDING POSITION

1. Two-arm barbell military press: The lifting action should be done rapidly to help develop explosive power.
2. Two-arm barbell snatch: Make very quick lifts with only average weight.
3. Curls: Be sure to start with arms extended and lift to a complete flexion.
4. Deep knee bends (not more than 90° bend): Be careful to bend the knees only to the position in which the thighs are parallel to the floor.
5. Combined deadlift and shoulder shrugs: Raise shoulders as high as possible and lower weight to floor after each shrug.
6. Upright rowing: Pull barbell up under chin.
7. Heel raises: Place toes on 2-inch board and raise up as high on toe as possible with weight on shoulders.
8. Bench press: Do with the back horizontal and on incline.
9. Twisting situps: While holding weight of 10 to 30 pounds behind neck, situp while sitting on incline board with feet and legs up.
10. Simulations of hang position: Using rubber stretch hose attached to base of goal post or other structure, simulate hang position and do 2 or 3 sets of 10 to 20 repetitions.

APPENDIX

a. motivating and handling track athletes

There are many ways to motivate and handle track athletes. How this is accomplished depends upon the personality and the methods of the coach and the personality and potential of the athlete. Of course, each person is an individual. The following suggestions are given with the idea that not all of them may be used by every coach or athlete.

1. Most athletes respond best to encouragement. However, a few put forth their best effort when discouraged, ignored, or rebuked by the coach.

2. One technique used by a prominent coach is to ignore completely those who have not been performing their best. This doesn't cause all athletes to perform at their best. The coach using such a technique may not gain respect from some of his athletes, while others may need to be handled this way.

3. Another coach uses a procedure in which he asks only that his track and field men try their best to improve. He takes on the trips only those he believes have tried to improve during a given period.

4. Self-suggestion (self-hypnosis) is a method used by many cham-

pions to help them do their best in a meet. They actually talk themselves into performing at a top level. Boys can be helped to start to utilize this procedure.

5. Usually the fastest learning takes place in situations in which errors are made to be unpleasant and correct performances are made to be pleasant. (This method is called *recognition.*)

6. Keeping accurate records of daily and meet performances is necessary if athletes are to know what they have done in the past and what may be expected of them in the future. Their interest will be heightened by the use of such a procedure.

7. If the athletes are somewhat introspective, they may use a technique called *self-criticism.* This means that they may make a list of all their faults and then proceed to correct them. However, some boys who are anxious to do well often need to be admonished against being too self-critical.

8. Some coaches have the happy faculty of being able to relax their performers with the use of stories, expressions, and actions. Others keep on the squad a "relaxer," a boy who is able to say funny things and be the clown. Some coaches and athletes have a routine they go through to bring about relaxation. Keeping mind and body occupied aids in becoming and remaining relaxed.

9. It is believed that much effort should be spent in developing a winning attitude and tradition. Athletes may perform far above their estimated ability just because it is a tradition at their school to win and excel.

10. The idea that they are being timed or that their work is being measured causes many athletes to put forth their best efforts. There are occasions in practice when it is best not to have a stop watch available, but most of the time a record of the efforts of each individual should be maintained.

11. It is usually best to have the experienced athlete perform at all-out effort gradually. In fact, the athletes in most events should be working on form and not maximum effort in the early part of the season. Early all-out performances may result in the development of bad habits and staleness. Pointing toward performing at a high level in 2 or 3 big meets, at least by the top performers, appears to be sound.

12. The coach should be enthusiastic and confident. This attitude is usually transferred to the athlete.

13. An athlete should compete against himself in trying to improve. This is especially true of the beginner.

14. The coach should keep in touch with the parents of most athletes. A winning attitude often begins in the home.

15. The appearance of the coach and his athletes before school

audiences, service club members, and other civic and community groups helps in maintaining the public's interest and support, as well as that of the school and the athletes.

16. Getting good publicity for the meets and performances helps maintain squad interest.

17. Organizing practices and meets in an efficient manner helps make participation enjoyable.

18. The more competitors out for the team in high school, the more chance a coach has of discovering top performers. If he can have at least 2 boys compete for the top position in each event, the boys will probably perform better than if there were only 1 outstanding performer.

19. Great performers of the past can often assist the coach in their specialty—and by their mere presence they stimulate greater effort on the part of the aspirants.

20. Constant study of films of top performers and of himself helps the athlete to acquire a knowledge of what to work on for improvement.

b. coaching strategy

Deciding how to employ the track and field men most effectively in dual, conference, state, or sometimes even national meets is like matching wits in a game of chess. Some moves or decisions are self-evident; others depend on what the opposition does. Only general suggestions may be offered when the particulars are unknown. Each meet's strategy must be planned for the specific contest. Some of the factors that may affect strategy follow.

1. Without much practice, dash men may be used as low hurdlers for extra points.

2. Good quarter-milers may double as 220 men, or even 880 runners, for extra points.

3. Low hurdlers can usually long jump.

4. Good 880 runners may double in the 440.

5. Milers usually can run the 880 in good time.

6. Sprinters can usually long jump.

7. High hurdlers may be able to high jump.

8. High jumpers can usually run the high hurdles.

9. Pole vaulters could be used as low hurdlers, since they constantly run low hurdles during their workouts.

10. The same may be said of long jumpers.

11. Sometimes pace setters are used to set so fast an early pace that inexperienced runners, and even experienced athletes who like to be front runners, are lured into running at too exhausting a pace.

12. Normally, key runners should run against the good runners of the opposing team; otherwise the opponents gain points with inferior runners.

13. When running into a strong wind in races longer than 220 yards, a smart runner lets the opposing runner of approximately the same ability shield him from the wind, if possible, by running behind him. He then tries to outkick him at the finish.

14. It may be wise in a relay race to match runners who have beaten their opponents in an open race at this distance. A psychological advantage may be gained.

15. If an all weather track surface is not available, the stronger runner should do the best on a muddy track. Grease or graphite should be placed on the shoes in such a situation to help prevent them from picking up mud.

16. It should be remembered that some field and track athletes perform best before a crowd. Meets have been won or lost for this reason.

17. Javelin throwers and other field performers need a reference point on which to focus when throwing. A field without trees surrounding it may be a handicap to the thrower used to having trees as a background.

18. Right-footed lead leg hurdlers have more difficulty keeping their balance than left-footed hurdlers in running the hurdles around a curve.

19. Some men are front runners and may expend a great deal of energy in trying to keep the lead if forced into doing so. They may slow up or even quit if they lose the lead.

20. Some runners can only run fast if they are behind.

21. A top performer (especially a field event man) practicing with poorer ones before a meet, or even during the week, may develop bad habits or have trouble with his timing and coordination.

22. Runners sometimes pick up the rhythm and tempo of the other runners in a race. This may be a benefit or a detriment. Procedures may be used to offset any detrimental effects.

23. The order of performance may affect the outcome. A good throw or jump by a performer just before his equally-capable opponent performs may cause his opponent to try too hard and, consequently, not do his best.

24. It is apparent that psychological factors play a leading role in coaching strategy. If possible, the track coach should study the members of the opposing team before the teams meet (through last year's results, scouting at other meets, talking to his own boys who know the opponents, and so on) and make decisions that may involve psychological aspects.

BIBLIOGRAPHY

books

Bannister, Roger, *The Four Minute Mile*. New York: Dodd, Mead & Co., 1964.

Bresnahan, George T., W. W. Tuttle, and Francis X. Cretzmeyer, *Track and Field Athletics*. St. Louis: The C. V. Mosby Co., 1956.

Bunn, John W., *Scientific Principles of Coaching*. Englewood Cliffs, N.J.: Prentice-Hall, Inc., 1955.

Cooper, John M., and Ruth B. Glassow, *Kinesology*, 2nd ed. St. Louis: The C. V. Mosby Co., 1968.

Cromwell, Dean B., *The Hurdles, 120-220-440*. Indianapolis: International Sports, Inc., 1939.

————, *The Javelin Throw and Relay Races*. Indianapolis: International Sports, Inc., 1939.

————, *The Sprint Races*. Indianapolis: International Sports, Inc., 1939.

Doherty, John K., *Modern Track and Field*. Englewood Cliffs, N.J.: Prentice-Hall, Inc., 1960.

258

————, *Modern Training for Running*. Englewood Cliffs, N.J.: Prentice-Hall, Inc., 1964.

Doherty, Ken, *Track and Field Moves on Paper*. Swarthmore, Penn.: A series of three publications published by the author, 1967.

Dyson, Geoffrey H. G., *The Mechanics of Athletics*. London: University of London Press, 1962.

Ecker, Tom, ed., *Championship Track and Field*. Englewood Cliffs, N.J.: Prentice-Hall, Inc., 1964.

Foreman, Ken, and Virginia Husted, *Track and Field*. Dubuque: W. C. Brown Co., 1966 (W. C. Brown Physical Education Activities Series).

Gilmour, Garth, *A Clean Pair of Heels*. London: Herbert Jenkins Ltd., 1963.

Gordon, James A., *Track and Field: Changing Concepts and Modern Techniques*. Boston: Allyn & Bacon, Inc., 1966.

Howell, Alfred B., *Speed in Animals*. New York: Hafner Publishing Co., Inc., 1965.

Hyman, Dorothy, *Sprint to Fame*. London: Stanley Paul & Co. Ltd., 1964.

Kinzle, Donn, *Practical Track Athletics*. New York: The Ronald Press Company, 1957.

Lawther, John S., *Psychology of Coaching*. Englewood Cliffs, N.J.: Prentice-Hall, Inc., 1965.

————, *The Learning of Physical Skills*. Englewood Cliffs, N.J.: Prentice-Hall, Inc., 1968.

Miller, Richard I., *Fundamentals of Track and Field Coaching*. New York: McGraw-Hill Book Company, 1952.

Miller, Kenneth D., *Track and Field for Girls*. New York: The Ronald Press Company, 1964.

O'Connor, Harold, *Coach's Guide to Winning High School Track and Field*. West Nyack, N.Y.: Parker Publishing Co., 1965.

Powell, John T., *Track and Field Fundamentals for Teacher and Coach*. Champaign, Ill.: Stipes Publishing Co., 1962.

Smith, George W., *All Out for the Mile; A History of the Mile Race: 1864-1955*. London: Forbes Robertson, 1955.

V-Five Association of America, *Track and Field*. Annapolis, Md.: United States Naval Institute, 1950.

Wakefield, Frances, Dorothy Harkins, and John M. Cooper, *Track and Field Fundamentals for Girls and Women*. St. Louis: The C. V. Mosby Co., 1966.

Watts, Denis Claude V., *Tackle Athletics This Way*. London: Stanley Paul & Co. Ltd., 1964.

periodical articles

Clohency, G., "Developing Sixty-foot Shot Putters," *Athletic Journal*, XLVI (February 1966), 16.

Cooper, J. M., "Key to Becoming a Fast Sprinter," *Athletic Journal,* XLIII (February 1963), 16.

Doherty, J. K., "Nature of Endurance in Running," *JOHPER,* XXXV (April 1964), 30.

Dyson, G. H. G., "Mechanics in Athletics," *JOHPER,* XLVII (January 1967), 46.

Ecker, T., "Clearing the High Jumper's Trail Leg," *Athletic Journal,* XLVI (February 1966), 38.

Hackett, H., "Training for the Long Jump and Triple Jump Double," *Athletic Journal,* XLVI (February 1966), 8-9.

Hay, J. G., "Pole Vaulting Energy Storage and Pole Bend," *Scholastic Coach,* XXXV (March 1966), 56.

Henry, F. M., "Research on Sprint Running," *Athletic Journal,* XXXII (February 1952), 30.

Jacoby, E., "Discus Mechanics," *Scholastic Coach,* XXXVI (February 1967), 7-9.

Larkin, R. A., "Improved Technique in Speed Relay Baton Exchanges," *Athletic Journal,* XLVII (January 1967), 8-9.

Masin, H. L., "Valeri Brumel's Blasting Spin-Roll," *Scholastic Coach,* XXXI (February 1962), 8-9.

Powell, J. T., "Willie Davenport: Hurdling's Mr. Form," *Scholastic Coach,* XXXVI (March 1967), 14-16.

Sylvia, A. J., "Body Mechanics of Sprinting," *Athletic Journal,* XLVI (March 1966), 14-15.

Timmons, B., "Clinical Analysis of Jim Ryun's Stride," *Scholastic Coach,* XXXVI (March 1967), 12-13.

research articles

Asprey, G. M., *et al.,* "Effect of Eating at Various Times on Subsequent Performances in the Two Mile Run," *Research Quarterly,* XXXVI (October 1965), 233-36.

Baacke, L. W., "Relationship of Selected Anthropometric and Physical Performance Measures to Performance in the Running Hop, Step, and Jump," *Research Quarterly,* XXXV (May 1964), 107-15.

Cearley, J. E., "Linearity of Contributions of Ages, Heights, and Weights to Prediction of Track and Field Performances," *Research Quarterly,* XXVIII (October 1957), 218-22.

Deshon, D. E., and R. C. Nelson, "Cinematographic Analysis of Sprint Running," *Research Quarterly,* XXXV (December 1964), 451-55.

deVries, H. A., "Looseness Factor in Speed and O_2 Consumption of an Anaerobic 100 Yard Dash," *Research Quarterly,* XXXIV (October 1963), 305-13.

Dintiman, G. B., "Effects of Various Training Programs on Running Speed," *Research Quarterly,* XXXV (December 1964), 456-67.

Henry, F. M., "Force-time Characteristics of the Sprint Start," *Research Quarterly*, XXIII (October 1952), 301-18.

——, "Note on Physiological Limits and the History of the Mile Run," *Research Quarterly*, XXV (December 1954), 483.

——, "Prediction of World Records in Running Sixty Yards to Twenty-six Miles," *Research Quarterly*, XXVI (May 1955), 147-55.

——, "Time-Velocity Equations and Oxygen Requirements of All-out and Steary-pace Running," *Research Quarterly*, XXV (May 1954), 164-77.

——, and I. R. Trafton, "Velocity Curve of Sprint Running with Some Observations on the Muscle Viscosity Factor," *Research Quarterly*, XXII (December 1951), 409-22.

Kihlberg, J., and M. J. Karvonen, "Comparison on Statistical Basis of Achievement in Track and Field Events," *Research Quarterly*, XXVIII (October 1957), 244-56.

Klissouras, V., and P. V. Karpovich, "Electrogoniometric Study of Jumping Events," *Research Quarterly*, XXXVIII (March 1967), 41-48.

Kronsbein, F., "Steady-pace vs. Variable Speed in High School 220-Yard Run," *Research Quarterly*, XXVI (October 1955), 289-94.

Mathews, D. K., "Aerobic and Anaerobic Work Efficiency," *Research Quarterly*, XXXIV (October 1963), 356-60.

Nagle, F. J., and T. G. Bedecki, "Use of the 180 Heat Rate Response as a Measure of Circulorespiratory Capacity," *Research Quarterly*, XXXIV (October 1963), 361-69.

Pierson, W. R., and R. J. Rasch, "Bruce Physical Fitness Index as a Predictor of Performance in Trained Distance Runners," *Research Quarterly*, XXXI (March 1960), 77-81.

Schultz, G. W., "Effects of Direct Practice, Repetitive Sprinting, and Weight Training on Selected Motor Performance Tests," *Research Quarterly*, XXXVIII (March 1967), 108-18.

Siegerseth, P. O., and V. F. Grinaker, "Effect of Foot Spacing on Velocity in Sprints," *Research Quarterly*, XXXIII (December 1962), 599-606.

Stock, M., "Influence of Various Track Starting Positions on Speed," *Research Quarterly*, XXXIII (December 1962), 607-14.

INDEX